# NEGRO VOICES IN AMERICAN FICTION

# NEGRO VOICES IN AMERICAN FICTION

HUGH M. GLOSTER

NEW YORK / RUSSELL & RUSSELL

REISSUED, 1965, BY RUSSELL & RUSSELL
A DIVISION OF ATHENEUM PUBLISHERS, INC.
BY ARRANGEMENT WITH THE UNIVERSITY OF NORTH CAROLINA PRESS
L. C. CATALOG CARD NO: 65-17895
ISBN: 0-8462-0577-7
PRINTED IN THE UNITED STATES OF AMERICA
BY SENTRY PRESS, NEW YORK

To
L. T. G.

# Preface

IN A "FOREWORD" to Harry Hartwick's *The Foreground of American Fiction* Harry Haydon Clark says that "there is no better index to the American mind during the last forty years than the American novel." The validity of this statement is well illustrated in American Negro fiction, for the thinking and experience of twentieth-century Negroes are reflected in their novels and short stories. In this body of writing are mirrored the psychology and interests of Negroes, their achievements and aspirations, and the problems arising from their juxtaposition with the white majority of the country.

Though often lacking enduring beauty and universal appeal, American Negro fiction reveals authors who, in literature as in life, are forced by environmental pressure to become race-conscious and to preoccupy themselves with the problems of adjustment to a resisting and sometimes antagonistic society. With racial considerations motivating most of their work, they write chiefly about their status as a segregated, oppressed, ridiculed, and exploited minority in the American social order. In degrees and manners varying with their individual temperaments, environmental surroundings, and philosophies of life, they not only deal with such injustices as discrimination, disfranchisement, peonage, and lynching, but also voice the achievements, potentialities, and aspirations of their people.

In view of the fact that a reliable mosaic of Negro life and thought in the United States is to be found in novels and short stories by Negro authors, this study of the themes, attitudes, and milieus of Negro writers of fiction from Charles W. Chesnutt to Richard Wright and of the relation of their published works to the broader cultural life of the country should be of sociological and literary value.

In the first place, this book should be of value to students of social history because it shows how the Negro mind—conditioned by time, place, and circumstance—has reacted to the problems of a racial minority in the United States. While some of the best transcripts of Negro experience have been made by white authors, much of the mass of writing about the American Negro has been external commentary and superficial generalization, often flavored by ethnic or sectional bias and sometimes more of a rationale of the color problem than an honest depiction of Negro behavior. This volume, undertaking to present the Negro as his own interpreter, furnishes first-hand evidence of what he thinks of America and how he reacts to what America thinks of him.

In the second place, this book should be of value to students of literature because it demonstrates that Negro novels and short stories, which are often discussed and sometimes disdained as alien creations, are really part and parcel of the main body of American authorship. While frequently influenced by racial temper and minority-group emphases, the fiction of Negroes nevertheless reflects the plantation tradition, Nordicism, realism, naturalism, primitivism, Freudianism, regionalism, proletarianism, and other movements in American literature. Along with his white confrere the Negro artist seeks literary maturity, universal values, and a significant expression of human life. Trends in modern Negro literature, therefore, are neither spasmodic nor fragmentary, but are inextricable patterns in the warp and woof of the American literary fabric.

In this work the author has tried to permit no theory—economic, political, social, or philosophical—to influence his approach. As far as possible, he has let Negro writers of fiction speak for themselves. The method has been to proceed directly to the themes, attitudes, and background of the works under examination. Since these three factors, rather than literary craftsmanship, are of major importance in this study, dragnet methods have been adopted in assembling fiction by Negroes, and eclectic procedures have been avoided. As a result, the works which are discussed illustrate a wide range of fictional skills and are frequently inferior examples of their form. Since this book is concerned not so much with literary appraisal as with racial expression, artistic evaluation has been avoided except for the occasional employment of terms indicating the quality of a work.

The author gratefully acknowledges indebtedness to the following in the preparation of this volume: to Dr. Oscar Cargill of the Department of English of New York University for advice and encouragement from the beginning to the completion of the study from which this book has developed; to the librarians of the Schomburg Collection of the New York Public Library, Atlanta University, Fisk University, Hampton Institute, Harvard University, Howard University, LeMoyne College, New York University, and the Library of Congress for helpful co-operation and for the use of their resources in Negro history and literature; to the General Education Board and the Alpha Phi Alpha Fraternity for fellowship grants; and to Miss Mildred Burch, Mrs. Louise Torrence Gloster, and Mr. Emanuel A. Bertrand for clerical assistance.

*May, 1947*

# Acknowledgments

PERMISSION has been granted by the following publishers and individuals to quote from the works listed below. The place and date of publication will be found in the Bibliography.

American Book Company: *The Foreground of American Fiction* by Harry Hartwick. The Associated Publishers: *The Negro in Our History* by Carter G. Woodson. The Associates in Negro Folk Education: *The Negro in American Fiction* by Sterling A. Brown. The Association for the Study of Negro Life and History: *The Journal of Negro History.* Sterling A. Brown, Arthur P. Davis, and Ulysses Lee: *The Negro Caravan,* edited by Sterling A. Brown, Arthur P. Davis, and Ulysses Lee.

Helen M. Chesnutt: *The Colonel's Dream, The House Behind the Cedars, The Marrow of Tradition,* and *The Wife of His Youth and Other Stories of the Color Line,* all by Charles W. Chesnutt.

The Christopher Publishing House: *Aunt Sara's Wooden God* by Mercedes Gilbert.

The Citadel Press: *River George* by George W. Lee; *A Long Way from Home* by Claude McKay; *Black No More* by George S. Schuyler; *The Blacker the Berry* and *Infants of the Spring,* both by Wallace Thurman.

Columbia University Press: *The Southern Plantation* by Francis Pendleton Gaines. The Crisis: *The Crisis.*

Dodd, Mead and Company: *The Negro in Literature and Art* by Benjamin G. Brawley; *The Fanatics, The Heart of Happy Hollow, The Sport of the Gods, The Strength of Gideon and Other Stories,* and *The Uncalled,* all by Paul Laurence Dunbar.

Doubleday and Company: *Let Me Breathe Thunder* by William Attaway; *The Clansman* and *The Leopard's Spots,* both by Thomas Dixon, Jr.; *The Responsibilities of a Novelist* by Frank Norris; *O Canaan!* by Waters E. Turpin; *My Larger Education* by Booker T. Washington.

Herman Dreer: *The Immediate Jewel of His Soul* by Herman Dreer.

W. E. B. DuBois: *The Quest of the Silver Fleece* and *The Souls of Black Folk,* both by W. E. B. DuBois.

Mrs. Sutton E. Griggs: *The Hindered Hand, Imperium in Imperio, Overshadowed, Pointing the Way,* and *Unfettered,* all by Sutton E. Griggs.

Harcourt, Brace and Company: *Black Reconstruction, Dark Princess,*

*Darkwater,* and *Dusk of Dawn,* all by W. E. B. DuBois; *The Beginnings of Critical Realism in America* by Vernon Louis Parrington; *Fighting Words,* edited by Donald Ogden Stewart.

Harper and Brothers: *One Way to Heaven* by Countee Cullen; *Banana Bottom* and *Banjo,* both by Claude McKay; *These Low Grounds* by Waters E. Turpin; *Native Son* and *Uncle Tom's Children,* both by Richard Wright.

Mrs. John H. Hill: *Princess Malah* by John H. Hill. Houghton Mifflin Company: *Letters 1850-1908* by Grover Cleveland. International Publishers: *The Negro and the Democratic Front* by James W. Ford.

Alfred A. Knopf: *The Walls of Jericho* by Rudolph Fisher; *The Big Sea, Not Without Laughter,* and *The Ways of White Folks,* all by Langston Hughes; *The Autobiography of an Ex-Coloured Man* by James Weldon Johnson; *Passing* and *Quicksand,* both by Nella Larsen; *Nigger Heaven* by Carl Van Vechten; *The Fire in the Flint* and *Flight,* both by Walter White.

J. B. Lippincott Company: *The Chinaberry Tree* by Jessie Fauset; *Moses: Man of the Mountain* by Zora Neale Hurston.

Liveright Publishing Corporation: *There Is Confusion* by Jessie Fauset; *Cane* by Jean Toomer; *Tropic Death* by Eric Walrond.

The Macmillan Company: *American Fiction 1920-1940* by Joseph W. Beach; *Drums at Dusk* by Arna Bontemps; *A Short History of the American Negro* and *A Social History of the American Negro,* both by Benjamin G. Brawley; *Intellectual America: Ideas on the March* by Oscar Cargill and *The Social Revolt 1888-1914,* edited by Oscar Cargill; *The American Novel 1789-1939* by Carl Van Doren.

The Nation: *The Nation.* Opportunity: *Opportunity.* William Pickens: *The Vengeance of the Gods and Three Other Stories of the Real American Color Line* by William Pickens. The Saturday Review of Literature: *The Saturday Review of Literature.* George S. Schuyler: *Slaves Today* by George S. Schuyler.

Charles Scribner's Sons: *The Liberation of American Literature* by V. F. Calverton; *The Negro: The Southerner's Problem, The Old South,* and *Red Rock,* all by Thomas Nelson Page.

Simon and Schuster: *Breaking into Print,* edited by Elmer Adler.

The Viking Press: *Brown America* by Edwin R. Embree; *American Stuff* by Federal Writers' Project; *Along This Way* by James Weldon Johnson.

# Contents

# NEGRO VOICES IN AMERICAN FICTION

CHAPTER I

# Backgrounds of Negro Fiction

## I. *RECONSTRUCTION & DISFRANCHISEMENT*

AT THE CLOSE of the Civil War the United States was confronted with one of the most perplexing problems of its history. The death knell had been sounded for the Southern agricultural regime, and an entire social and economic system was in ruins. Not only were the states of the Confederacy to be restored to their former places in the Union, but radical readjustment and reorganization had to be accomplished in the lives of the inhabitants of the South. "Here undoubtedly," as Benjamin Brawley has observed, "was a difficult situation—one calling for the highest quality of statesmanship, and of sportsmanship on the part of the vanquished."[1]

The aftermath of the Civil War left the Southern aristocracy bitter and poverty-stricken. In numerous instances Confederate soldiers returned home to find their women and children sick and undernourished, their dwellings devastated or plundered, their livestock reduced or confiscated, their slaves released from further obligation as bondmen, their currency and investments rendered worthless and unnegotiable, and their relatives and friends maimed or killed during the conflict. Approximately four million slaves had been manumitted by a stroke of the Presidential pen, many cities had been shelled and burned, transportation facilities had been put out of commission, and considerable private property had been seized by Federal authorities.[2] Further aggravating the former slaveholders were the activities of "carpetbaggers" and "scalawags," the meteoric ascendance of Negroes and poor whites, and the passing of political power and national leadership to the farmers and industrialists of the North.

The plight of the freedmen was not much better than that of their former masters. Though liberated by the Thirteenth Amendment, accorded citizenship by the Fourteenth, and protected in the right to vote by the Fifteenth, the ex-bondmen were both bewildered and alienated by the circumstances of their new status in society. Like the dispossessed plantation owners, they were living in a land whose social and economic foundations had been wrecked. In a move to educate the freedmen and to prepare them for citizenship, Northern philanthropists and missionary agencies sent teachers into the South and established schools for their training. "This philanthropic scheme," as Woodson has noted, "presupposed that education in the classical field was the urgent need of Negroes, in that it was essential to a proper understanding of the problems of government, and that when this was supplied, the masses thus enlightened would have an advantage by which they could triumph over all opposition."[3] In a further effort to protect the Negro and bring order out of chaos, the government established the Freedmen's Bureau, which, as DuBois states, "set going a system of free labor, established a beginning of peasant proprietorship, secured the recognition of black freedmen before courts of law, and founded the free common school in the South."[4]

The white South, however, resented the intrusion of Northern missionaries and regarded any legislation in behalf of the emancipated Negro as an additional dose of humiliation. Especially disliked by the ex-landholders was the widespread participation of former slaves in Reconstruction politics and government. This aversion to the Negro in public office grew out of the inveterate belief that he was inherently inferior and therefore unworthy to enjoy the full measure of citizenship. Coupled with this prejudice was the fear that political equality would lead to social equality, which would involve intermarriage, and to economic equality, which would abolish wage differentials. As a result of this attitude toward the native capacity of the Negro and his newly acquired power, a widening gulf grew between the two races, and the majority of Southern whites sought ways and means of divesting the freedmen of political influence and of superimposing a new type of domination in the South. In this action the former landlords were joined by the poor whites, who likewise opposed racial equality and resented Negroes attending school, holding office, and making laws.[5]

The failure of the Freedmen's Bureau to establish good will between whites and blacks, caused largely by inefficient local administration and blundering Federal supervision, accelerated the anti-Negro campaign of Southerners who were determined to keep the former slave states "a white man's country." One of the first steps taken was the organization in 1865 of the Ku Klux Klan, a group of white men sworn to keep the Negro servile and to maintain racial absolutism in the South. Preying upon the ignorance and superstition of former bondmen, the Klan intimidated Negroes at the polls and terrorized them with marauding, mutilation, and lynching. Though sometimes affording temporary relief, Congressional measures to protect the Negro citizen and officeholder generally added fuel to the fire and sometimes resulted in interracial clashes. The South finally succeeded, however, in diminishing the political strength of the Negro and in gaining control of courts and legislative bodies. With severe penalties for vagrancy instituted, black men often found themselves convicted for minor offenses and leased to farmers and business men.[6] Furthermore, through the pressure of legislation and group mores, segregation was effected in transportation facilities as well as in schools and other public establishments.[7]

The success of the South in curtailing the rights of Negro citizens was largely due to the changed attitude of the victorious North. Though spasmodic efforts were made through Congressional action to adjust unbalanced conditions in the former slave states, the North did not work so industriously to reconstruct the

South as it did to overthrow the plantation economics of that section. "After the Civil War was over," as Calverton says, "the social energy invested in the Abolitionist movement dissipated itself into ineffectual channels."[8] During the post-bellum period, moreover, as Cargill observes, the North was more interested in money than in spiritual elevation:

> The Civil War, waged undeniably on the strength of the passionate idealism of the combatants, had outmoded idealism and had taught, as wars always do, the cash value of opportunism. Romantic faith, as well as Romantic phraseology, died on the battlefield.[9]

The North, then, increasingly occupied itself with industrial and commercial enterprises, even courting the favor of the South if such were financially expedient. The withdrawal of Federal troops by President Rutherford B. Hayes thus left the handling of the Negro problem largely in the control of the petty bourgeoisie, a new ruling class closely affiliated with Northern capitalism.[10] In a memorable address before the New England Society of New York in 1886 Henry W. Grady, a Georgian speaking on "The New South," emphasized his section's desire for a free rein in making racial adjustments:

> To liberty and enfranchisement is as far as the law can carry the Negro. The rest must be left to conscience and common sense. It must be left to those among whom his lot is cast, with whom he is indissolubly connected, and whose prosperity depends upon their possessing his intelligent sympathy and confidence.[11]

Grady's speech received extensive publicity as well as popular favor; and thereafter the North, waxing increasingly indifferent to the status of the freedmen, gradually yielded concessions which gave the South virtually unchecked prerogative in contriving further oppressive policies and statutes which Grady would hardly have condoned.

Considering vigorous intervention of the North in behalf of the Negro as only a remote possibility, the dominant Southern middle class proceeded not only to convert freedmen into wage slaves but also to add disfranchisement to earlier repressive measures applied to Negroes. In 1890 Mississippi denied suffrage to the majority of her Negro citizens by establishing literacy and the poll tax as prerequisites for casting the ballot.[12] South Carolina took similar steps in 1895. Three years later Louisiana devised the widely adopted "grandfather clause," an enactment which limited the ballot to the descendants of citizens who had exercised suffrage in ante-bellum times. Painstakingly wording their restrictive provisions so as to evade flagrant violation of the Fifteenth Amendment, North Carolina in 1890, Virginia and Alabama in 1901, Georgia in 1907, and Oklahoma in 1910 virtually excluded Negroes from the electorate. Though somewhat varying in details, the disfranchising clauses of the several states were similar in that they deprived Negroes of the ballot, admitted white citizens to suffrage, and delegated administrative duties to agencies that were fully aware of the purposes of the legislation.

## II. *THE PLANTATION TRADITION AND RACIALISM*

Running parallel to the suppression and disfranchisement of the Negro were the literary misrepresentations of the black man by the plantation school of Thomas Nelson Page and the racist cult of Thomas Dixon. Though the plantation motif received emphasis before the Civil War in the work of John Pendleton Kennedy, W. A. Carruthers, John Esten Cooke, James W. Hungerford, William Gilmore Simms, and others of their coterie, it was not until after the conflict that the literary vogue of the so-called "sweetest, purest, and most beautiful civilization" enjoyed its greatest popularity. As Gaines notes:

> We come with 1870 to a new age. There is not a new tradition. This is a new appreciation for the old tradition, there are striking enlargements of it. What makes this age new is a two-fold fact: the surprising

increase in the number of writers who turn to the plantation or some characteristic representation exclusively for the value of the material; and the prevalence among these writers of as romantic an attitude as ever characterized the most rapturous of the early sustainers of the tradition.[13]

Among a group of post-bellum writers including Grace Elizabeth King, Ruth McEnery Stuart, James Lane Allen, Maurice Thompson, Harry Stillwell Edwards, Joel Chandler Harris, Walter Hines Page, and F. Hopkinson Smith, Thomas Nelson Page stood out as the leading portrayer of what E. C. Stedman sentimentally termed "the unspeakable charm that lived and died with the old South." In such volumes as *In Ole Virginia, or Marse Chan and Other Stories* (1887), *The Old South: Essays Social and Political* (1892), and *Social Life in Old Virginia* (1897), Page, adopting a condescending and smiling attitude, creates an appealing plantation scene. On a broad canvas he paints a stately mansion presided over by lovely ladies and gallant gentlemen who wear imported finery, enjoy horse-racing and other gentle diversions, and dispense prodigal hospitality. The attitude of these cavaliers toward their slaves is cordial, kindly, benign, and sometimes devoted. The contented bondmen appear proudly engaged as servants in the big house or as laborers in the fields. Near the quarters are prankish pickaninnies romping gleefully in youthful abandon and black veterans resting comfortably in their declining years. Particularly emphasized is the loyal relationship between the master and the servant, the mistress and the maid, and the Negro mammy and her charges. The slave receives commendatory treatment for showing courage, fortitude, and self-sacrifice in relieving the destitution and distress of the Southern aristocracy during and after the war. In general, however, the Negro is presented as a simple, contented, comic, credulous, picturesque, and sometimes philosophical character, gifted in singing, dancing, tale-telling, and reuniting estranged white lovers. Such, then, is the picture of the Southern plantation provided by Page, of whom Gaines says, in comparing him with Harris:

The Virginian is, however, far more passionate in the maintenance of a hypothesis of departed glory, paints in more glowing colors, is uniformly more idealistic, descends less frequently—if ever—from the heights of romantic vision; in short, he expresses the supreme glorification of the old regime, he 'wrote the epitaph of a civilization.'[14]

Despite obvious tricks of literary endearment, the sentimental plantation vogue sponsored by Page and his associates attracted an extensive reading public, including a large number of reconciled and kindly disposed Northerners, and literally submerged the limited pro-Negro literature of the time. "Abolitionism," as Gaines notes, "was swept from the field; it was more than routed, it was tortured, scalped, 'mopped up.' "[15] During Reconstruction the plantation tradition gained as signal a victory in the literary wars as did *Uncle Tom's Cabin* in the ante-bellum period.

Page, however, was more than the retrospective romancer of a vanished civilization; he was also the partisan defender of the patriarchal South. In the latter capacity he helped to bring about disfranchisement and other restrictions applied to Negroes, who were portrayed as maladjusted or dangerous after emancipation. "How Andrew Carried the Precinct," a short story which appears in *Pastime Stories* (1894), presents a mulatto politician who would have won an election over a white man if the latter's black servant had not intervened. *Red Rock* (1898), a novel, berates scalawags, carpetbaggers, Negro politicians, and Northern missionaries and idealizes Southern blue-bloods for nobility in adversity as well as in prosperity. In *Red Rock* Moses, a mixed-blood character depicted as the incarnation of the black peril, is eventually lynched after several crimes "sufficiently heinous to entitle him to be classed as one of the greatest scoundrels in the world." In "The Negro Question," an essay in *The Old South* (1892), Page marshals references in an effort to demonstrate that the black man, being unprogressive as well as mentally and socially inferior, is unprepared to assume the unlimited enjoyment of citizenship:

These examples cited, if they establish anything, establish the fact that the Negro race does not possess, in any development which he has yet attained, the elements of character, the essential qualifications to conduct a government, even for himself, and that if the reins of government be intrusted to his unaided hands, he will fling reason to the winds and drive to ruin.

However, because he was convinced that schooling made freedmen more useful members of society, Page advocated elementary education for all Negroes and higher training for those who proved themselves worthy.[16] He was particularly fond of Booker T. Washington, to whom he refers as "one who is possibly esteemed at the South the wisest and sanest man of color in the country, and who has, perhaps, done more than any other to carry out the ideas that the Southern well-wishers of his race believe to be the soundest and most promising of good results."[17] The Negro in a superior position, however, was more than Page could tolerate:

> We have educated him; we have aided him; we have sustained him in all right directions. We are ready to continue our aid; but we will not be dominated by him. When we shall be, it is our settled conviction that we shall deserve the degradation to which we have sunk.[18]

Though demanding Anglo-Saxon supremacy, Page at least looked with favor upon Negroes like Booker T. Washington, felt that the two races could thrive in a system of social separation, and never attempted to excuse the Invisible Empire of responsibility for lawlessness. On the other hand, in the writings of Thomas Dixon and his school we have uncompromising Negrophobia and unrivaled vituperation. Dixon expressed his racial creed in two novels which he describes as follows:

> *The Leopard's Spots* was the statement in historical outline of the conditions from the enfranchisement of the Negro to his disfranchisement.
>
> *The Clansman* develops the true story of the "Ku Klux Klan Conspiracy," which overturned the Reconstruction régime.[19]

As a matter of fact, neither of the two works is a realistic rendering of history. Betraying incendiary sensationalism by such chapter titles as "A Thousand-Legged Beast" and "The Black Peril," *The Leopard's Spots: A Romance of the White Man's Burden 1865–1900* (1902), perhaps the most bigoted of American novels, is mainly concerned with complimenting the slaveholding aristocracy; attacking carpetbaggers, scalawags, the Freedmen's Bureau, Northern missionaries, and educated Negroes; ridiculing Yankees who do not practise racial theories in actual social situations; attempting to establish the Negro as a degenerate, inferior, irresponsible, and bestial creature "transformed by the exigency of war from a chattel to be bought and sold into a possible beast to be feared and guarded"; decrying miscegenation as a process that would destroy through Africanization the racial integrity of the Anglo-Saxon; and extolling the Invisible Empire as the defender of the weak, the expeller of thieves and parasites, the preserver of Aryan culture, and "the old answer of organized manhood to organized crime." The main target of Dixon's attack in *The Leopard's Spots* is George Harris, son of Eliza Harris of *Uncle Tom's Cabin,* who, after being educated at Harvard by a Northern philanthropist and given a Custom House clerkship in Boston by an American Senator, insults the lawmaker by asking permission to pay court to his daughter. The eulogy of the Invisible Empire is more elaborately developed in *The Clansman: An Historical Romance of the Ku Klux Klan* (1905), a work dedicated to the author's uncle, a former Grand Titan of the hooded order, and converted in 1916 by D. W. Griffith into *The Birth of a Nation,* one of the most inflammatory box-office attractions in the history of the American motion picture industry. *The Clansman* follows *The Leopard's Spots* in vilifying Yankees and Negroes as well as in assailing the commingling of blood. In the novel Lydia Brown and Silas Lynch represent the threat of the mulatto concubine and of the politician, respectively, to national welfare.

## III. *THE TRAGIC MULATTO*[20]

In the fiction of Thomas Nelson Page and Thomas Dixon the mixed-blood is portrayed as the embodiment of the worst qualities of both races and hence as a menace to the dominant group. To these propagandists the mulatto woman is the debaser of the white aristocrat, while the mulatto man is the besmircher of white virginity and the dangerous intruder in the political scene. On the contrary, other writers in varying degrees were sometimes sympathetic toward the Negro-white hybrid because of his possession of Caucasian blood, which they often considered as a factor that automatically made this character the superior of the darker Negro and therefore a more pitiable individual. Hence the mulatto, thwarted in social progress because of Negro blood, became one of the popular characters of American fiction; and it was in portrayals of this personage that white writers made their most significant departures from the plantation tradition.

A native of New Orleans and a Confederate veteran, George W. Cable, for example, was an understanding novelist of a restricted phase of racial life. The first major Southern writer of fiction to undertake an impartial representation of Negro experience, he was particularly fascinated, not by the freedmen of Reconstruction, but by the exotic *gens de couleur* of Louisiana during the early 1800's. In the lives of these persons of mixed blood, as *Old Creole Days* (1879) and *The Grandissimes* (1880) illustrate, Cable discovered distinctive subjects for local color and romance. A collection of short stories, *Old Creole Days* contains two narratives which are noteworthy for their interpretation of problems of the color line. The first is " 'Tite Poulette," in which quadroon Madame John, former mistress of a Louisiana gentleman, pretends that her beautiful near-white daughter, 'Tite Poulette, is the child of Spaniards in order that the girl may marry a Dutchman. A dramatic situation develops in the conflict between the worldly-wise mother, who is resolved that her daughter shall not bear the burden of color, and self-sacrificing 'Tite Poulette, who is not inclined to wed a white man because of customs and laws forbidding intermarriage. The second is "Madame Delphine," in which a mother again conceals the African blood of her daughter so that the girl may wed a white suitor. When the relatives of the man threaten to reveal his criminal record as a pirate if he will not renounce his fiancée, the girl resignedly grieves but later gains happiness when Madame Delphine offers affidavits to disprove her motherhood and thus to safeguard her daughter's marriage to a white man. Madame Delphine is doubtless the most awe-inspiring mulatto character in the American short story. *The Grandissimes,* a novel, provides further sympathetic treatment of mixed-bloods in old Louisiana. A grandee, Numa Grandissime, has two sons, the older illegitimate and colored and the younger legitimate and white, each bearing the name Honoré. Numa educates both and, unwilling to discriminate against the former, bequeaths the larger share of his property to the elder son. Although the brothers get along well together as business operators in New Orleans, Honoré, free man of color, miserable because of his racial status and his unsuccessful wooing of Palmyre, an irresistible mulatto beauty, eventually ends has own life. Palmyre, a cunning and seductive woman, is as significant a mulatto personage in the American novel as is Madame Delphine in the American short story. Unlike the practitioners of racialism and the plantation tradition, Cable unblinkingly faced the facts of race and caste in the Southern setting which he described.

Like Cable, Mark Twain (Samuel Langhorne Clemens) was of Southern extraction, served in the Confederate Army, spent much of his life in the North, and showed better knowledge of the South than did the writers of the plantation school. Twain veered sharply from the chivalric tradition in the handling of the Roxana legend in *The Tragedy of Pudd'nhead Wilson* (1894). In this novel Roxana, who is indistinguishable from white, becomes the mother of a boy, Valet de Chambre, by a white aristocrat on the same day that her mistress gives birth to a son, Thomas à Becket Driscoll. In an effort to save her child from bondage Roxy exchanges the infants, who are almost identical. This deception results in the white boy succumbing to the degrading influence of slavery, Roxy's son growing up as a dissolute and criminal aristocrat, and Roxy herself being sold down the river by her own offspring. The Roxana narrative furnishes not only a penetrating study of the influence of heredity and environment in determining the development of a person but also a telling picture of the limitations of bondage and the circumscriptions of caste in the South.

Several Southern short-story writers followed Cable in the treatment of Louisiana mixed-bloods, but wrote principally of such characters in the post-bellum period and frequently showed a penchant for racial bias. Grace Elizabeth King, for example, wrote stories which dramatize the position of the New Orleans mulatto. In "Monsieur Motte" quadroon Marcélite Gaulois, pretending to receive financial assistance from her former master, through industry and self-sacrifice rears and educates a young white girl to whom she is devoted. "Madrilène" illustrates how an elderly voodooist frustrates the plan of an octoroon procuress to convert a white girl into a prostitute. In "The Little Convent Girl" a twelve-year-old girl drowns herself upon discovering that her mother has Negro blood. In certain tales of *Bayou Folk* (1894) Kate Chopin gives more convincing transcripts of Louisiana life. "Désirée's Baby" introduces Armand Aubigny, a proud Creole who renounces his wife when their colored child is born but later discovers that the infant's African blood came from his own mother. In "La Belle Zoraïde" an exotic slave goes insane after bearing a child for a black lover who is disapproved as a suitable husband by her white mistress.

Outside the Louisiana setting the mulatto was not a popular character in Southern short stories, and hence we find few instances of the use of this type elsewhere in the region. In "Where's Duncan?" Joel Chandler Harris, the creator of Uncle Remus and usually a spokesman for Southern traditions, sets forth a grim and bloody tale of Georgia life. Infuriated at being sold to a trader, Featherstone, a mulatto slave, returns to incite his mother to slay his white father. At the end of the story the vengeful son and his parents are destroyed in a raging fire. "The Case of Mary Ellen," by the same author, presents a near-white girl, the offspring of the usual union of an aristocrat and a mulatto slave woman, who becomes a close friend of her master's daughter, receives an education in New England, and later becomes an artist of international repute. Matt Crim's "Was It an Exceptional Case?" treats a light-skinned woman who, upon learning of her mother's Negro blood, rejects her Northern fiancé and subsequently dies in misery. In "Ishmael" Richard Malcolm Johnston delineates an affluent, refined near-white who is the product of the conventional patrician-slave relationship.

Turning to the North, we find that Abolitionist fervor subsided after the Civil War and that in the post-bellum fiction of this section there was only slight use of tragic mulatto types employed frequently in antislavery novels published prior to 1865. The three most important Northern novelists of the late nineteenth century to treat mulatto characters were Rebecca H. Davis, Albion W. Tourgée, and William Dean Howells. In *Waiting for the Verdict* (1867) Mrs. Davis introduces a near-white who gains status in the majority group before being exposed as the possessor of Negro blood. In several tractlike novels Tourgée, an Ohio-born Union officer who settled in North Carolina after the war, was a caustic critic of the Southern gentleman and a militant champion of Negro rights. In *A Royal Gentleman* (1881), which appeared in 1874 as *'Toinette,* Tourgée illustrates, through the amours of Arthur Lovett and Geoffrey Hunter, the anguish and tragedy which two blue-bloods experience as a result of their entanglements with beautiful mulatto women. Lovett's passion is directed toward Belle, his sister's privileged maid; while Hunter becomes involved with 'Toinette, one of the illegitimate children of Lovett and Belle. Tourgée's attitude toward 'Toinette's passing in order to seek her white lover is uncensuring. After describing the post-bellum South in the semi-autobiographical *A Fool's Errand* (1879) and the well-documented *Bricks without Straw* (1880), both of which set forth the terrorism of the Ku Klux Klan and Southern hostility to Yankees and progressive Negroes, Tourgée probed the reaction of representative mulattoes to their racial position in *Pactolus Prime* (1890). It is a far cry from Tourgée's turbulent reform novels to William Dean Howells' *An Imperative Duty* (1892). In this book Rhoda Aldgate, the daughter of a white physician and an octoroon woman, is reared in the North and kept uninformed of her Negro blood by her father's sister, Mrs. Meredith. When Rhoda promises to wed a white minister, Mrs. Meredith feels morally obligated to disclose the facts concerning her niece's racial extraction and, disregarding the objections of her physician, Dr. Olney, reveals the secret to the girl. Subsequently Rhoda breaks her engagement, and her aunt commits suicide. Later Dr. Olney, having fallen in love with Rhoda despite her background, weds her and carries her to Rome, where she passes as an Italian but nevertheless suffers mental tortures because she is not white. The author's main purpose is not to crusade for racial reform but to indicate that "Puritan civilization has carried the cult of the personal conscience into mere dutiolatry" and to support this thesis by showing how Rhoda's happiness was sacrificed and Mrs. Meredith's life was lost as a result of the aunt's morbid devotion to duty. A survey of fiction by Northern writers during the Reconstruction period reveals that Tourgée was the only major Northern white novelist of his time who vigorously campaigned for justice for the Negro.

In brief, although several white writers undertook to portray the Negro realistically in fiction written after the Civil War, their works are chiefly sympathetic approaches to the problems of mulattoes in American society. Unmistakable again and again is the hypothesis that white-Negro hybrids have acumen and attractiveness because of their white ancestry, that they deserve pity because the blood of Caucasian fathers flows in their veins, and that their misery, bitterness, defiance, and ambition are traceable to proud paternal forebears. This color-biased approach to Negro character kept many white writers from painting the whole picture. For example, only few upstanding characterizations are made of the dark-skinned Negro, who also suffers, hates, rebels, and aspires. Liaisons involving colored men and white women—which O'Neill, Waldo Frank, Faulkner, Caldwell, and others treat today—and the experiences of their offspring are glossed over by virtually all these authors. Few bothered to explain or imply that when mulattoes surpass they do so not because of white paternity but because of superior parentage and better opportunities. It thus became chiefly the responsibility of Negro writers of the time to tell the known but neglected truths and to counteract the propaganda of racialism and the plantation tradition.

## IV. *THE WASHINGTON-DUBOIS CONTROVERSY*

During these years of disfranchisement and fictional propaganda, Negro leadership was not idle. In the post-bellum period Frederick Douglass, who had played an important role in the campaign that led to the abolition of slavery, strove aggressively to gain political power and unqualified citizenship for his people. The efforts of militant race leaders, however, met the disapproval of Booker T. Washington, who thought that these agitators were not furnishing the guidance needed to prepare Negroes "for the opportunites and responsibilities of freedom" and that black folk "needed something more than to be reminded of their sufferings and of their political rights; that they needed to do something more than merely to defend themselves."[21] Accordingly, in 1895, a few months after Douglass' death, Washington announced his racial manifesto in a memorable address at the Cotton States Exposition in Atlanta. The main propositions of this speech were, first, that the fates of Negroes and whites of the South are inextricably interlocked; second, that the two races, sympathetically co-operating, should work out their common destiny in the South; third, that Negroes should stress industrial rather than professional education; and, fourth, that black men should not vigorously agitate for social and political equality. The keynote of the address was contained in the following utterance: "In all things that are purely social we can be as separate as the fingers, yet one as the hand in all things essential to mutual progress."[22]

The reception of Washington's speech, which attracted the interest of the majority of the informed citizens of the country, was generous. Washington had provided a declaration of racial policy on which the North and South could agree. The North, preoccupied with commercialism, was tiring of the Negro problem; and the South, determined to disfranchise and segregate the black man, was willing to co-operate with a placable, conciliatory Negro leader not strongly inclined toward political agitation and social equality. In a telegram to *The New York World* on September 19, 1895, Clark Howell, editor of *The Atlanta Constitution,* speaking for the New South, said:

> The speech is a full vindication from the mouth of a representative Negro of the doctrine so eloquently advanced by Grady and those who have agreed with him that it is to the South that the Negro must turn for his best friend, and that his welfare is so closely identified with the progress of the white people of the South, that each race is mutually dependent upon the other, and that the so-called "race problem" must be solved in the development of the natural relations growing out of the association between the whites and blacks of the South.
>
> The question of social equality is eliminated as a factor in the development of the problem. . . .[23]

The stamp of approval was also given to Washington's proposals by President Grover Cleveland, who wrote thus to the Tuskegee principal:

> Your words cannot fail to delight and encourage all who wish well for your race; and if our colored fellow citizens do not from your utterances gather new hope and form new determination to gain every valuable advantage offered them by their citizenship, it will be strange indeed.[24]

Although Washington's Atlanta address gave the North and the South a common ground from which to approach the Negro problem, the speech did not enjoy unanimous acceptance among colored people themselves. It is true that many Negroes, cowed by Southern controls and in some instances still inhibited by a slave psychology, looked with favor upon a racial policy characterized by social separation, economic entrenchment, and political subordination. The majority of educated Negroes, however, took strong exception to Washington's views; and among these dissenters W. E. B. DuBois, then professor of sociology at Atlanta University, was most influential and soon found himself the standard-bearer of the militant faction. Insisting upon suffrage, civic equality, and education according to ability as racial objectives, DuBois called attention to "the triple paradox" of Washington's career:

> 1. He is striving nobly to make Negro artisans business men and property-owners; but it is utterly impossible, under modern competitive methods, for workingmen and property-owners to defend their rights and exist without the right of suffrage.
>
> 2. He insists on thrift and self-respect, but at the same time counsels a silent submission to civic inferiority such as is bound to sap the manhood of any race in the long run.
>
> 3. He advocates common-school and industrial training, and depreciates institutions of higher learning; but neither the Negro common-schools, nor Tuskegee itself, could remain open a day were it not for teachers trained in Negro colleges, or trained by their graduates.[25]

With the organization of *The Boston Guardian* by Monroe Trotter and George Forbes in 1901, the opposition to Washington was augmented. The anti-Washington movement gained additional momentum in 1905 and 1906, when the Niagara Movement was initiated by DuBois with the following platform:

1. Freedom of speech and criticism.
2. Unfettered and unsubsidized press.
3. Manhood suffrage.
4. The abolition of all caste distinctions based simply on race and color.
5. The recognition of the principles of human brotherhood as a practical present creed.
6. The recognition of the highest and best human training as the monopoly of no class or race.
7. A belief in the dignity of labor.
8. United effort to realize these ideals under wise and courageous leadership.[26]

After holding annual meetings at Fort Erie in 1905, at Harper's Ferry in 1906, in Boston in 1907, and in Oberlin in 1908, the Niagara Movement merged with the National Association for the Advancement of Colored People, which was started in 1909 and incorporated two years later.

The National Association for the Advancement of Colored People continued to oppose the compromises of Booker T. Washington and to demand the full participation of the Negro in American democracy. In November, 1910, its official organ, *The Crisis,* appeared, with DuBois as editor, and announced the following platform:

The object of this publication is to set forth those facts and arguments which show the danger of race prejudice, particularly as manifested today toward colored people. It takes its name from the fact that the editors believe that this is a critical time in the history of the advancement of men. Catholicity and tolerance, reason and forbearance can today make the world-old dream of human brotherhood approach realization; while bigotry and prejudice, emphasized race consciousness and force can repeat the awful history of the contact of nations and groups in the past. We strive for this higher and broader vision of Peace and Good Will.

The policy of *The Crisis* will be simple and well-defined:

It will first and foremost be a newspaper: it will record important happenings and movements in the world which bear on the great problem of inter-racial relations, and especially those which affect the Negro-American.

Secondly, it will be a review of opinion and literature, recording briefly books, articles, and important expressions of opinion in the white and colored press on the race problem.

Thirdly, it will publish a few short articles.

Finally, its editorial page will stand for the rights of men, irrespective of color or race, for the highest ideals of American democracy, and for reasonable but earnest and persistent attempt to gain these rights and realize these ideals. The magazine will be the organ of no clique or party and will avoid personal rancor of all sorts. In the absence of proof to the contrary it will assume honesty of purpose on the part of all men, North and South, white and black.[27]

By 1918 *The Crisis* had reached a paid monthly circulation in excess of a hundred thousand copies, and DuBois later made the following evaluation of the accomplishments of this periodical and of its sponsoring agency:

With this organ of propaganda and defense we were able to organize one of the most effective assaults of liberalism upon reaction that the modern world has seen. We secured extraordinary helpers; great lawyers like Moorfield Storey and Louis Marshall; earnest liberals like Villard, Milholland, John Haynes Holmes, Mary Ovington, Jane Addams, the Spingarns, Charles Edward Russell, and William English. We gained a series of court victories before the highest courts of the land which perhaps have never been equalled, beginning with the overthrow of the vicious Grandfather Clauses in 1915 and the breaking of the backbone of segregation in 1917. Above all we could, through *The Crisis* and our officers, our secretaries and friends, place consistently and continuously before the country a clear-cut statement of the legitimate aims of the American Negro and the facts concerning his condition. We organized his political power and made it felt and we started a campaign against lynching and mob law which was the most effective ever organized and at long last seemed to bring the end of the evil in sight.[28]

During the twenty years between his Atlanta speech of 1895 and his death in 1915 Booker T. Washington, making numerous lectures and writing several volumes including the autobiographical *Up from Slavery* (1901), was a formidable opponent for Negro intellectuals who championed equalitarianism. At Tuskegee Institute he attained national prestige by developing educational practices that antedated John Dewey's experiments and helped to produce a revolution in pedagogical procedures. Backed by whites of the North and South, he used his personal popularity to influence the appointment of Negroes to political and educational positions. Defending his social concepts, he argued that the self-styled "Talented Tenth" of his people "understand theories, but they do not understand things," that they "know books, but they do not know men," that they are "ignorant in regard to the actual needs of the masses of the coloured people in the South today," and that such crusaders are therefore merely "fighting windmills."[29] The outbreak of the World War in 1914 and the death of Washington in the following year, however, not only spelled the doom of conciliation and submissiveness as a racial policy, but also gave the militant Negro intellectuals an advantage which they have not since relinquished.

CHAPTER 2

# Negro Fiction to World War I

AS THE foregoing chapter indicates, the defeat of the Confederacy neither solved the race problem nor gave the Negro security as a citizen. After the war, reconciliation replaced Abolitionist fervor in the North; and in the South the new leadership proceeded to divest the Negro of gains made during the conflict and Reconstruction. The Ku Klux Klan organized to intimidate Negroes and hold them in a subordinate position. Courts and legislative bodies reverted to Southern control. Disfranchising legislation handicapped black men in the exercise of the ballot. The South took steps to insure the social separation of the races and to control employment through discriminatory measures that permeated the economy of the entire section.

The treatment of the Negro in literature was similar to his treatment in life. The portrayers of the tragic mulatto handled this character with more sympathy than they accorded the black Negro because of their self-adulatory assumption that the mixed-blood demonstrates upstanding character and deserves commiseration because of his possession of Anglo-Saxon blood. Viewing the feudal South in sentimental retrospect, the plantation school of Thomas Nelson Page won a literary triumph rivaling that of the antislavery writers of the 1850's by submitting the thesis that the Negro is best adjusted as a slave and is inherently incompetent to undertake the responsibilities of citizenship. Going a step further, the white-supremacy cult of Thomas Dixon propagated doctrines of unadulterated Negrophobia and sponsored the removal of the colored population from contact with the majority group. The following account of the literary treatment and national status of the Negro near the turn of the century is given by Charles W. Chesnutt, one of the leading colored authors of the period:

> Thomas Dixon was writing the Negro down industriously and with popular success. Thomas Nelson Page was disguising the harshness of slavery under the mask of sentiment. The trend of public sentiment at the moment was distinctly away from the Negro. He had not developed any real political or business standing; socially he was outcast. His musical and stage successes were still for the most part unmade, and on the whole he was a small frog in a large pond, and there was a feeling of pessimism in regard to his future.[1]

Negro fictionists reacted in various ways to American caste as expressed in letters and in life. Some, choosing in certain cases to give little or no attention to controversial racial issues, wrote narratives about white people or plantation tales about Negroes. Others, the majority, undertook to defend the black man and to make a case for social justice. Paul Laurence Dunbar dealt entirely with white characters in three novels—*The Uncalled* (1898), *The Love of Landry* (1900), and *The Fanatics* (1901)—as well as in "Ohio Pastorals," a series of five short stories which appeared in *Lippincott's Monthly Magazine* beginning in August, 1901, and concluding in December of the same year. The titles of these stories are "The Mortification of the Flesh," "The Independence of Silas Bollender," "The White Counterpane," "The Minority Committee," and "The Visiting of Mother Danbury." Also a portrayal of white life is Chesnutt's superbly constructed tale, "Baxter's Procrustes," which appeared in *The Atlantic Monthly* for June, 1904. Furthermore, both Dunbar and Chesnutt produced short stories which conformed, except for minor alterations and innovations, to the main outlines of the plantation tradition. Frankly admitting indebtedness to Joel Chandler Harris, Chesnutt wrote *The Conjure Woman* (1899), a collection of tales adopting the usual plantation motif but showing cruelty and oppression as occasional practices in slave life. After writing *The Conjure Woman* Chesnutt turned from the plantation tradition, but Dunbar imitated the idyllic romancing of Page and Harris in four books of short stories—*Folks from Dixie* (1898), *The Strength of Gideon* (1900), *In Old Plantation Days* (1903), and *The Heart of Happy Hollow* (1904). Though a few of Dunbar's short stories attempt a realistic rendition of Negro life, the Harris-Page formulas and implications are usually adopted. Others who chose to avoid American racial issues in their fiction were Dunbar's wife, now known as Mrs. Alice Dunbar-Nelson, who as Alice Moore wrote *Violets and Other Tales* (1895) and as Alice Dunbar produced *The Goodness of St. Rocque and Other Stories* (1899), the latter book inspired by the work of Cable and concerned principally with Creole life in the New Orleans area; John S. Durham, writer of "Diane, Priestess of Haiti," a romance published in *Lippincott's Monthly Magazine* for April, 1902; and George W. Ellis, author of *The Leopard's Claw* (1917), an account of the adventures of British aristocrats in England and West Africa just before World War I.[2]

While a few Negro writers in certain instances chose to neglect the realities of race relations in order to treat the lives of white people or the experiences of black folk on the legendary Southern plantation, the majority attempted to idealize the Negro, plead his cause, and remove the impediments before him. Stirred by problems of Reconstruction and memories of slavery as well as by the literary libels of Page and Dixon, most Negro authors answered propaganda with counterpropaganda. The post-bellum period was not the time of the first experience of Negro writers in the nation's literary wars over the status of the black man. During the 1850's the ranks of antislavery campaigners included at least four Negroes who published novels or short stories—namely, William Wells Brown, Frank J. Webb,[3] Martin Delany, and Frances E. W. Harper—and these authors' works of fiction, which generally exhibit the methods and materials of Abolitionist propaganda, will be briefly described before further attention is given to their successors who were active after the Civil War.

Brown's *Clotel, or The President's Daughter: A Narrative of*

*Slave Life in the United States* (1853), the first novel by an American Negro, was published in London and is similar to much other antislavery fiction in its depiction of the hard lot of near-whites having only a slight admixture of African blood. Capitalizing upon rumors concerning Thomas Jefferson's interracial amours and mulatto progeny,[4] the novel presents Currer, a colored woman of Richmond, as the President's discarded mistress and the mother of his two talented children, Clotel and Althesa. The body of the narrative recounts the unhappy experiences of Currer and her daughters after the death of their benevolent owner. The most dramatic and ironical scene in the book is Clotel's escape from slave-chasers by hurling herself into the Potomac River "within plain sight of the President's house and the Capitol of the Union." In American editions of the novel which appeared in 1864 and 1867—the former as *Clotelle: A Tale of the Southern States* and the latter as *Clotelle, or The Colored Heroine: A Tale of the Southern States*—there are many revisions, including the substitution of an anonymous Senator for Jefferson. The hastily moving plot of the 1867 edition begins with the sale into slavery of Agnes, a mulatto whose father was a Senator, and Isabella and Marion, her daughters by a Southern scion. Henry Linwood, a Richmond aristocrat, purchases Isabella, who subsequently becomes his mistress and the mother of his child Clotelle. Later Linwood's mother-in-law, upon discovering his extra-marital affair, separates Isabella and Clotelle and returns them to bondage. Trapped by slave hunters during an attempt to join her daughter, Isabella chooses suicide in the Potomac rather than surrender. Subsequently a French officer liberates Clotelle and carries her as his wife to India, where he is killed in military service. Afterwards Clotelle marries Jerome, her slavery-time black lover whom she meets in Europe. At the outbreak of the Civil War the couple return to the United States, where Jerome meets a soldier's death in the Union Army and Clotelle acts as a nurse and secret agent. At the end of the conflict Clotelle starts a school for freedmen in

Mississippi. The lives of Agnes and Marion end more tragically, the former dying in Natchez before her manumission and the latter reverting to bondage along with her two daughters after her white husband passes away. In this novel the author's primary concern is to accumulate pity-evoking hardships for his heroines, the "impassioned and voluptuous daughters of the two races,—the unlawful product of the crime of human bondage." It should be noted that Marion is perhaps the first colored character in American fiction to become the legal wife of a white citizen in this country. Brown's second novel, *Miralda, or The Beautiful Octoroon* (c. 1855), to which references are made in mid-century commentaries, has not been found by modern scholars; but the title suggests that the volume, if actually written, is another account of the trials of a near-white woman of remarkable loveliness.

The theme of the tragic mulatto is repeated in Webb's *The Garies and Their Friends* (1857), which was published in London. The second edition included an introduction by Mrs. Stowe, which had failed to arrive in time for the first printing, as well as a dedication to Lady Noel Gordon. Treating the aftermath of interbreeding in the urban North, the novel sets forths the misfortunes undergone by a mixed couple and their offspring. Mr. Garie, an affluent white gentleman, marries his mulatto mistress and provides a family home in Philadelphia. Their happiness is short-lived, however, for the discovery of Mrs. Garie's Negro ancestry and the labeling of Mr. Garie as an Abolitionist lead precipitously to mob violence during which the husband is murdered and the wife dies of premature childbirth. Thereafter the curse of color plagues the Garie children. In contradistinction to the Garies, a humble dark-skinned family struggles to a degree of mediocre security and contentment. *The Garies and Their Friends* is unlike most other early fiction by Negroes in that it analyzes the effects of race prejudice above the Mason-Dixon line.

Delany's fragmentary "Blake, or The Huts of America," which appeared serially in seven installments in *The Anglo-African*

*Magazine* in 1859, differs from *Clotelle* and *The Garies and Their Friends* through its idealization of black characters and its sympathetic interpretation of the Negro masses of the South. The hero, Henry Holland, slave of Colonel Stephen Franks of Natchez, is described as follows:

> Henry was black—a pure negro—handsome, manly but intelligent, in size comparing well with his master, but neither so fleshly nor heavy built in person. A man of good literary attainments—unknown to Colonel Franks, though he was aware he could read and write—having been educated in the West Indies, and decoyed away when young. His affection for wife and child was not excelled by Colonel Franks for his. He was bold, determined and courageous, but always mild, gentle and courteous, though impulsive when an occasion demanded his opposition.

Minor characters extolled in the book include Ailcey, "a handsome black girl, graceful and intelligent," who is "true to her mistress and her honor," and Sampson, "a black, tall, stoutly built, and manly, possessing much general intelligence, and a good looking person." Of the same complexion as Sampson are his wife, "a neat, intelligent, handsome little woman," and his "five pretty children." In New Orleans during Mardi Gras festivities the black beauty is hailed as the equal of other lovely women: "Here might be seen the fashionable lady of French or American extraction, and there the handsome, and frequently beautiful maiden of African origin, mulatto, quadroon, or sterling black. . . ." The novel is mainly an account of the adventures and activities of Henry as a slave insurrectionist. After Colonel Franks sells Maggie, Henry's wife, who had been promised freedom, Henry vows that he will "never again serve any white man living!" Becoming a runaway, he travels through Mississippi, Louisiana, Arkansas, Missouri, and Indiana as the organizer of a general uprising to overthrow slavery. Henry's attitude toward Christianity is not common among Negro characters in American fiction. For example, when counseled by his father-in-law to seek comfort in his faith after the sale of Maggie, Henry replies rebukingly:

"Religion! . . . that's always the cry with black people. Tell me nothing about religion when the very man who hands you the bread at communion, has sold your daughter away from you."

Unlike many other polemicists of his time, Delany discovered good and evil in both races and in both sections. The Northern opportunist and the Negro drunkard appear in the same gallery with the slave trader and the arrogant aristocrat. Delany also voiced the restiveness and resentment of the black masses of the feudal South.

Mrs. Harper's "The Two Offers"—which appeared in *The Anglo-African Magazine* for September and October, 1859, to become perhaps the first published short story by an American Negro—is a tribute to a Northern white woman who, after a friend's unhappy experience as a wife, sacrifices marriage and motherhood in order to participate in the antislavery crusade, "an unpopular cause but not an unrighteous one."

The foregoing paragraphs indicate that post-bellum Negro authors of novels and short stories received a ready-made supply of stock characters and arguments for use in the campaign against repression and the plantation tradition from Brown, Webb, Delany, and Mrs. Harper as well as from more prominent Abolitionist propagandists. In some cases these characters and arguments are closely imitated; but in other instances important revisions and innovations, most of which developed naturally from American life and thought after the Civil War, are introduced. Generally speaking, post-bellum Negro writers of fiction attribute the retardation of their people to slavery and Jim-Crowism and their concomitant evils. Interested in the controversy between compromising and militant Negro leaders, they give their support in most cases to the apostles of the doctrine of challenge. While complimenting individual white citizens for supporting democracy and justice, these authors nevertheless blame the majority group for such oppressive practices as lynching, chain gangs, peonage, disfranchisement, segregation, and the misuse of

Negro women. Wishing to paint a flattering picture of racial life and character so as to elicit justice from whites and provide inspiration for blacks, they skim over instances of Negro poltroonery, poverty, and crime. They generally present decorous, educated, aspiring heroes who surmount the stumbling blocks of race to become successful politicans, lawyers, teachers, journalists, ministers, and physicians. For leading female roles they select beautiful mulattoes, the progeny of Southern gentlemen and slave women. While handling interracial romance with sympathy, they usually state or imply that passing and interbreeding have direful consequences for white and Negro alike. Defying the conventions of the time, a few writers treat love affairs involving white women and colored men. The remaining pages of this chapter will provide a more detailed examination of fiction by Negro authors between the Civil War and World War I.

## Frances Ellen Watkins Harper

Both in the time of its publication and in the nature of its contents Frances Ellen Watkins Harper's *Iola Leroy, or Shadows Uplifted* (1892) is a transitional novel. Appearing eight years before the turn of the century and treating both the ante- and postbellum period, it was the first published novel by an American Negro after the Civil War and the first to treat the era of Reconstruction.

There is little question about the source of *Iola Leroy:* it is almost wholly the product of reading Brown's *Clotelle*. Like *Clotelle, Iola Leroy* is a study of the color line, the principal characters being either white or light enough to pass. Eugene Leroy, a wealthy Creole planter, educates, frees, and marries Marie, a beautiful mulatto. To this couple are born Iola, Harry, and Gracie, who, along with their mother, are disinherited and remanded to slavery after Eugene dies of yellow fever. Later Gracie also succumbs to this disease; and Iola, refusing a marriage proposal from a New England physician because of racial considerations, is sold into bondage in North Carolina. Becoming a nurse in the Union Army at the outbreak of the war, Iola finds Robert Johnson, her long-lost uncle. After Lee's surrender the family reunites in North Carolina, Iola becomes the wife of a successful doctor, and Harry the principal of a thriving school.

In *Iola Leroy* Mrs. Harper—who before the Civil War was the best-known Negro writer of Abolitionist verse as well as the author of "The Two Offers"—helped to establish the precedent of developing well-mannered, educated colored characters to offset the stock figures of the plantation tradition. The novel suggests that near-whites should cast their lot with the minority group. Frankly admitting the propagandistic nature of her work, Mrs. Harper writes in a note on the last page of the book:

> From threads of fact and fiction I have woven a story whose mission will not be in vain if it awaken in the hearts of our countrymen a stronger sense of justice and a more Christlike humanity in behalf of those whom the fortunes of war threw, homeless, ignorant and poor, upon the threshold of a new era. Nor will it be in vain if it inspire the children of those upon whose brows God has poured the chrism of that new era to determine that they will embrace every opportunity, develop every faculty, and use every power God has given them to rise in the scale of character, and to add their quota of good citizenship to the best welfare of the nation.

In the attempt to prepare a novel that would inspire justice among whites and emulation among blacks, Mrs. Harper handles characters and situations with sentiment and idealism rather than with objectivity and realism. Nevertheless, *Iola Leroy* is historically significant as an attempt to counteract stereotypes and as a transitional novel showing the shift from the slavery background to the Reconstruction setting.

## J. McHenry Jones

Like *Iola Leroy,* J. McHenry Jones's *Hearts of Gold* (1896) presents decorous characters and probes the consequences of interbreeding in the Reconstruction period. The action deals with the love affairs of two Negro couples—Clement St. John and Lucile Malone, and Lotus Stone and Regenia Underwood. After establishing *The Events,* a successful newspaper dedicated to the promotion of Negro efforts in politics and literature, St. John marries Lucile. The romance of Stone and Regenia is fraught with troubles. Regenia, adopted by her white maternal grandparents after the death of her ex-slave colored father and high-born white mother, who were legally married, is heiress to the Underwood fortune. Though related by blood to the Underwoods, Dr. Frank Leighton wishes to marry Regenia but hesitates to become a suitor because of her ancestry. He grows madly jealous of Stone, however, and separates the lovers by intercepting their letters. He also dispossesses Regenia by forging Mrs. Underwood's will in his favor and allowing the old lady to die of a curable ailment. Accepting a teaching position, Regenia meets Stone, with whom she becomes reconciled. After several unsuccessful attempts to kill the lovers Leighton himself meets an accidental death. The close of the novel finds the friendly couples enjoying family life and Regenia in possession of her legacy.

In *Hearts of Gold* Jones takes pains to show Negroes to advantage. For example, in describing a reunion of the black Knights Templars, the author writes: "A like number of no other race in the country, their equals financially, could approach these Afro-Americans in gallantry and orderly demeanor." In addition to depicting prepossessing aspects of Negro life and character, Jones calls attention to legal injustice, the convict peonage system, lynching, the exploitation of women, and other disadvantages suffered by the colored population. By no means a commendable book, *Hearts of Gold* is nevertheless noteworthy as perhaps the first American novel to offer as a leading character a person who is the offspring of the lawful marriage of a white woman and a colored man.

PAULINE E. HOPKINS

In *Contending Forces: A Romance Illustrative of Negro Life North and South* (1900) Pauline E. Hopkins, actuated by the desire to do all she could "in an humble way to raise the stigma of degradation from my race," followed Mrs. Harper and J. McHenry Jones in placing the case of worthy but oppressed Negroes before the American bar of justice. The author thus expressed her belief in fiction as an instrument of racial uplift:

> Fiction is of great value to any people as a preserver of manners and customs—religious, political and social. It is a record of growth and development from generation to generation. No one will do this for us; we must ourselves develop the men and women who will faithfully portray the inmost thoughts and feelings of the Negro with all the fire and romance which lie dormant in our history, and, as yet, unrecognized by writers of the Anglo-Saxon race.

The overplotted action of the novel follows the experiences of Charles Montfort, his near-white British wife Grace, who recalls Cora Munro of Cooper's *The Last of the Mohicans,* and their descendants. Moving from Bermuda to a North Carolina plantation with his wife and two sons, Charles and Jesse, Montfort decides to liberate his slaves within twenty-five years and retire with his family to England. Learning of Grace's Negro blood and of Montfort's intention to free the bondmen, Anson Pollock, a white neighbor, takes steps which lead to the murder of Montfort, the suicide of Grace, the hiring of Charles to an English mineralogist, and the reduction of Jesse to slavery. After escaping to New England, Jesse marries mulatto Elizabeth Whitfield and thus joins "that unfortunate race, of whom it is said that a man had better be born dead than to come into the world as part and parcel of it." The rest of the novel traces the love affairs and economic struggles of Jesse's grandchildren, Dora and William Smith.

In an introductory note Mrs. Hopkins, asserting that her novel was based upon experiences described in public addresses as well as upon occurrences with which she was personally familiar, stated that she had "tried to tell an impartial story, leaving it to the reader to draw conclusions." This effort was unsuccessful, however, for *Contending Forces,* like *Iola Leroy* and *Hearts of Gold,* is characterized by the usual exaggerations of its genre. Perhaps the best comment that may be made about the book is that it provides interesting sidelights on the struggles of a middle-class Negro family for education, employment, and social adjustment in post-bellum Boston.

### CHARLES W. CHESNUTT

To move from Mrs. Harper, J. McHenry Jones, and Mrs. Hopkins to Charles W. Chesnutt is to proceed from untalented narrators to a gifted novelist, for Chesnutt is one of the significant figures in American Negro literature. Paving the way for the so-called Renascence of the 1920's, he overcame the double standard by which Negro literary work is sometimes appraised, scaled the barriers placed before colored writers by publishers not too eager to contravene the racial conventions then accepted by the American reading public,[5] counteracted the anti-Negro propaganda of writers like Page and Dixon, and either used or foreshadowed many of the themes treated by race novelists of the present century.

The publication of Chesnutt's folk stories in *The Atlantic Monthly*, representing the first time this periodical had accepted the contributions of a colored American, may be said to mark the coming-of-age of Negro literature in the United States. Before Chesnutt the fiction of Negro authors had been customarily received with the tacit understanding that it was inferior to that of white writers. To Chesnutt, however, the stigma of Negro inferiority was not applied. His emancipation from the hypothetical yoke of racial limitation is clearly indicated in William Dean Howells' criticism of his early short stories:

> It is not from their racial interest that we could first wish to speak of them though that must have a great and very just claim upon the

critic. It is much more simply and directly, as works of art, that they make their appeal, and we must allow the force of this quite independently of the other interest.[6]

Chesnutt's first book, *The Conjure Woman* (1899),[7] a collection of seven folk tales suggestive of the work of Joel Chandler Harris, made its appearance twelve years after "The Goophered Grapevine," the initial story in the volume, was published in *The Atlantic Monthly*. To say that Chesnutt wrote somewhat after the fashion of Harris does not signify that he was a slavish imitator,[8] for *The Conjure Woman* occasionally probes beneath the rosy surface of the conventional plantation setting. The plan of *The Conjure Woman* is simple enough. Uncle Julius, a cunning mulatto ex-slave quite different from the fawning "uncles" portrayed by the school of Thomas Nelson Page, tells seven folk tales to a prosperous white couple who have hired him after settling in North Carolina to engage in grape culture. These tales, showing the weal and woe of the ante-bellum plantation and highlighting the conjuration of old Aunt Peggy, have their raison d'être in Uncle Julius' shrewd maneuvers to promote his own welfare and that of his friends. Remembering his lucrative income from a neglected vineyard, Uncle Julius tries to forestall the purchase and culture of the plot by telling the story of "The Goophered Grapevine." In "Po' Sandy" he prevents the wrecking of the old schoolhouse which his fellow parishioners wished to use as a church. He effects the re-employment of his shiftless grandson in "Mars Jeems's Nightmare." In "The Conjurer's Revenge" he persuades his employer to purchase a worthless horse and obtains a good commission from the seller in the deal. "Sis' Becky's Pickaninny" convinces the wife of his employer that the left hind foot of a rabbit is a sure bringer of good luck. In "The Gray Wolf's Ha'nt" he endeavors to prevent the clearing of a swampy tract where he obtains honey in large quantities. Finally, in "Hot-Foot Hannibal" he brings about the reconciliation and marriage of two young white lovers. In these stories are occasionally unfolded the tragedy and injustice of bondage—the cruelty of master and overseer, the estrangement of husband and wife, the separation of mother and child, and commercial traffic in human life. These themes, which mirror social misery as an integral part of slavery, were handled by Chesnutt with such objectivity and detachment that for a long time many readers were unaware that his work was that of a Negro.[9] As a result of Chesnutt's more comprehensive vision, his stories are more realistic and lifelike:

> They are new and fresh and strong, as life always is, and fable never is; and the stories of *The Conjure Woman* have a wild, indigenous poetry, the creation of sincere and original imagination, which is imparted with tender humourousness and a very artistic reticence.[10]

It is noteworthy that Chesnutt exposed the sordid side of the plantation with the folk tale, the same literary form that was frequently chosen to portray the Negro as a contented bondman and as an inferior being. In *The Conjure Woman* Chesnutt probably wrote seriously for a purpose, although many of his ideas are expressed through situations and in dialect.

In *The Wife of His Youth and Other Stories of the Color Line* (1899) Chesnutt turned to the problems of near-whites and mulattoes, feeling that the more involved lives of Negroes of mixed blood furnish superior subject matter for fiction.[11] The volume achieves artistic unity through the presentation in each story of a serious problem arising from the Negro's position in the American social order. The title story, "The Wife of His Youth," a masterful study of the Blue Vein Society of Groveland (Cleveland), presents a cultured mulatto who respectfully but not enthusiastically acknowledges an ignorant black woman whom he married before the Civil War and who helped him to escape to freedom. This narrative is a pioneering transcript of upper-class Negro circles in the urban North. In "Her Virginia Mammy," a tale which suggests Cable's "Madame Delphine" and " 'Tite Poulette," a colored mother keeps silent concerning the Negro ancestry of her daughter so that the young woman may marry an aristocratic young white Southerner. "The Sheriff's Children" is a tragic story of a vengeful illegitimate mulatto who is fatally wounded by his white half-sister before he can take the life of his father, a North Carolina sheriff. "A Matter of Principle" presents Cicero Clayton, a proud mulatto who preaches the brotherhood of man but who nevertheless exhibits a deep-seated prejudice toward black people. "Cicely's Dream" is the pathetic account of the unfulfilled love of a colored girl for a white Federal soldier who was accepted as a Negro after receiving a head wound which resulted in temporary loss of memory. "The Passing of Grandison" introduces a crafty slave who, by pretending to abhor Abolitionists, succeeds in duping his gullible master and getting himself and his family into Canada. "Uncle Wellington's Wives," one of the early treatments of the marriage of a colored man and a white woman, is the story of an elderly Negro who finds more discomfort with an Irish mate in Cleveland than with a dark spouse in a small North Carolina town. "The Bouquet" reveals the devotion of a little colored girl for her deceased white teacher and shows how ingrained prejudice frustrates childish affection. "The Web of Circumstance" sets forth the consequences of the miscarriage of justice in a small Southern town.

In *The Wife of His Youth and Other Stories of the Color Line* Chesnutt delves into intra-racial as well as inter-racial problems. When this volume was finished, not only had he treated many aspects of slavery and Reconstruction, but he had also used a number of the themes which Negro novelists of the twentieth century were to employ. Outstanding among these were the prevalence of color prejudice within the Negro group, the dangers of passing, the bitterness of the mulatto offspring of interracial mating, the pitfalls of urban life and intermarriage in the North, and the maladministration of justice in small towns of the South. In almost every case the implications are tragic, and at the conclusion of the last story in the volume the author deserts his customary objective method to express a hope for good will among mankind:

> Some time, we are told, when the cycle of years has rolled around, there is to be another golden age, when all men will dwell together in love and harmony, and when peace and righteousness shall prevail for a thousand years. God speed the day, and let not the shining thread of hope become so enmeshed in the web of circumstance that we lose sight of it; but give us here and there, and now and then, some little foretaste of this golden age, that we may the more patiently and hopefully await its coming.

In 1899, the year in which *The Wife of His Youth and Other Stories of the Color Line* was issued, Chesnutt temporarily interrupted his production of fiction to publish a biography of Frederick Douglass. With the turn of the century, however, he reverted to fiction and produced three race-conscious novels which tell of the hard lot of the Negro during the Reconstruction period. Veering from the Southern servant-master literary pattern of Negro-white relationships, he probed the consequences of segregation and miscegenation in a manner distinctly different from that of Thomas Nelson Page and Thomas Dixon. In these works Chesnutt discarded the relaxed plantation scene for that of the tense Southern small town. Characteristic of this setting is a run-down economic condition and a bitter anti-Negro attitude provoked chiefly by the Civil War and the carpetbag regime. Dr. Green, one of the minor characters of Chesnutt's first novel, *The House Behind the Cedars* (1900), expresses the representative white sentiment toward colored citizens of the community:

> "They may exalt our slaves over us temporarily, but they have not broken our spirit, and cannot take away our superiority of blood and breeding. The Negro is an inferior creature; God marked him with the badge of servitude, and has adjusted his intellect to a servile condition. We will not long submit to his domination."

Emphasizing the difficult struggles and the luring temptations of a young mulatto woman fair enough to join the white group, *The House Behind the Cedars,* which Carl Van Vechten calls "perhaps the first authentic study on the subject of passing,"[12] is essentially a study of crossing the color line in a small North Carolina town. Rena Walden, the heroine, leaves her mother, the former concubine of a deceased Southern gentleman, to seek superior advantages in the home of her brother John, who had previously moved into the white race, started the practice of law in South Carolina, and married a refined white woman. In John, who anticipates the hero of James Weldon Johnson's *Autobiography of an Ex-Coloured Man,* and in Rena, who is a prototype of Helga Crane of Nella Larsen's *Quicksand,* Chesnutt shows two typical attitudes of those who pass:

> With [John], the problem that oppressed his sister had been in the main a matter of argument, of self-conviction. Once persuaded that he had certain rights, or ought to have them, by virtue of the laws of nature, in defiance of the customs of mankind, he had promptly sought to enjoy them. This he had been able to do by simply concealing his antecedents and making the most of his opportunities, with no troublesome qualms of conscience whatever. But . . . Rena's emotions, while less easily stirred, touched a deeper note than his, and dwelt upon it with greater intensity.

In her new home Rena and George Tryon, a young aristocratic friend of her brother, soon fall in love and become engaged. Eventually Tryon, learning of Rena's racial background, renounces her hand but subsequently seeks her as a mistress. To escape him, Rena obtains employment in a nearby Negro school, where she is molested by Jeff Wain, a rakehell school principal who is one of Chesnutt's few dissolute mulattoes. In an effort to avoid the advances of Tryon and Wain, Rena tries to flee to her mother but faints on the way. After being rescued by Frank Fowler, a devoted and self-sacrificing black admirer, Rena dies in his arms, saying, ". . . my good friend—my best friend—you loved me best of them all."

*The House Behind the Cedars* represents Chesnutt's initial large-scale attempt to counteract the propaganda of race-baiting writers and to establish the novel of Negro life on a sound esthetic foundation. In this work the passer is not censured, and the attachment between the colored heroine and her white lover is exhibited as decent and respectable. This method of handling such a relationship furnishes sharp contrast to that in Dixon's novels, which consistently depict interracial sexual contacts as sensual and demoralizing.

In his second novel, *The Marrow of Tradition* (1901), Chesnutt studies the plight of the professional Negro in the small Southern town, the tragic outcome of interbreeding, and the struggle of Negro citizens for political power. One of the most interesting characters in the book is Dr. William Miller (the probable prototype of Dr. Kenneth Harper of Walter White's *Fire in the Flint*), a cultured Negro who has studied medicine in leading universities of America and Europe. Though having the opportunity to practice in the North and thereby avoid oppression, Miller turns to Wellington, where he feels that he can render valuable service by founding a hospital and a medical college. Neither radical nor militant in racial issues, he is willing to compromise:

> Miller was something of a philosopher. He had long ago had the conclusion forced upon him that an educated man of his race, in order to live comfortably in the United States, must either be a philosopher or a fool; and since he wished to be happy, and was not exactly a fool, he had cultivated philosophy.

Furthermore, Miller is hopeful for a time of racial understanding, considering the strife of Reconstruction a social evil which will eventually pass away:

> He liked to believe that the race antagonism which hampered his progress and that of his people was a mere temporary thing, the outcome of former conditions, and bound to disappear in time, and that when a colored man should demonstrate to the community in which he lived that he possessed character and power, that community would find a way in which to enlist his services for the public good.

Despite his willingness to compromise and co-operate, Miller becomes disheartened upon discovering racial enmity within the medical profession and losing his little son in an avoidable race riot.

The half-sister relationship between Dr. Miller's octoroon wife Janet and white Mrs. Olivia Merkell Carteret, both legitimate daughters of the same father, afforded Chesnutt an opportunity to probe the intra-family problems of whites and their mulatto relatives. The mere sight of Janet's boy, whose resemblance to the patrician Merkells is striking, shocks Olivia so much that she gives premature birth to a child, almost losing her own life in the process. On the other hand, Janet, wanting to be friendly with her high-born half-sister, had always yearned in vain "for a kind word, a nod, a smile, the least thing that imagination might have twisted into a recognition of the tie between them." During the aforementioned riot Olivia is brought to her knees when her son's life depends upon whether Janet will let Dr. Miller take the case. In this crisis Janet rejects the name and riches which Olivia offers and which are rightfully hers, and, in spite of the recent death of her own son, requests Dr. Miller to use his medical skill to insure the boy's recovery:

> "I throw back your father's name, your father's wealth, your sisterly recognition. I want none of them,—they are bought too dear! Ah, God, they are bought too dear! But that you may know that a woman may be foully wronged, and yet may have a heart to feel, even for one who has injured her, you may have your child's life, if my husband can save it! Will," she said, throwing open the door into the next room, "go with her!"

The professional tribulations of Dr. Miller and the difficulties of his wife with the white members of her family are but a phase, however, of the racial dissonance and strife in Wellington. The white citizens are vexed because of the political influence of Negroes, who constitute two-thirds of the town's population; and Major Carteret, Olivia's husband, voices his sentiments concerning the Negro in state affairs through the columns of *The Morning Chronicle:*

Taking for his theme the unfitness of the Negro to participate in government,—an unfitness due to his limited education, his lack of experience, his criminal tendencies, and more especially to his helpless mental and physical inferiority to the white race,—the major had demonstrated, it seemed to him clearly enough, that the ballot in the hands of the Negro was a menace to the commonwealth. He had argued with entire conviction, that the white and black races could never attain social and political harmony by commingling their blood; he had proved by several historical parallels that no two unassimilable races could ever live together except in the relation of superior and inferior....

Especially objectionable to the majority group is the prominence of colored men in Reconstruction government. Therefore the murder of Mrs. Polly Ochiltree, an act which is impulsively attributed to an innocent Negro named Sandy Campbell, is all the provocation that is needed to fan the fires of racial hate into an all-consuming flame. *The Morning Chronicle* at once makes an issue of the killing, and unconscionable George McBane voices popular sentiment when he declares:

"We seem to have the right nigger, but whether we have or not, burn *a* nigger. It is an assault upon the white race, in the person of old Mrs. Ochiltree, committed by the black race, in the person of some nigger. It would justify the white people in burning *any* nigger. The example would be all the more powerful if we got the wrong one. It would serve notice on the niggers that we shall hold the whole race responsible for the misdeeds of each individual."

With incendiary speeches like this coming from leaders of the town, mob spirit quickly develops and a riot is set in motion.[13] The whites appear on the streets, spreading insult, terror, punishment, and death. When neither Lawyer Watson nor any other professional Negro will lead the blacks in the conflict, Josh Green, a vengeful man from the masses, assumes command and fatally stabs McBane before meeting his own violent death.

*The Marrow of Tradition* embraces many aspects of interracial life in the South during Reconstruction. Here are presented the intra-family strife sometimes occasioned by miscegenation, the affection of the white gentleman for the black servant, the contrast between Northern and Southern opinion regarding social contacts with the Negro, the disadvantages of Jim-Crowism, the handicaps of the colored professional man in a prejudice-ridden environment, the destructive course of mob passion, and the seeming futility of Negro efforts to acquire full civil rights. It is interesting to note that in this novel, as in *The House Behind the Cedars,* Chesnutt prescribes no panacea for the ills which he exposes; and the implication is that he was not very hopeful for harmonious race relations in the Southern states.

In his last novel, *The Colonel's Dream* (1905), Chesnutt again uses the small-town locale and white leading characters. Colonel Henry French, an aristocrat who fought with the Confederacy during the Civil War, gains wealth and broader social vision in the North and thereafter comes South with his motherless son Philip to find Clarendon, his home town, under the control of Bill Fetters, a former poor white, and in the grip of social and economic disintegration. Of the backwardness of Clarendon, Chesnutt writes:

> There were no mills or mines in the neighborhood, except for a few grist mills, and a sawmill. The bulk of the business consisted in supplying the needs of an agricultural population, and trading in their products. The cotton was baled and shipped to the North, and reimported for domestic use, in the shape of sheeting and other stuffs. The corn was shipped to the North, and came back in the shape of corn meal and salt pork, the staple articles of diet. Beefsteak and butter were brought from the North, at twenty-five and fifty cents a pound respectively. There were cotton merchants, and corn and feed merchants; there were dry-goods and grocery stores, drug stores and saloons —and the usual proportion of professional men. Since Clarendon was the county seat, there were, of course, a courthouse and a jail. There were churches enough, if all filled at once, to hold the entire population of the town, and preachers in proportion. The merchants, of whom a number were Jewish, periodically went into bankruptcy; the majority of their customers did likewise, and thus a fellow-feeling was promoted, and the loss thrown back as far as possible. The lands of the large farmers were mostly mortgaged, either to Fetters, or to the bank, of which he was the chief stockholder, for all that could be borrowed on

them; while the small farmers, many of whom were coloured, were practically tied to the soil by ropes of debt and chains of contract.

Appalled by the town's decay, French determines to devote his efforts to the rescue of the community from Fetters and begins his reform by erecting a modern cotton mill and providing for the enlightenment of the people, white and colored. When Dr. McKenzie, pastor of the Presbyterian Church, opposes the education of Negroes with the contention that to a divinely doomed race "ignorance is euthanasia, and knowledge is but pain and sorrow," French replies that colored people may logically anticipate a prosperous future in the United States, that they have earned their right to liberty through labor, and that they deserve equal treatment since they were brought here through no fault of their own. French, furthermore, champions not social equality but simple justice:

> In principle the Colonel was an ardent democrat; he believed in the rights of man, and extended the doctrine to include all who bore the human form. But in feeling he was an equally pronounced aristocrat. A servant's right he would have defended to the last ditch; familiarity he would have resented with equal positiveness.

French's projects for the development of Clarendon run smoothly for a while but hit a snag when labor troubles arise because of the promotion of a capable Negro worker to the foremanship of the masons. Further difficulties develop when French orders a joint funeral and burial for his son Philip and Peter, an elderly ex-slave who lost his life in an effort to save the boy's. Jim Green, the discharged white foreman of the masons, expresses the sentiments of the majority of his townsmen:

> "Colonel French is an enemy of his race," he declared to his sympathetic following. "He hires niggers when white men are idle, and pays them more than white men are earning. And now he is burying them with white people."

After the incensed citizens disinter Peter's corpse, French, having become hopeless and disillusioned, leaves for New York to bury his son and servant near his deceased wife. Once in the North, he abandons the cotton mill project but continues to provide for the welfare of his friends in Clarendon.

*The Colonel's Dream* illustrates the conflict between entrenched prejudice and idealistic reform in a representative Southern small town during the Reconstruction period. In this book Chesnutt describes the social tensions caused by the endeavors of philanthropists to assist Negroes, the rise of poor whites to political and financial power, and the efforts of dispossessed aristocrats to retain some semblance of their former station. In Southern post-war economy he notes the prevalence of bankruptcy and indebtedness, the maladministration of agriculture and industry, the inhuman treatment of women and children in factories, the evils of peonage and the convict lease system, and the unfair allocation of funds for popular education. He shows freedmen hampered at the polls, suffering discrimination in labor unions, feared as would-be social equals, and denied security of life and property. In the last paragraph of the book, following the exposure of these social ills, Chesnutt leans to pessimism in contemplating the future of Clarendon and of the Negro:

> But Clarendon has had its chance, nor seems yet to have another. Other towns, some not far from it, lying nearer the main lines of travel, have been swept into the current of modern life, but not yet Clarendon. . . . White men go their way, and black theirs, and these ways grow wider apart, and no one knows the outcome. But there are those who hope, and those who pray, that this condition will pass, that some day our land will be truly free, and the strong will cheerfully help to bear the burdens of the weak, and Justice, the seed, and Peace, the flower, of liberty, will prevail throughout all our borders.

After *The Colonel's Dream* Chesnutt did not publish another book. A news article in *The Pittsburgh Courier* for June 30, 1928, announced a novel by Chesnutt which was to be published during the following winter, but this book did not appear. Chesnutt was quoted as having made the following statement concerning the volume: "The book is a novel dealing with Negro life of the present day, just as my former novels dealt with the same subject twenty-five years ago." Perhaps his silence was due, partly at least, to disappointment in the results of his campaign for the betterment of social conditions in the South.[14]

Whether disappointed in his campaign or not, Chesnutt was an important trail-blazer in American Negro fiction. In his early stories of plantation life he not only made the folk tale a more faithful transcript of actual conditions but also became the first colored writer of fiction whose work was generally criticized without consideration of race. In *The Wife of His Youth and Other Stories of the Color Line* he experimented with racial subject matter which he subsequently handled at greater length in *The House Behind the Cedars, The Marrow of Tradition,* and *The Colonel's Dream.* All four of these books are favorably disposed toward the mulatto, who ostensibly represented for Chesnutt the most accomplished character in the Negro group. In treating the complexities of caste and color during the Reconstruction period, Chesnutt sometimes seems to accept the racial myths of his time; but he had a keen eye for social injustice and, before laying down his pen, he had either used or suggested many of the themes of the fiction of Negro life as we know it today.

### Paul Laurence Dunbar

Catering to the demands of publishers and readers of his time, Dunbar generally evaded themes such as those presented in Chesnutt's novels and usually specialized either in the treatment of white American life or in the perpetuation of the plantation tradition. Three of his novels—*The Uncalled* (1898), *The Love of Landry* (1900), and *The Fanatics* (1901)—deal almost entirely with white characters; and the fourth, *The Sport of the Gods* (1902), though a promising naturalistic study, illustrates the plantation-school concept that the Negro becomes homesick and demoralized in the urban North. With a few exceptions, moreover, the short stories comprising *Folks from Dixie* (1898), *The Strength of Gideon* (1900), *In Old Plantation Days* (1903), and *The Heart of Happy Hollow* (1904) follow the formulas of Thomas Nelson Page.

Dunbar's first novel, *The Uncalled* (1898), appeared complete in *Lippincott's Monthly Magazine* for May, 1898, and was published in book form later in the same year. Reflecting Dunbar's contemplation of a ministerial career,[15] the novel traces the life of Frederick Brent, a small-town orphan boy who is compulsorily educated for the clergy. Brent obtains a Methodist pastorate voluntarily relinquished by the elderly father of his fiancée but resigns rather than preach openly against a woman who had digressed from virtue. In Cincinnati, where he later obtains a clerical position, he joins the Congregational Church.

Distinctly a shallow novel, *The Uncalled* attacks the religious bigotry of the small town. Discussing Hester's determination to train Brent for the church, Dunbar writes:

> Poor, blind, conceited humanity! Interpreters of God, indeed! We reduce the deity to vulgar fractions. We place our own little ambitions and inclinations before a shrine, and label them "Divine messages." We set up our Delphian tripod, and we are the priests and oracles. We despise the plans of Nature's Ruler and substitute our own. With our short sight we affect to take a comprehensive view of eternity. Our horizon is the universe. We spy on the Divine and try to surprise his secrets, or to sneak into his confidence by stealth. We make God the eternal a puppet. We measure the infinite with a foot-rule.

In the metropolitan environment of Cincinnati, however, Brent breathes a freer air, as the following passage from one of his letters shows:

> "I feel that I am growing. I can take good full breaths here. I couldn't in Dexter: the air was too rarefied by religion."

Dunbar also answers the small-town concept of the immorality of the large city:

> It is one of the defects of the provincial mind that it can never see any good in a great city. It concludes that as many people are wicked,

where large numbers of human beings are gathered together there must be a much greater amount of evil than in a smaller place. It overlooks the equally obvious reasoning that, as some people are good, in the larger mass there must be also a larger amount of goodness.

*The Love of Landry* (1900), the weakest of Dunbar's novels, is a tedious and pointless account of the journey of tubercular Mildred Osborne to Colorado for her health. While in the West, Mildred falls in love with Landry Thayer, a well-born Philadelphian. The only Negro character in the story is a train porter who thinks that white people delight in "trampling on, and making a fool of, the black man." Perhaps the main importance of *The Love of Landry* is its suggestion of Dunbar's residence in Colorado and sympathy for fellow-sufferers with lung ailments. Certainly the book has no literary distinction.

Of *The Fanatics* (1901), a more successful handling of white characters, Dunbar writes: "You do not know how my hopes were planted in that book, but it has utterly disappointed me."[16] Mirroring intersectional strife among relatives and friends in a small Ohio town during the Civil War period, the novel opens with two former friends—Bradford Waters, a Unionist, and Stephen Van Doren, a Confederate supporter—alienated as a result of conflicting ideologies. When Van Doren's son Bob joins the Southern forces, Waters insists that his daughter Mary end her courtship with the young rebel; but the girl refuses:

> She loved Bob, not his politics. What had she to do with those black men down there in the South, it was none of her business? For her part, she only knew one black man and he was bad enough. Of course, Nigger Ed was funny. They all liked him and laughed at him, but he was not exemplary. He filled, with equal adaptability, the position of town crier and town drunkard. Really, if all his brethren were like him, they would be none the worse for having masters.

Exasperated by Mary's loyalty to her lover, Waters ejects his daughter. At the close of the war, however, the Waters and Van Dorens are reconciled; and Nigger Ed becomes more than the town buffoon:

There were men who had seen that black man on bloody fields, which were thick with the wounded and dying, and these could not speak of him without tears in their eyes. There were women who begged him to come in and talk to them about their sons who had been left on some Southern field, wives who wanted to hear over again the last words of their loved ones. And so they gave him a place for life and everything he wanted, and from being despised he was much petted and spoiled, for they were all fanatics.

In his last and most promising novel, *The Sport of the Gods* (1902), which had previously appeared in *Lippincott's Monthly Magazine* for May, 1901, Dunbar describes the misfortunes of a Negro family that migrates from a small Southern town to New York City. The first paragraph of the book suggests Dunbar's awareness of the repeated romanticizing of the ante-bellum South and his intention to depart from the tradition in portraying the family whose members are the main characters of the story:

Fiction has said so much in regret of the old days when there were plantations and overseers and masters and slaves, that it was good to come upon such a household as Berry Hamilton's, if for no other reason than that it afforded a relief from the monotony of tiresome iteration.

Not all continues well with the Hamiltons, however, for Berry receives a ten-year sentence for the alleged theft of money from Francis, the irresponsible half-brother of his employer, Maurice Oakley. Because of community ill will, Fannie, Kit, and Joe Hamilton—Berry's wife, daughter, and son respectively—move to New York City. In Harlem, Joe disintegrates, and Dunbar comments as follows upon the change in his character:

Whom the gods wish to destroy they first make mad. The first sign of the demoralization of the provincial who comes to New York is his pride at his insensibility to certain impressions which used to influence him at home. First, he begins to scoff, and there is no truth in his views nor depth in his laugh. But by and by, from mere pretending, it becomes real. He grows callous. After that he goes to the devil very cheerfully.

Becoming a frequenter of the Banner Club, "a social cesspool, generating a poisonous miasma and reeking with the stench of decayed and rotten moralities," Joe meets and later murders yellow-skinned Hattie Sterling. In contemplation of the fate of the youth, Dunbar states that "the stream of young Negro life would continue to flow up from the South, dashing itself against the hard necessities of the city and breaking like waves against a rock,—that, until the gods grew tired of their cruel sport, there must still be sacrifices to false ideals and unreal ambitions." After Joe is sent to the penitentiary, Francis confesses use of the money supposedly stolen by Berry and urges the acquittal of the Negro; but Maurice determines to protect the honor of his relative. Eventually, however, a New York newspaper reporter conducts an investigation which results in Berry's release. At the close of the novel Kit is dancing on the stage for a living, Maurice is mentally deranged because of an obsessive determination to maintain Francis' innocence, and Berry is living with his wife in their former home on the Oakley place. Of the old couple's re-establishment in the South, Dunbar writes fatalistically:

> It was not a happy life, but it was all that was left to them, and they took it up without complaint, for they knew they were powerless against some Will infinitely stronger than their own.

Though amateurish in execution, *The Sport of the Gods* is Dunbar's worthiest effort in fiction and suggests abilities which possibly did not achieve fruition because of the author's early death. Written under the influence of naturalism, which Parrington defines as "pessimistic realism,"[17] *The Sport of the Gods* follows Emile Zola's *Nana* (1880), Stephen Crane's *Maggie: A Girl of the Streets* (1893), Frank Norris' *McTeague* (1899), and other novels in which man is conceived as a powerless figure in an amoral and careless world. Showing race prejudice as an all-destructive virus, the book reveals social corruption in the South as well as in the North. In the Southern small town, interracial distrust is exposed, and the vaunted chivalry of Dixie gentlemen is debunked through the characterization of Francis and Maurice Oakley. In the New York setting, inexperienced Negro youth are pictured in a treacherous environment which deterministically produces degeneration and disaster. By treating the challenging and comparatively unworked Harlem low-life scene, Dunbar analyzed a background that was later to intrigue Claude McKay, Carl Van Vechten, and other writers of the 1920's. As a matter of fact, Van Vechten expresses the indebtedness of *Nigger Heaven* to *The Sport of the Gods* by saying that in the latter novel Dunbar "described the plight of a young outsider who comes to the larger New York Negro world to make his fortune, but who falls a victim to the sordid snares of that world, a theme I elaborated in 1926 to fit a newer and much more intricate social system."[18]

To move from Dunbar's novels to his short stories is to enter a different field. Three of the novels sentimentally treat white characters in their conventional setting, and the fourth is a naturalistic study of a post-bellum Negro family in a small Southern town and in Harlem. However, in most of the short stories comprising *Folks From Dixie* (1898), *The Strength of Gideon and Other Stories* (1900), *In Old Plantation Days* (1903), and *The Heart of Happy Hollow* (1904), Dunbar becomes a successful imitator of the plantation school. Like other resuscitators of the legendary South, he presents "the big house," peopled by high-spirited and indulgent blue-bloods, and "the quarters," inhabited by spoiled and satisfied slaves whose lives are made picturesque by conjuration, gambling, feasting, rivalries, love affairs, mimicry, and primitive religion. In this environment move such familiar types as the proprietary mammy, the pompous butler, the pretentious coachman, and the plantation exhorter. A wide social gulf divides the slaves in "the big house" from those in "the quarters." The relationship between master and slave is idealized as one of mutual affection and loyalty, and the best masters do not buy and sell slaves unless forced to do so because of financial strain. Furthermore, the patricians generally avoid flogging by delegating this unpleasant assignment to overseers or supervised Negroes. The overseer, being in most cases a representative of "poor white trash," is not portrayed sympathetically. A purveyor of these expected themes, Dunbar avoids penetrating social analysis of the South and suggests that Negroes who migrate to the North become maladjusted and demoralized individuals who remember the years before emancipation with pitiable nostalgia.

*Folks from Dixie,* Dunbar's first collection of short stories, contains twelve tales treating action before and after the Civil War. The majority of the narratives conform to the postulates of the plantation tradition. "Anner Lizer's Stumblin' Block" presents a slave woman who will not become converted until sure of the marital intentions of her lover. "A Family Feud" is a story of ante-bellum days told to the author by Aunt Joshy. "The Intervention of Peter" shows how an old Negro prevents a duel between two Southern gentlemen. "The Colonel's Awakening" mirrors the loyalty of two ex-slaves to their elderly demented master who has lost his wealth and sons in the Civil War. "The Ordeal at Mount Hope," "The Trial Sermons on Bull-Skin," and "Mt. Pisgah's Christmas Possum" furnish glimpses of Negro church life. Anticipating *The Sport of the Gods,* "Jimsella" describes the struggles of a Negro couple in New York, where "it was all very different: one room in a crowded tenement house, and the necessity of grinding day after day to keep the wolf—a very terrible and ravenous wolf—from the door." Several stories in *Folks from Dixie,* however, tend to diverge from plantation prescriptions. "Aunt Mandy's Investment" treats the machinations of a Negro shyster who fleeces gullible black folk. "The Deliberation of Mr. Dunkin" unfolds the wooing of a teacher by an affected member of the school board. "Nelse Hatton's Revenge" sets forth the kindness of an ex-slave to a former master whom he had earlier vowed to kill. Veering from plantation requirements more than any other story in the volume, "At Shaft 11" recounts the heroic part played by Sam Bowles, a Negro foreman, in a West Virginia mine strike and race riot.

The imprint of the plantation tradition is also strong upon

*The Strength of Gideon and Other Stories,* a collection of twenty narratives. The title story and "Mammy Peggy's Pride" depict the loyalty of ex-bondmen to their former masters. "Viney's Free Papers," "The Fruitful Sleeping of the Rev. Elisha Edwards," "The Case of 'Ca'line': A Kitchen Monologue," "Jim's Probation," and "Uncle Simon's Sunday Out" portray various experiences of plantation life. Illustrative of the unfitness of the Negro to cope with the inhospitable environment of the Northern metropolis are "An Old Time Christmas," "The Trustfulness of Polly," "The Finding of Zach," "The Faith Cure Man," "Silas Jackson," "The Finish of Patsy Barnes," and "One Man's Fortunes." The last-named story records the failure of a Negro lawyer who learns "that the adages, as well as the books and the formulas, were made by and for others than us of the black race." Several stories of the volume, however, break rather sharply from typical plantation subject matter. "Mr. Cornelius Johnson, Office Seeker," "A Mess of Pottage," and "A Council of State" present the Negro in politics. "The Ingrate" portrays a slave who yearns for freedom:

> To him his slavery was deep night. What wonder, then, that he should dream, and that through the ivory gate should come to him the forbidden vision of freedom? To own himself, to be master of his hands, feet, of his whole body—something would clutch at his heart as he thought of it; and the breath would come hard between his lips.

Escaping to Canada, he rejoices in the work of the Abolitionists and joins the Union Army during the Civil War.[19] A bloody tale of lynching and mob passion, "The Tragedy of Three Forks" is social protest that is a far cry from Dunbar's usual treatment of the Southern scene. After Jane Hunster, a white girl of a small Kentucky town, commits arson because of jealousy, her father hastily attributes the crime to a Negro:

> "Look a here, folks, I tell you that's the work o' niggers. I kin see their hand in it."

Thereafter incendiary newspaper articles result in the seizure and lynching of two innocent Negroes. In a struggle for pieces of the mob's rope to be kept as souvenirs, Dock Heaters fatally stabs Jane's fiancé; and the one-sided justice of the South is indicated in the following persuasive reply to a demand that the murderer also be lynched: "No," cried an imperious voice, "who knows what may have put him up to it? Give a white man a chance for his life."

Most of the stories of *In Old Plantation Days* follow the pattern of those in Page's *In Ole Virginia* and have their setting on the plantation of Stuart Mordaunt, a typical master of the legendary South. "Aunt Tempy's Triumph" shows how a proprietary mammy, who thinks she owns the "plantation with all the white folks and niggers on it," succeeds in giving away the master's daughter in marriage. "Dizzy-Headed Dick," "A Lady Slipper," and "Who Stand for the Gods" present slaves who intervene to assist white lovers. "Aunt Tempy's Revenge," "The Trouble about Sophiny," "Ash-Cake Hannah and Her Ben," "The Conjuring Contest," "Dandy Jim's Conjure Scare," "The Memory of Martha," and "The Easter Wedding" deal principally with the love affairs of bondmen. The old-fashioned exhorter and plantation religious life are described in "The Walls of Jericho," "How Brother Parker Fell from Grace," "The Trousers," and "The Last Fiddling of Mordaunt's Jim." Slave loyalty is exemplified in "A Blessed Deceit" and "The Stanton Coachman." "The Brief Cure of Aunt Fanny" reveals the rivalry between two plantation cooks, while "A Supper by Proxy" pictures a lavish feast prepared by Negroes in "the big house" in the absence of the master. "Mr. Groby's Slippery Gift" unfolds the loyalty of two slave brothers and the cruelty of an overseer. The last five stories of the volume shift to post-bellum times and urban scenes. "The Finding of Martha," highly suggestive of Chesnutt's "The Wife of His Youth," sets forth the successful quest of a Negro preacher for his wife of slavery times. "The Defection of Mary Ann Gibbs," "A Judgment of Paris," "Silent Samuel," and "The Way of a

Woman," all having their locale in the Negro ghetto of a Northern city, are chiefly concerned with competition in love.

In *The Heart of Happy Hollow* Dunbar gives the following description of the setting of the stories:

> Wherever Negroes colonize in the cities or villages, North or South, wherever the hod carrier, the porter, and the waiter are the society men of the town; wherever the picnic and the excursion are the chief summer diversion, and the revival the winter-time of repentance, wherever the cheese cloth obtains at a wedding, and the little white hearse goes by with black mourners in the one carriage behind, there—there—is Happy Hollow. Wherever laughter and tears rub elbows day by day, and the spirit of labour and laziness shake hands, there—there—is Happy Hollow, and of some of it may the following pages show the heart.

Though dealing chiefly with post-bellum Negro life, many of the sixteen tales of *The Heart of Happy Hollow* do not escape the influence of the plantation tradition. "Cahoots" sentimentalizes the life-long devotion of a slave to his master. "The Wisdom of Silence" portrays an ex-slave who, having grown prosperous and boastful, is humbled and thereafter aided by his former owner. "One Christmas at Shiloh" and "A Matter of Doctrine" present Negro ministers as suitors. "Old Abe's Conversion" traces the transformation of an old-fashioned exhorter into a progressive pastor. "A Defender of the Faith" and "The Interference of Patsy Ann" mirror the pathos of Negro life in a big city. "The Mission of Mr. Scatters," "The Promoter," and "Schwalliger's Philosophy" expose colored swindlers. "The Scapegoat" describes the craft of a Negro politician, while "The Home-Coming of 'Rastus Smith" limns a young Negro lawyer who adopts a supercilious attitude toward his mother and former sweetheart. "The Boy and the Bayonet" illustrates a lesson in military discipline. Misleadingly titled, "The Race Question" is the soliloquy of an old colored man at a race track. In "The Lynching of Jube Benson" a white physician, defending his opposition to mob violence, recounts the murder of a loyal and innocent Negro friend.

In his short stories, therefore, Dunbar generally accepts the limitations and circumscriptions of the plantation tradition. Glorifying the good old days in the accepted manner, he sentimentalizes master-slave relationships and implies that freedom brings social misery to the black man. Negro migrants to the urban North are usually represented as nostalgic misfits, some of whom fall prey to poverty, immorality, or disease, and others to disillusionment occasioned by political or professional reverses. "The Ingrate" and "The Tragedy at Three Forks," both of which are effective examples of the use of irony, are possibly the only stories in the four volumes that entirely escape the tendency to idealize Dixie. Furthermore, the narratives give an unauthentic recording of life because of their neglect of the unpleasant realities of the Southland. These considerations lead directly to the observation that Dunbar usually catered to the racial preconceptions of his publishers and readers by employing the themes and stereotypes of the plantation tradition. Nevertheless, his literary reputation itself constituted a strong argument against Negro inferiority; and he helped to prepare the American audience for succeeding authors possessing greater originality and deeper social understanding.

### Sutton E. Griggs

While Dunbar was acquiescent and uncontroversial, Sutton E. Griggs was challenging and militant. Not only did he exalt Negro character and attack oppression after the fashion of Frances Ellen Watkins Harper, J. McHenry Jones, and Pauline E. Hopkins, but he also made his novels handbooks of group promotion and political strategy for his people. Most outspoken among the glorifiers and defenders of his race in twentieth-century American fiction, he chronicled the departure of the servile black man and hailed the advent of the new Negro: "The cringing, fawning, sniffling, cowardly Negro which slavery left, had disappeared, and a new Negro, self-respecting, fearless and determined in the assertion of his rights, was at hand." Embittered by the doctrines of Thomas Dixon, Griggs was the most vocal and didactic of those novelists who explained the black man's failings as natural consequences of savagery and enslavement and who applauded his achievements as indications of talent and ability. If Dixon's fear and hatred of the Negro led to derogation in *The Leopard's Spots* and *The Clansman,* Griggs's admiration and sympathy for his people resulted in apotheosis in *Imperium in Imperio* (1899), *Overshadowed* (1901), *Unfettered* (1902), *The Hindered Hand* (1905), and *Pointing the Way* (1908). Because Griggs was industrious enough to establish his own publishing company and to promote the sale of his books among the black masses of the country, his novels, though virtually unknown to white American readers, were probably more widely circulated among Negroes than the fiction of Chesnutt and Dunbar.

Griggs's first novel, *Imperium in Imperio,* is a fantastic account of a national Negro political organization. The main characters are dark-skinned Belton Piedmont and mulatto Bernard Belgrave, graduates of Stowe (Roger Williams?) and Harvard Universities, respectively. Invited by Piedmont, Belgrave joins the Imperium in Imperio, a militant agency secretly formed "to unite all Negroes in a body to do that which the whimpering government childishly but truthfully" said it could not do. Elected president of the Imperium, Belgrave proposes during a meeting of the organization in Waco that Negroes engage in open revolt as a means of accomplishing the surrender of Texas and Louisiana, the former to be retained and the latter to be ceded to foreign allies in return for aid. After making the unpopular counterproposal that Negroes voluntarily segregate themselves in Texas in order to work out their destiny, Piedmont chooses death by execution in preference to co-operation in Belgrave's treasonous plan. In the last paragraph of the novel Griggs points to the truth that human beings, regardless of race or social status, will not complacently endure oppression and bondage: "When will all races and classes of men learn that men made in the image of God will not be the slaves of another image?"

Though weakened by melodramatic situations, idealized characters, and stilted conversation, *Imperium in Imperio* is the first political novel by an American Negro. Besides exposing miscegenation, oppression, and Jim-Crowism, it attacks the exploitation of the black man in American politics and points out the need for an agency to protect Negro interests not safeguarded by the government. While extravagant in conception, *Imperium in Imperio* suggests the philosophy that produced the National Association for the Advancement of Colored People and other organizations striving for the full participation of the Negro in American democracy.

In *Overshadowed* Griggs, considering the Negro as an unincorporable member of the social order, surveys the American scene with a feeling of futility. In the preface he sees a hard road ahead for the Negro, "whose grandfather was a savage and whose father was a slave," in a social order developed and dominated by "the most cultured, aggressive and virile type of all times, the Anglo-Saxon." With Richmond, Virginia, as its main background, *Overshadowed* traces the love of Erma Wysong and Astral Herndon. While Herndon is in college, John Benson Lawson, an ex-governor's son, engages Dolly Smith to attempt to procure Erma as a mistress. Dolly, who happens to be Erma's maternal aunt, makes no effort to arrange a meeting between her niece and the young aristocrat. Actually Dolly is a sworn enemy of the Lawson family because of the ex-governor's mistreatment and non-support of her sister, his former mistress and the mother of his illegitimate child Erma. To obtain revenge, she eventually brings young Lawson to court, where she makes public the illicit intimacies of both father and son. As a result of the trial, the ex-governor loses his mind, Dolly is tarred and feathered, and young Lawson receives a jail sentence. Some time later, Herndon and Erma, who have married, are surprised one winter night by the coming of Erma's brother

John, escaped from a chain gang to which he had been sentenced for the murder of a master workman who insisted that labor unions exclude Negroes. Soon afterwards John dies of exposure, and Erma suddenly succumbs to shock and grief. A white friend advises the grieved husband that the adoption of a viewpoint similar to that of Booker T. Washington would ease his suffering:

> "Your status here is but due to conditions inherent in the situation. Why not bow to the inevitable, accept conditions as you find them, extract from life as much good as can come from well-directed efforts, and beyond this point have no yearnings? Develop character, earn money, contribute to the industrial development of the country, exercise your wonderful capacity for humility, move continuously in the line of least resistance and, somehow, all will be well."

Rejecting this counsel and later discarding the idea of emigration to Africa because "it, too, is overshadowed," Herndon buries his wife in mid-ocean, where "there abides no social group in which conditions operate toward the overshadowing of such elements as are not deemed assimilable."

The thesis of *Overshadowed* is that in all parts of the world, and particularly in the United States and Africa, the Negro must bear an encumbrance because of his race. Attention is focused upon the American scene, where miscegenation causes the death of Erma and her mother, the suicide of Dolly, the insanity of ex-Governor Lawson, the imprisonment of his son John, and the loss of a wife and a mother by Herndon. The novel also exposes the instability of Negro employment, the exclusion of the Negro by labor unions, and the maladministration of justice in Southern courts. Especially interesting in *Overshadowed* is the subtle attack upon the philosophy of Booker T. Washington. It is after hearing an optimistic speech by Washington that Erma advises her brother John to confess the crime for which he is sentenced. A further veiled thrust at the Tuskegee educator's program is made when Astral Herndon rejects the Washingtonian argument for remaining in America and severs relations with all lands in which the

Negro is oppressed. On the whole, *Overshadowed* paints a gloomy picture of race relations and does not offer the prospect of adjustment in the immediate future.

"It is the aim of *Unfettered,*" states Griggs in an introductory note, "to lead the reader into the inner life of the Negro race and lay bare the aspirations that are fructifying there." The novel opens with the death of a benevolent Tennessee plantation owner who leaves the bulk of his wealth to a nephew, Lemuel Dalton, but provides liberally for an old Negro nurse and a beautiful mulatto girl named Morlene. After dispossessing the colored beneficiaries of his uncle's will, Lemuel almost provokes a riot by wounding Harry Dalton, a young Negro who had overcome him some years earlier. Concluding that formal training had induced Harry and his sister Beulah to assume social equality, angered whites drive the pair out of the community and thereby cause a mass exodus of black folk. Later Beulah, believed to be a ringleader of the migration, is killed during an attack by a group of young white men. In order to avoid further bloodshed, the whites draft as a mediator a Negro school teacher, a representative of the type which Griggs calls perhaps "the greatest conservator of peace in the South, laboring *for* the Negroes by the *appointment* of the whites, being thus placed in a position where it was to his interest to keep on good terms with both races." After reluctantly marrying Harry, Morlene goes with him to a nearby city, where she meets Dorlan Warthell, a successful Negro politician, who is at once attracted by her intelligence and beauty. Warthell, at odds with the Republican Party, plans to use the Negro vote to force the United States to grant political independence to the Philippine Islands. Angered by Warthell's intention, a venal Congressman engages Harry to take the Negro politician's life; but Morlene overhears the plot, warns the intended victim, and deserts her husband. Left by his wife and repudiated by his party, Harry sacrifices himself to save the lives of a woman and her children. Thereupon Warthell proposes to Morlene, who promises to consent if he will outline a plan which will unfetter the mind of the Negro and enable the two races to live together in peace and harmony. When Warthell submits his project, entitled "Dorlan's Plan," Morlene agrees to become his wife. Meanwhile Lemuel's young Northern bride, who has been taught by her husband to hate and fear the Negro, becomes hysterical upon seeing a colored boy and is fatally wounded in a fall from horseback. Sorrowfully aware of the dire effects of misinstructing his wife, Lemuel realizes that good will is necessary for the happiness and welfare of both races in the South.

*Unfettered,* like *Overshadowed,* provides a dismal picture of race relations. The opposition of prejudiced whites to the education of the Negro is set forth, and an analysis is made of the motives underlying intimidation and segregation. Worthy of passing note are the political views of Warthell, who, though distrustful of the Democrats because their "chief tenets are the white man's supremacy and exclusiveness in government," nevertheless recognizes no unseverable party ties. In his concern for the progress of the Philippines, moreover, Warthell expresses interest in the world-wide advancement of darker races.

Griggs's views on racial policy are given in an appended essay called "Dorlan's Plan: Sequel to *Unfettered*: A Dissertation on the Race Problem." This essay, a serious approach to the problem of racial adjustment in the United States, points out that the major task is to institute merit and not color as the standard of preferment. Since the oppression of the Negro derives from unfortunate circumstances of the past, the race is urged to "meet and combat the timorous conservatism that has hitherto impeded our progress." The Negro is advised not to rely wholly upon the Republican Party. Listed as necessary in the task of preparing the race for a better future are character development, worthy home life, public school education for the masses, technological schools for industrial workers, and universities for the training of "men capable of interpreting and influencing world movements, men able to adjust the race to any new conditions that may arise." Land ownership and a back-to-the-farm movement are recommended. Good government and simple justice, not race supremacy and partisan patronage, are defined as desirable goals of political action. Cultivation of the friendship of the Southern white man as well as of the citizens of other sections of the country and of other nations is also emphasized as a *sine qua non* of enlightened racial policy. In the promotion of this program the support of the orator, journalist, literary artist, painter, sculptor, and composer is invoked. As a statement of desirable procedure for the colored people of the United States, "Dorlan's Plan" is a precursor of James Weldon Johnson's *Negro Americans, What Now?* (1934) and of numerous other guides to interracial harmony.

In his next novel, *The Hindered Hand,* Griggs portrays the harsh aspects of miscegenation in the South and attacks the biased portrayal of the Negro in Thomas Dixon's *The Leopard's Spots.* The tragedy and disaster consequent upon interbreeding is shown in the lives of a near-white couple's three children. Because of her dark complexion the first, Tiara Merlow, is early separated from her family in order to make passing easier for her parents, brother, and sister. The second, the Reverend Percy G. Marshall, when seen holding his sister Tiara in his arms, is killed by a Negro. After being forced into an unhappy marriage with a white man, the third, Eunice Seabright, becomes demented when her racial identity is revealed. Concerning Eunice's insanity a Northern specialist says:

> "The one specific cause of her breakdown is the Southern situation which has borne tremendously upon her. That whole region of the country is affected by a sort of sociological hysteria, and we physicians are expecting more and more pathological manifestations as a result of the strain upon the people."

The plight of the Negro is suggested in Tiara's defense of her mother, who becomes a suicide after fanatical but fruitless efforts to establish herself and her family in the majority group:

"My mother is dead and paid dearly for her unnatural course. But do not judge her too harshly. You people who are white do not know what an awful burden it is to be black in these days of the world. If some break down beneath the awful load of caste which you thrust upon them, mingle pity with your blame."

The maladministration of justice in the South is illustrated by the unwarranted lynching of Foresta Crump and Bud Harper in Mississippi. An investigator, upon asking a white native whether mob action against the couple was caused by "the one crime," receives the following explanation:

"That's all rot about one crime. We lynch niggers down here for anything. We lynch them for being sassy and sometimes lynch them on general principles. The truth of the matter is the real 'one crime' that paves the way for a lynching whenever we have the notion, is the crime of being black."

At a subsequent trial of the lynchers a young prosecuting attorney becomes a political outcast for demanding justice, and the jury sets the mobbers free.

In the first and second editions of *The Hindered Hand* a review of Thomas Dixon's *The Leopard's Spots* appears in the form of a conversation between two of the characters of the novel, but in the third edition the review is amplified into an article at the end of the book. Even in the third edition, however, *The Leopard's Spots* is mentioned in the body of the novel when A. Hostility, in an unsuccessful effort to enlist Negro aid in a Slav movement against the Anglo-Saxon, calls the attention of Tiara's lover, Ensal Ellwood, "to the book written for the express purpose of thoroughly discrediting the Negro race in America." Elwood is perturbed by the literary campaign against the Negro:

Ensal thought of the odds against the Negro in this literary battle: how that Southern white people, being more extensive purchasers of books than the Negroes, would have the natural bias of the great publishing agencies on their side; how that Northern white people, resident in the South, for social and business reasons, might hesitate to father books not in keeping with the prevailing sentiment of Southern white people; how that residents of the North, who essayed to write in defense of the Negro, were laughed out of school as mere theorists ignorant of actual conditions; and, finally, how that a lack of leisure and the absence of general culture handicapped the Negro in fighting his own battle in this species of warfare.

In "A Hindering Hand, Supplementary to *The Hindered Hand*: A Review of the Anti-Negro Crusade of Mr. Thomas Dixon, Jr.,"[20] Griggs avers that Dixon's malice derives from the traditional dislike of the Southern poor white for the Negro and that his purpose is to promote the expulsion of those having African blood from the United States. To accomplish this aim, according to Griggs, Dixon attempts "to thoroughly discredit the Negroes, to stir up the baser passions of men against them and to send them forth with a load of obloquy and the withering scorn of their fellows the world over, sufficient to appall a nation of angels." Among the propagandistic techniques allegedly used by Dixon are the delineation of the Negro as the lustful despoiler of white womankind, the offering of degenerates as representative types of black men, and the attribution of natural inferiority to those of African extraction. Griggs denies that the consuming desire of the Negro is to wed a white woman, as indicated by Dixon in the portrayal of George Harris in *The Leopard's Spots*. In consideration of Dixon's methods and materials, Griggs submits the following epitaph for the white author:

> This misguided soul ignored all of the good in the aspiring Negro; made every vicious offshoot that he pictured typical of the entire race; presented all mistakes independent of their environments and provocations; ignored or minimized all the evil in the more vicious elements of whites; said and did all things which he deemed necessary to leave behind him the greatest heritage of hatred the world has ever known. Humanity claims him not as one of her children.

Though weak according to artistic standards, *The Hindered Hand* is the most elaborate attack upon Thomas Dixon in American Negro fiction. In addition, the book treats the well-worn themes of miscegenation and injustice and shows the Negro mind weighing open revolt and emigration to Africa[21] against bearing the hardships of an ethnic minority in the United States. The denial of political rights is designated as the chief factor which "causes the Ethiopian in America to feel that his is indeed 'The Hindered Hand.'"

Like *The Hindered Hand*, *Pointing the Way* is concerned primarily with interbreeding and politics, but ends upon a more hopeful note. Letitia Gilbreath, spinster daughter of a white man and his ex-slave mistress, considers it "a shocking crime for two dark persons to marry each other" and therefore undertakes to induce her niece Clotille to become the wife of Baug Peppers, a mulatto lawyer. Clotille, however, loves Conroe Driscoll, her dark-skinned college sweetheart, and, while studying in Boston, invites a beautiful English-Spanish-Indian girl named Eina Rapona to her Southern home in Belrose with the hope that the visitor will marry Peppers and thus leave her free to wed the young man of her choice. After reaching Belrose, Eina becomes seriously interested in Peppers; but Seth Molair, a white attorney and also an admirer of Eina, warns the attractive newcomer that "to work, to eat, to sleep, to die is the utmost programme that organized society in the South offers" the Negro, and instructs her that she may not mingle socially with both races:

"In the South social freedom is not permitted, for reasons that I need not discuss here. Whoever affiliates socially with the one race in the South is denied the social life of the other."

When Eina asks whether there is any hope for interracial harmony, Molair replies:

"The one thing needed in the South is political cooperation between the better elements of whites and the Negroes, but the manner of the coming of emancipation, enfranchisement, and elevation to high public station seems to have riveted the Negro into one party, while the terror of being ruled by an alien and backward race has chained the real strength of the white race into an opposing party. . . . As long as there is a bitter political war between the Negroes and the whites of the South, how can the condition change?"

Resolving to try to bring about better race relations in Belrose, and aligning herself with the Negro group, Eina persuades Peppers to ask Molair to run for mayor on a platform pledging justice to all. Moved by the ruthless murder of a Negro youth by a white chain-gang guard, Molair enters the race and wins the election. Molair's impartial and progressive administration, during which Driscoll becomes a captain in the municipal fire department, not only draws national attention and Presidential commendation, but also elicits the enthusiastic interest and financial support of a millionaire ex-Southerner who is not pleased with the steady northward migration of Negroes and wishes to improve the status of blacks and poor whites in the South. Successful in her campaign for better race relations in Belrose, Eina persuades Peppers to test Southern disfranchising legislation before the Supreme Court. Assisted by funds bequeathed by Letitia, who earlier died in a fire in which Driscoll made a fatal effort to save her, Peppers carries a test case to the highest tribunal, before which he makes an eloquent plea for the enfranchisement of his people. The novel closes with endorsement of the Belrose experiment and with Peppers winning the hand of Eina, who is unique as an individual not possessing African blood but passing as a Negro.

Illustrating how the happiness of lovers is thwarted by an old maid afflicted by color mania, *Pointing the Way* sets forth the tragic consequences of intraracial prejudice. The novel also seeks to show that the political co-operation of the races in the South contributes not only to the solution of the problems of that section but also to the general improvement of conditions throughout the country. While deficient according to standards of art, *Pointing the Way* is another example of Griggs's pioneering work in political fiction.

At this point it might be well to draw certain comparisons between Griggs and Chesnutt, the two most prominent propagandists in American Negro fiction during the first decade of the present century. Both writers employ the well-exploited subject matter of miscegenation, prejudice, and oppression. Unlike Chesnutt, however, Griggs recommends a way to a better life for his people. Rejecting open revolt, exodus to Africa, and the racial platform of Booker T. Washington, he offers a program of political co-operation with the white South and alignment with whatever party offers the Negro the maximum participation in government. Unlike Chesnutt again, Griggs tends to exalt black pigmentation, especially for his heroes, as the following description of Warthell, the protagonist of *Unfettered*, indicates: "As to color he was black, but even those prejudiced to color forgot that prejudice when they gazed upon this ebony-like Apollo." Chesnutt, on the other hand, while ridiculing the color line within his race, shows a predilection for mulattoes and occasionally uses black stereotypes which most of his Negro contemporaries tabooed. As an artist, however, Chesnutt is the superior in every way, for deficiencies in plot, characterization, and diction loom obtrusively in the novels of Griggs.

### G. Langhorne Pryor

G. Langhorne Pryor's *Neither Bond nor Free* (1902) is similar to the fiction of Griggs in its emphasis upon racial and political issues as well as in its complimentary portrayal of dark-complexioned Negroes. Having only a thin thread of action, which traces the wooing of Merna Attaway by Toussaint Ripley, the novel is composed chiefly of tedious discussions of the race problem by respectable, educated Negroes. For example, a chapter on "Literary Life in the Capital" reproduces verbatim the papers read and discussed at a session of the Blyden Historical and Literary Society. In this meeting James M. Hughes, speaking on "The Status of the American Negro," echoes the program of Booker T. Washington:

> "I will conclude by saying you must quit politics, put behind you all dreams of literary and scholastic attainments, acquire practical industrial knowledge, court and deserve the friendship of the best white people in your neighborhood. Heed the advice of Oscar Richards: 'Leave the Negro problem to the South.'"

The chapter on "Politics in the South" deals with Ripley's experiences as a campaigner for the Republican Party, and that on "The Black Republic" contains Merna's advocacy of the colonization of Liberia by American Negroes. After a chapter called "Race Problems," which treats an antilynching conference held at the Southern Industrial Institute, come three chapters in which the author expresses his own views on conditions in the South. The following statement is typical of Pryor:

> And yet, after all, there is no serious friction between the whites and blacks of the South. . . . The educated Negro makes for peace, and his industrial training is the sure foundation of future usefulness. Let him make friends with the people with whom his destiny is involved. Let him divide intelligently in politics, but never rest content until his ballot is counted as cast. The self-interest of the whites—a ruling passion with all men—will protect the ballot in the black hand when it becomes a potent factor, determining, as the balance of power, the authority of men in political affairs.

### George Marion McClellan

George Marion McClellan's *Old Greenbottom Inn and Other Stories* (1906) is a collection of five narratives treating life in rural Alabama. The Inn and its surroundings—the site of a slave market in ante-bellum times but of the Industrial and Normal School for Negroes in the years after the war—provide the stories with a common background. Except for the last tale, which describes the devotion of an old slave to a famous horse, the stories set forth the bitter experiences of Negro women.

The title piece deals with the old theme of miscegenation. John McBride, an aristocratic slaveholder, and Lucinda, a mulatto, have a child named Daphne. Upon the insistence of his white wife, McBride sells Lucinda but allows Daphne to remain in the home as the companion of his legitimate daughter, Eunice. After the Civil War, during which McBride loses his life, Daphne falls into a liaison with Joseph Cramer, Eunice's fiancé. Discovering the secret lovers in a rendezvous, John Henry, Daphne's Negro suitor, kills Cramer and is subsequently lynched. At the end of the story Daphne, having become the mother of Cramer's posthumous child, is demented; and Eunice and her mother, bereft of worldly possessions, are classed as "pore white trash."

"For Anniston's Sake," which extols virtuous Negro womanhood, presents a student of the Industrial and Normal School who chooses to commit suicide rather than yield to the lust of a ruffian whose character is revealed in his remarks:

> "When I asked you to come and live with me you called me a thief and the low-down scrapings of poor white trash. When I told you any sort of a white man was good enough for a nigger, you spat in my face and got knocked down. . . . The Giant's cave is not as good as the cabin I invited you to, but you won't mind that, my fine lady."

"The Creole from Louisiana" recounts the unwavering affection of Lizzie Story, a public school teacher of the Old Greenbottom Inn district, for Bertie Stein, a mulatto student eight years her junior. Though educated by Lizzie at Fisk University, Stein marries a Creole classmate, Stella Jerome. After graduation the couple spend a year of study in Europe, where they become the parents of a boy. Returning to Nashville with her husband and son, Stella drowns herself rather than resume an illicit relationship with a former white paramour from Louisiana. Thereafter Stein returns with his son to Old Greenbottom Inn, where he resignedly marries Lizzie.

In the fourth story, "Essie Dortch," the octoroon heroine goes to Fisk University, where she meets John Walters, the leading man in a troupe of Negro actors. When Essie refuses to submit to Walters outside the bonds of matrimony, he arranges a sham wedding. Learning of his earlier marriage, she stabs him and takes refuge in a New Orleans convent. Walters recovers, but Essie rejects a worthy suitor because of her conviction that a second marital venture might be overcast by her earlier unhappy experiences.

*Old Greenbottom Inn and Other Stories*—with the exception

of "The Death of Hanover," the fifth and final narrative in the volume—describes the difficult position of Negro women. Though handicapped by bastard birth, illicit cohabitation, insult, inadequate protection, and limited opportunities, they are nevertheless depicted as capable of virtue, honor, fortitude, and self-sacrifice. The stories mirror the transition of the race from bondage to freedom and embody a more authentic picture of Negro college life than any preceding volume. The degrading influence of race prejudice upon Southern whites is indicated. In an introductory note to *Old Greenbottom Inn and Other Stories* McClellan declares that "many pitiable tragedies" of Southern Negro life—"concerning which now exist only silence, unbelief, and indifference"—deserve to be told. It is regrettable that he himself did not further exploit the rich literary mine of which he was aware.

### James E. McGirt

James E. McGirt's *The Triumphs of Ephraim* (1907), a collection of eight inferior short stories, reveals the Negro to advantage but also shows the imprint of the plantation tradition. "At the Mercy of a Slave," which the author declares "will tear the black skin from the Negro's bosom and lay bare his very soul, that you may see and dissect it," eulogizes a bondman for loyalty to the wife and child of a Southern gentleman who was absent fighting in the Civil War. "Lifting the Veil" is a tribute to Aunt Diana, who accommodates her former mistress by successfully rearing the illegitimate son of a young Southern blue-blood and a poor white girl. "The Triumphs of Ephraim" and "The Test that Failed" provide glimpses of Negro society. In the former a coachman wins the hand of the daughter of the president of a large Negro school, while in the latter two Greensboro college men prove their affection for an attractive girl. "In Love as in War," an apotheosis of the Negro soldier, presents a colored sergeant who outstrips the scion of an aristocratic New Orleans family to win the love of a Filipino princess. Though weak in technique, *The*

*Triumphs of Ephraim* is less propagandistic than most Negro fiction of its time.

## J. W. Grant

In *Out of the Darkness, or Diabolism and Destiny* (1909) J. W. Grant is disturbed because of the ridicule and vilification accorded the Negro:

> The historical and literary libels, the minstrel shows, the "rag time" music and advertising designs have all, at all times, held the Negro up to contemptuous gaze, and pictured him as a fawning fool!

Convinced that writers of other races will not recognize the accomplishments of the black man, Grant avows that "if the Negro wishes the truths of the history of his thralldom, persecution, degradation, ostracism, and his successes and triumphs over his enemies and calumniators told, he himself must tell it!" In *Out of the Darkness,* therefore, he undertakes "to strike one blow in justice's cause" and "to say something in exculpation and commendation of my people."

The main characters of *Out of the Darkness* are Lucius Storms, Julius Jarnigan, and Harold Scott, Livingstone College alumni who later become physician, lawyer, and minister, respectively. Storms, a medical graduate of Harvard and the discoverer of a cure for yellow fever, falls in love with a white patient whose life he saves but is lynched before an intimate relationship develops. On the other hand, Scott and Jarnigan attain domestic and professional success but manifest divergent views on racial policy:

> Harold Scott, being a minister, became a devout apostle of the gospel of salvation through industrial and political acquiescence. He preferred to work along the line of least resistance.
>
> Julius Jarnigan, being a lawyer, a combative calling, took up the cudgel in defense of the propaganda, "Universal Educational and Political Opportunity" for all men, whether black, white, red, brown or yellow—for "all men up, and not some men down."

In this matter of choice between the program of Booker T. Washington and that of W. E. B. DuBois, Grant leaves no doubt as to his position by expressing contempt for the recommendations of the former: "What are houses, land and money to men who are *women?*"

*Out of the Darkness* also describes the disadvantages of the Negro before and after the Civil War. On the plantation of Storms' white father we observe slave-trading in its most repulsive form, and during Reconstruction we see the South using disfranchisement and terrorism in an effort to divest the Negro of power. Southern tolerance of the incendiary propaganda of Thomas Dixon is implied in the following quotation from an editorial in a white newspaper:

> One writer, who has done more than any other in moulding public sentiment against the Negro, has declared that it is his mission to drive the Negro from this country. While we of the South know that his fabrications are emanations from a diseased brain, yet since they help our cause, what care we?

The despoilment of colored women by white men is likewise held in the spotlight. In connection with the yielding of Storms' mother to her master, for example, Grant writes:

> That was then and is now the fate of many Negro house-girls in the South. They were considered the legitimate prey of either the fathers or sons in the families where they served.

In developing the character of Storms, moreover, Grant examines the psychology of the bitter near-white who, rejected by one race because of a small percentage of Negro blood, nevertheless shrinks from the insult, persecution, and degradation which are the lot of the other. The strained relationship between Storms and his white half-brother recalls the half-sister bond between Janet Miller and Olivia Carteret in Chesnutt's *The Marrow of Tradition,* while Storms' determination to keep his purchased residence in a white neighborhood anticipates a similar stand by Fred Merrit in Rudolph Fisher's *The Walls of Jericho* (1928).

Written to exalt Negro character, *Out of the Darkness* has the artificialities and extravagances of its species. To show the unfairness of prejudice and discrimination, Grant presents Negroes who are models of decorum in social and professional life. He exerts himself to commend the attire and refinement of well-to-do Negroes, and includes political speeches, commencement addresses, and newspaper editorials designed to display the educational attainments of colored people.

ROBERT L. WARING

In *As We See It* (1910) Robert L. Waring extols the Negro at the expense of the poor white. Assuming that poor whites "*present the true problem of the South,*" Waring sets out "to reveal two sides of Southern life which are carefully obscured, intentionally avoided, or deliberately misstated by newspaper and magazine writers." The first is the successful Negro, "whom calamity howlers are careful to keep in the background, and whom the Southern press persists in misrepresenting even to the point of malicious lying." The second is the poor white, "another class, lower, both morally and mentally, than the Negro." Waring lists incest, illiteracy, heavy infant mortality, and crime as bases of his aversion for the poor white.

At the beginning of the novel a benevolent Alabama planter of the old regime sends his son, Malcolm A. Overley, Jr., and his ex-slave's son, Abe Overley, Jr., to Oberlin College. At the same time Buck Lashum, son of a former slave overseer who profited from the collapse of the Confederacy, enters the Ohio school. Malcolm and Abe not only make good scholastic records but also fall in love with two respectable girls. In a poorly executed effort to discredit Abe, Buck and his friend, Squealer Bloxum, are apprehended by college authorities and expelled. Returning to Alabama, Buck, with the aid of several associates, gets revenge by whipping Abe's mother and sister to death. Abe later hears of the double murder and disposes of the killers one by one. At the close of the novel Abe and Malcolm are happily married to their college sweethearts.

Poorly written and constructed, *As We See It* is obviously planned to belittle the poor white and to compliment the progressive Negro and the plantation aristocrat. Sympathy with the ideology of Booker T. Washington is indicated in Abe's explanation that his Oberlin fiancée, like himself, thinks "that no good can possibly come by the mingling of the races socially." Like other works of its class, *As We See It* has the usual blemishes and shortsightedness of impassioned counterpropaganda.

### W. E. B. DuBois

W. E. B. DuBois's *The Quest of the Silver Fleece* (1911), an ably documented sociological novel, is a study of the American cotton industry. This work was probably influenced by Frank Norris' *The Octopus* (1901) and *The Pit* (1903), the first and second novels of a trilogy designed to treat the growing, marketing, and consumption of wheat, as well as to substantiate the author's theory that the best novel "proves something, draws conclusions from a whole congeries of forces, social tendencies, race impulses, devotes itself not to a study of men but of man."[22] Just as wheat is the motivating influence in Norris' works, so is cotton in *The Quest of the Silver Fleece*. For example, in Toomsville, Alabama, the main setting of the novel, "cotton was currency; cotton was merchandise; cotton was conversation." That cotton is also the master of the black man's fate is thus indicated:

> When cotton rose, the tenants had already sold their cotton; when cotton fell the landlords squeezed the rations and lowered the wages. When cotton rose again, up went the new Spring rent contracts. So it was that the bewildered black serf dawdled in listless inability to understand.

But cotton is likewise a determining force in the lives of Southern landlords, for Northern capitalists, grasping for financial gain, seek to monopolize the industry by establishing a dictatorship over the planters, merchants, and bankers of the South. To aggravate matters, Northern philanthropists subsidize private Negro schools and thus imperil the continued availabilty of ignorant, cheap, tractable labor. On this point Colonel St. John Cresswell, a blue-blood of the feudal South, asserts:

> "American cotton-spinning supremacy is built on cheap cotton; cheap cotton is built on cheap niggers. Educating, or rather *trying* to educate niggers, will make them restless and discontented—that is, scarce and dear as workers."

DuBois demonstrates close sociological observation in his description of Toomsville, an Alabama community elevated "above the cotton and the corn, fringed with dirty, straggling cabins of black folk." In the commercial center of the town "great bales of cotton, yellow-white in its soiled sacking, piled in lofty, dusty mountains, lay listening for the train that, twice a day, ran out to the greater world." The cotton warehouse, the seed mill, and the cotton gin are hubs of business and, like everything else except the main store, have "a general sense of dilapidation." In this setting, where cotton is the chief topic of discussion and the principal source of income, race relations are tense. Black tenant farmers are thrown into chain gangs for the slightest offenses, and the general pattern of Negro behavior is to cringe in submission and suffer in silence. Evidence of interbreeding is abundant. Within the white group, sharp social and ideological differences separate the aristocrats, the Yankee teachers, and the poor whites. The land barons fear the vote of the poor white and the infiltration of his blood, and at the same time resent the economic power and racial views of the Northerner. One poor white woman, aware that her class and Negroes are played against one another, anticipates Richard Wright's "Bright and Morning Star" by saying: "Durned if I don't think these white slaves and black slaves had ought ter git together." As a rule, however, the poor-white attitude toward Negroes is that of Tolliver, who hated "niggers only a shade more than he hated white aristocrats of the Cresswell type."

The main plot of *The Quest of the Silver Fleece* recounts the fantastic romance of Bles Alwyn and Zora Cresswell. In order to secure the money necessary for Zora's education, the young couple secretly grow in a nearby swamp the finest cotton ever seen in Tooms County. Learning that Zora had been deflowered some years previously by her young master, Harry Cresswell, Alwyn abruptly deserts her. Repelled in a subsequent attempt to enjoy Zora, Cresswell refuses payment for her swamp-grown cotton and calculates that her living expenses leave her in his debt. Upon the recommendation of Miss Smith, principal of the private school for Negroes, Zora gets work as maid to wealthy Mrs. Vanderpool and goes to New York, where she does considerable studying. In the meantime Alwyn, again through Miss Smith's intercession, obtains a clerkship in Washington and quickly gains political power, which he loses because of his own integrity and his opponents' craft and guile. Eventually Zora and Alwyn join Miss Smith's faculty, participate in the stabilization and development of the school, and marry.

The Cresswells give the author an opportunity to satirize the Southern landowning aristocracy. St. John Cresswell, a high-born gentleman of the old school, is antagonistic to Yankees and educated Negroes. After the Civil War he disregards the right of the black man to own property and disapproves the marriage of his children, Helen and Harry, to Northerners. Just before death, however, he bequeaths a large share of his estate to Miss Smith's school and recognizes Harry's child by a colored woman as his granddaughter. Harry, though having the prejudices of his father, is less militant and more yielding before the new demands of the Reconstruction period. Both father and son are adept in fleecing Negro tenants. Helen is depicted as physically attractive but intellectually vacuous.

John Taylor, a Wall Street speculator who marries Helen, makes no secret of his cupidity as an investor in cotton:

He purposed going into business neither for his own health nor for the health or clothing of the peoples, but to apply his knowledge of the world's nakedness and of black men's toil in such a way as to bring himself wealth.

Disdainful of Southern caste and color distinctions, this practical Yankee scorns pretensions based on lineage:

The caste way of thinking in the South, both as applied to poor whites and to Negroes, he simply could not understand. The weak and ignorant of all races he despised and had no patience with them.

In contrasting John's sister Mary, who becomes Harry's wife, and Miss Smith, DuBois discloses divergent Northern attitudes toward Negro education. Mary, a Wellesley graduate teaching Negroes only because of financial necessity, abhors contact with dark folk. Disapproving the liberal education of Negro youth, she thinks freedmen and their children should be trained for farming or domestic service and favors the administration of colored schools by Northern philanthropists and Southern bluebloods. On the other hand, Miss Smith, in the face of suspicion and opposition, advocates taking culture to the masses, feels that Negroes need more than elementary and manual training to survive in an organized plantation system, and believes that the Southern aristocracy is inimical to the best interests of colored people.

Among the Negro characters Alwyn and Zora, who are developed at greater length, are idealized and thus may be added to that gallery of portraits designed to instill race pride in Negroes and evoke justice from whites. Zora's rise from the Alabama cotton fields to a position of race leadership is incredible in its swiftness, and the same may be said of Alwyn's meteoric climb to such influential standing that he is seriously considered for the position of Secretary of the Treasury. A much more convincing character is Johnson, whom DuBois describes in these words:

Johnson was what Colonel Cresswell called "a faithful nigger." He was one of those constitutionally timid creatures into whom the servility of his fathers had sunk so deep that it had become second-nature. To him a white man was an archangel, while the Cresswells, his father's masters, stood for God. He served them with dog-like faith, asking no reward, and for what he gave in reverence to them, he took back in contempt for his fellows—"niggers!" He applied the epithet with more contempt than the Colonel himself could express. To the Negroes he was a "white folk's nigger," to be despised and feared.

By carrying false reports of a radical labor movement to Taylor and spreading malicious rumors among Negroes, Johnson seeks to destroy a co-operative farming project promoted by Zora and Alwyn. Ironically, however, he is lynched, along with an impetuous young Negro, by a Tooms County mob.

*The Quest of the Silver Fleece* also satirizes black and white politicians in Washington. Alwyn falls from the graces of his party because of refusal to support a crooked educational measure; and Caroline Wynn, his fiancée, who anticipates Sara Andrews of *The Dark Princess* (1928), marries one of the Negro shysters who plotted his decline from political power. Race-baiting and chicanery in national politics are exemplified in Mrs. Vanderpool's prevention of Harry's appointment as Ambassador to France by prompting prejudiced Americans to believe that Caroline's prize-winning sculpture, "The Outcasts," was sponsored by Mary Taylor Cresswell in the All-Southern Art Exhibit "to force social equality."

Subordinating character and plot to the study of the influence of the cotton industry upon American life, DuBois's *The Quest of the Silver Fleece* surpasses earlier novels by Negroes in the moulding of the facts of scholarly investigation with the feelings of a sensitive participant in the interracial struggle. Objects of attack are avaricious Northern industrialists with the dream of controlling the cotton-growing South and prejudiced Dixie land-owners with an "aristocratic pose and pretensions built on the poverty, crime, and exploitation of six generations of serfs." Interesting glimpses are given of political maneuvers in Washington and of the administration of the Negro private school. In "L'Envoi" DuBois petitions the reader to "lift thine eyes upon the Horror in this land—the maiming and mocking and murdering of my people, and the prisonment of their souls." Such an entreaty suggests that the author was aware of the polemical power of fiction.

### James Weldon Johnson

Published anonymously in 1912 with a preface by Brander Matthews and reissued under the author's name in 1927 with an introduction by Carl Van Vechten, *The Autobiography of an Ex-Coloured Man*[23] is noteworthy because of its restraint, its comprehensiveness, and its adumbration of the Negro Renascence of the 1920's. At a time when most Negro fictionists were giving blow for blow and painting extravagantly favorable pictures of members of the race, Johnson set out neither to glorify Negroes nor to malign whites but to interpret men and conditions as he knew them. This unbiased approach was immediately noted by Brander Matthews, who commented:

> This vivid and startlingly new picture of conditions brought about by the race question in the United States makes no special plea for the Negro, but shows in a dispassionate, though sympathetic, manner conditions as they actually exist between the whites and blacks today. Special pleas have already been made for and against the Negro in hundreds of books, but in these books either his virtues or his vices have been exaggerated.[24]

Besides being more detached than any preceding novel of American Negro life, *The Autobiography of an Ex-Coloured Man* is ground-breaking in its introduction of a well-realized cosmopolitan milieu. Unlike most earlier Negro fiction, it is not localized in the South but moves out into the broader field of European and Northern urban life. In the beginning of the book the hero accompanies his mother, the mistress of a wealthy Southerner, from agricultural Georgia to urban Connecticut, where he attends high school and shows talent as a pianist. Thwarted in his plan to enter Atlanta University, he proceeds to Jacksonville, Florida, and obtains a job in a cigar factory. Later he goes to New York City and mingles with Harlem cabaret society until a murder compels him to accept work as the entertaining musician and traveling companion of a millionaire introvert. After touring the principal cities of Europe with his eccentric employer, the hero resolves to return to the United States for the purpose of studying and transcribing the folk music of the American Negro. Nauseated by a Georgia lynching, however, he returns to New York and joins the white race in order to escape the shame and financial disadvantage of being a member of a defenseless minority. Within a few years he attains economic security and marries a respectable white woman who bears him two children before her untimely death.

We see in this novel an array of characters including Connecticut school children, Negro pullman porters, Cuban cigar factory workers, educated and well-to-do colored people, habitués of New York's Bohemian centers, Manhattan aristocrats, German musicians, preaching and singing leaders of Southern "big meetings," and New York's white bourgeoisie. In a word, *The Autobiography of an Ex-Coloured Man* signalizes the liberation of the Negro novelist from the habitual practice of using the South as a principal setting. As Van Vechten notes:

> Mr. Johnson, however, chose an all-embracing scheme. His young hero, the ostensible author, either discusses (or lives) pretty nearly every phase of Negro life, North and South and even in Europe, available to him at that period.[25]

In addition to being more impartial and more comprehensive than any earlier novel of American Negro life, *The Autobiography of an Ex-Coloured Man* is a milestone because of its forthright presentation of racial thought. Admitting the dual personality which some Negroes assume—one role among their own group and the other in the presence of whites—Johnson is himself not guilty of such a two-sided character. Not attempting to "wear the mask," he gives a calm, dispassionate treatment of people and situations as he sees them. This frank self-expression caused Brander Matthews to feel that "it is as though a veil had been drawn aside: the reader is given a view of the inner life of the

Negro in America, is initiated into the freemasonry, as it were, of the race."[26]

In discussing the American race problem, the author contrasts typical attitudes of Northern and Southern white people toward the Negro:

Northern white people love the Negro in a sort of abstract way, as a race; through a sense of justice, charity, and philanthropy, they will liberally assist in his elevation. . . . Southern white people despise the Negro as a race, and will do nothing to aid in his elevation as such; but for certain individuals they have a strong affection, and are helpful to them in many ways. With these individual members of the race they live on terms of the greatest intimacy; they intrust to them their children, their family treasures, and their family secrets; in trouble they often go to them for comfort and counsel; in sickness they often rely upon their care. This affectionate relation between the Southern whites and those blacks who come into close touch with them has not been overdrawn even in fiction.

Nevertheless, the continuous interracial strife in the South is shown to be exhausting to the energies of both groups. Upon the Negro operates a "dwarfing, warping, distorting influence" which forces him "to take his outlook on all things not from the viewpoint of a citizen, or a man, or even a human being, but from the viewpoint of a coloured man." Simultaneously the Southern white man is encumbered and retarded because of his preoccupation with racial issues:

The same thing may be said of the white man of the South; most of his mental efforts run through one narrow channel; his life as a man and a citizen, many of his financial activities, and all of his political activities are impassably limited by the ever present "Negro question."

In view of the South's record of oppression and injustice, Johnson feels that the leadership of the section should not be permitted to deal with the Negro problem:

I do not see how a people that can find in its conscience any excuse whatever for slowly burning to death a human being, or for tolerating such an act, can be entrusted with the salvation of a race.

He further believes that American Negroes have made at least four contributions that disprove their alleged inferiority:

> It is my opinion that the coloured people of this country have done four things which refute the oft-advanced theory that they are an absolutely inferior race, which demonstrate that they have originality and artistic conception, and, what is more, the power of creating that which can influence and appeal universally. The first two of these are the Uncle Remus stories, collected by Joel Chandler Harris, and the Jubilee songs, to which the Fisk singers made the public and the skilled musicians of both America and Europe listen. The other two are rag-time music and the cake-walk.

Turning to the hitherto inflammatory subject of miscegenation, Johnson manifests no bitterness. As a matter of fact, he censures neither the liaison between the hero's colored mother and white father, nor passing and intermarriage in the hero's own life. At one point, passing is justified not as an expedient aroused by "fear or search for a larger field of action and opportunity" but as a means of evading the "unbearable shame" of being "identified with a people that could with impunity be treated worse than animals." As a white man watching self-sacrificing Negroes fighting for the full emancipation of their race, however, the hero sometimes feels like "a coward, a deserter," and "possessed by a strange longing for my mother's people," he "cannot repress the thought that, after all, I have chosen the lesser part, that I have sold my birthright for a mess of pottage."

In brief, *The Autobiography of an Ex-Coloured Man,* like the novels of Chesnutt, is an important precursor of the Negro Renascence, for, as John Chamberlain notes, "it certainly caught the tempo of the future, and it explored problems that remain as portentous today as they were in 1912."[27] Carl Van Vechten, the author of *Nigger Heaven* (1926), the book that attracted the interest of the nation to Harlem, admits that he "discovered the Autobiography to be an invaluable source-book for the study of Negro psychology."[28] The Negro Renascence novels that closely follow the tradition of *The Autobiography of an Ex-Coloured*

*Man* are Jessie Fauset's *There Is Confusion* (1924) and *Plum Bun* (1929), Walter White's *Flight* (1926), and Nella Larsen's *Quicksand* (1928) and *Passing* (1929). All these novels show a preference for the Northern urban scene, especially New York City, and present in a leading role a refined and sensitive mulatto who, being more of a silent sufferer than a social reformer, passes in order to escape the discomforts of a racial minority and thereafter is in a quandary as to whether he has chosen the better part.

### Yorke Jones

Yorke Jones's *The Climbers: A Story of Sun-Kissed Sweethearts* (1912), which lacks the restraint of Johnson's *The Autobiography of an Ex-Coloured Man,* is another attempt to extol Negro education and culture. Wade, Fairfax, Holt, and Wilson are college schoolmates; and after graduation the first becomes a physician in the Southern city of Rockford, the second accepts a teaching position in a Gulf state, and the third and fourth enter the ministry in the North. Later, through the influence of Wade, Wilson obtains a church in Rockford and Holt a professorship in the Normal and Industrial College of the same city. After Holt is promoted to the presidency of the school, Fairfax joins the faculty and marries Holt's daughter Julia.

The racial views of the author are expressed at various points in the volume. Resentment is shown toward the minstrel concept of Negro character:

> Fairfax's people are America's butt of fun. They, too, are thought to be very light-hearted because they seem amusing; but while the black man is hopeful (because his present is new and his future is full of promise), yet it is a grave mistake to imagine that the child of Ham feels free of care, because, to his brother in white, he seems amusing.

On the other hand, pride is taken in the appearance of the audience at the graduating exercises of a Negro college:

> Have you ever attended a commencement of a Southern colored institution for higher learning? If you have, you do not need to be

told of the large, well-dressed, self-respecting crowd that gathered to witness Rockford's closing—the cream of the race in that region.

Like other novels written to compliment the Negro, *The Climbers* exaggerates the virtues of the upper class of the race and deplores the oppression of black folk in the South. Artificial characters, slow action, and shallow thinking render the book relatively inconsequential as a work of art.

### Joseph S. Cotter

In the serious stories included in *Negro Tales* (1912) Joseph S. Cotter shows a preference for sordid rather than flattering aspects of racial life, but his failure as a literary artist is just as obvious as that of Yorke Jones in *The Climbers.* Three of the more earnest selections in the volume are "Rodney," a characterization of the bitter mulatto son of a Negro woman and a white man; "Tesney, the Deceived," a study of a neurotic near-white girl who drifts into an unfortunate mésalliance with a drunken brawler; and "A Town Sketch," a contrast between the progressiveness of the white and the backwardness of the colored population of a small Southern town. The first two stories inexpertly handle the trite theme of the tragic mulatto, while the third suffers from amateurish excesses and generalizations.

### Oscar Micheaux

Avoiding both pride and bitterness in his treatment of interracial subject matter, Oscar Micheaux writes somewhat autobiographically of the experiences of an enterprising Negro in Chicago, the South Dakota farm lands, and the urban South. His first novel, *The Conquest: The Story of a Negro Pioneer* (1913), based largely on the author's own life and dedicated to Booker T. Washington, relates the experiences of Oscar Devereux in Illinois and South Dakota. In the latter state Devereux, after acquiring a homestead and becoming a prosperous farmer, falls in love with a Scottish girl but evades matrimony because of the racial barrier. Later marrying Orlean McCraline, daughter of a Negro preacher of Chicago, he finally leaves her because of frequent disagreements with her father.

In *The Conquest,* for the first time in American Negro fiction, a leading colored character appears in the role of a pioneer; and settlement in the Northwest is proposed as an approach to the alleviation of racial tension in the South. Admitting that the black man suffers injustice in the United States, Micheaux nevertheless asserts that this "should be no reason why the American Negro should allow obvious prejudice to prevent his taking advantage of opportunities that surround him." Recommending the Northwest as an area where the Negro might work out a successful future, the author continues:

> . . . for years I have felt constrained to deplore the negligence of the colored race in America, in not seizing the opportunity for monopolizing more of the many million acres of rich farm lands in the great Northwest, where immigrants from the old world own many acres of rich farm lands; while the millions of blacks, only a few hundred miles away, are as oblivious to it all as the heathen of Africa are to civilization.

In didactic chapters entitled "Where the Negro Fails" and "Progressives and Reactionaries" Micheaux advances opinions concerning the shortcomings and leadership of his race. He affirms that "the greatest of all the failings" of his people, both ignorant and educated, is the lack of "that great and mighty principle which characterizes Americans, called the initiative." In amplification of this idea, he says:

> Colored people are possible in every way that is akin to becoming good citizens, which has been thoroughly proven and is an existing fact. Yet they seem to lack the "guts" to get into the Northwest and "do things." In seven or eight of the great agricultural states there were not enough colored farmers to fill a township of thirty-six sections.
>
> Another predominating inconsistency is that there is that "love of luxury." They want street cars, cement walks, and electric lights to greet them when they arrive.

In an evaluation of the two conflicting schools of Negro leadership, Micheaux expresses a preference for the racial platform of Booker T. Washington:

> The Progressives, led by Booker T. Washington and with industrial education as the material idea, are good, active citizens; while the other class, distinctly reactionary in every way, contend for more equal rights, privileges, and protection, which is all very logical, indeed, but they do not substantiate their demands with any concrete policies; depending largely on loud demands, and are too much given to the condemnation of the entire white race for the depredations of a few.

A further examination of Micheaux's views on the Washington-DuBois controversy reveals, however, that he is not altogether in agreement with the views of the Tuskegee educator. He proposes the Northwest for Negro settlement, while Washington advised the black man to remain in the South. In addition, Micheaux is incorrect in the observation that DuBois was not a leader of the anti-Washington movement and that this movement did not gain momentum with the passing of the years.

*The Forged Note: A Romance of the Darker Races* (1915), largely autobiographical like *The Conquest,* is also a trail-blazing novel in its treatment of the experiences of a Negro writer in selling his own book in the urban South. Sidney Wyeth, author of a novel called *The Tempest* (really *The Conquest*), and Mildred Latham are promoting the sale of *The Tempest* among colored people in Southern cities. Wyeth goes to Attalia (Atlanta) and Effingham (Birmingham), while Mildred works in Memphis. At the close of the novel the couple, reunited in New Orleans, set out for South Dakota, the part of the country that Wyeth prefers and calls home.

Much of *The Forged Note* is direct criticism of Negro life in the urban South, "wherein people and environment are so different from the rest, that a great problem is ever at issue." Though aware of prejudice and persecution, Micheaux is chiefly concerned with the black man's own delinquencies. For example, one character in the book makes the following comment concerning the colored population of Effingham:

"These Negroes in Effingham are niggers proper. They think nothing about reading and trying to learn something; they only care for dressing up and having a good time."

A further indictment of Negroes, especially the leaders of the race, is given in an article which Wyeth contributes under the following headline to a Southern daily newspaper:

> Negro Says Race Faces Dreadful Conditions, Due to Lack of Leaders. Says Selfishness Is So Much the Order That There Is No Interest Whatever Toward Uplift. Professional Negro the Worst.

A sordid picture of the criminality and profligacy of colored Memphians is painted for Mildred by a minister:

"The city has a preponderance of ignorant, polluted people among the Negroes. They flock into this town from all around, and represent the low, polluted, and depraved element of our race. They settle about the levee district, spend their earnings for the worst whiskey, give the remainder of their time to gambling and all kinds of vice, and murder is the natural consequence."

Though indicating the degeneracy of Negro life in Southern cities, Micheaux offers no panacea and fails to exhibit the optimism and enterprise which characterize *The Conquest.*

Except for an intensification of the theme of intermarriage and a more detailed analysis of the main character's difficulties with his Negro wife because of her father's interference, *The Homesteader* (1917)[29] is quite similar to *The Conquest.* The novel is an account of the love of a Negro farmer of South Dakota for the daughter of a neighbor who has recently migrated from Indiana. When the lovers are brought together in a driving snowstorm, the author comments:

But what he was yet to know, and which is the great problem of our story, the girl, his dream girl, Agnes Stewart, happened to be white, while he, Jean Baptiste, The Homesteader, was a Negro.

Although strongly attracted to Agnes, Baptiste concludes that their marriage could not be consummated in the United States since

. . . *between him and his dream girl was a chasm so deep socially that bridging was impossible.* Because she was white while he was black, according *to the custom of the country and its law,* she could never be anything to him. (Italics by Micheaux.)

Moreover, he feels that such a union would not be for the best interests of the girl and himself:

> But to marry out of the race to which he belonged, especially into the race in which she belonged, would be the most unpopular thing he could do. He had set himself in this new land to succeed; he had worked and slaved to that end. He liked his people; he wanted to help them. Examples they needed, and such he was glad he had become; but if he married now the one he loved, the example was lost; he would be condemned, he would be despised by the race that was his. Moreover, last but not least, he would perhaps, by such union bring into her life much unhappiness, and he loved her too well for that.

For these reasons, therefore, Baptiste decides to marry a woman of his own race and eventually weds Orlean McCarthy (note the similarity of the name to that of the wife of the hero in *The Conquest*), a Chicago minister's daughter, whom he carries to his homestead in South Dakota. The Reverend McCarthy succeeds in alienating his daughter's affections and causing her to sell property which her husband had given her. After Orlean, tormented by conscience, commits patricide and suicide, Baptiste is accused of a double murder but is later acquitted because of findings of a detective hired by Agnes. Baptiste and Agnes are brought together through the use of *deus ex machina,* a device frequently used in American fiction to solve the difficulties of interracial romance. Returning to South Dakota, Baptiste learns that Agnes has Negro blood and marries her without anxiety concerning American mores and law.

Though unimpressive in technique, Oscar Micheaux's novels introduce characters and settings far removed from the well-trod paths of American Negro fiction. The problem of intermarriage, the cardinal interest in *The Conquest* and *The Homesteader,* is left dangling in the former work but is solved in the latter through the hackneyed device of revealing that the supposedly white heroine is a mixed-blood. *The Conquest,* which attempts to defend the program of Booker T. Washington, proposes Negro migration to the Northwest as a means of improving race relations in the South. In *The Forged Note* the author missed an unusual opportunity to probe the life of the Southern urban Negro. With all their inadequacies, however, Micheaux's novels stand in contrast to much of the complimentary fiction produced by many Negro writers before the World War.

### William M. Ashby

In *Redder Blood* (1915) William M. Ashby went a step further than Oscar Micheaux in *The Conquest* and *The Homesteader* by stressing that no social or legal restrictions are strong enough to keep two lovers apart:

> The book [*Redder Blood*] does say, however,—and, I hope, strongly, —that where two persons love each other deeply neither custom, nor convention, nor law are great enough barriers to keep them apart, else we should never have had Othello and Desdemona.

To illustrate this theory, Ashby brings together in marriage Stanton Birch, a prominent white New Yorker, and Zelda Marston, a colored woman who is passing in order to gain "a chance to live—an equal chance." After the couple become the parents of a son named Adrian, Birch expresses liberal racial views. While reading of an attack upon a Negro at a Southern convention, for example, he comments:

> "I don't see why a people that have proved themselves thriving, earnest, and willing since we've freed them should not always be allowed civil and human rights without always being attacked by fanatics."

When Zelda suggests that the Negro problem should possibly be worked out in the South, he replies:

> "It's not a Negro problem, it is not a Southern problem, it is a human, live American problem. Should the settlement of the 'Immigration Question' be left to New York because most of the immigrants come to New York's harbor and because so many of them settle in that city? No; just so, then, with these people."

Asked by his wife if he approves intermarriage, he answers:

> "I am sure I would always abide by the laws of nature, justice, and God; they are indestructible and irrefutable."

Birch impulsively deserts Zelda, however, upon learning many years later that she is the daughter of an aristocratic Virginian and a mulatto woman; but Adrian, after receiving this report, loyally remains with his mother. When Adrian confesses to his fiancée, Wanda Croydon, that he has Negro blood, she exclaims:

> "You leper! You cancer in a man's form, you imp let loose from limbo! You deceived me. Acid-like you ate into my pure soul, knowing all the time what you were, knowing that you were black as midnight. Let me wipe away your kisses, let me tear my flesh from my frame. I was pure; your black skin has corrupted me, polluted me. Get out of my sight forever."

Though Wanda later regrets this outburst of temper, Adrian refuses to renew their engagement because of the possibility that their offspring might be dark. On the other hand, Birch, unable to forget his wife during extensive travels abroad, returns to her waiting arms.

In its emphasis upon the theme of passing, *Redder Blood* follows the tradition of Chesnutt's *The House Behind the Cedars* and Johnson's *The Autobiography of an Ex-Coloured Man* and anticipates the novels of Jessie Fauset and Nella Larsen. One of the pitfalls of passing is illustrated in the desertion of Zelda by her husband. Although Adrian's refusal to wed the woman of his choice is a common resolution of this particular type of dilemma, *Redder Blood* does not inveigh against intermarriage when lovers are aware of the various problems that they will likely face.

### F. Grant Gilmore

Similar to *Redder Blood* in its stress upon miscegenation, F. Grant Gilmore's *The Problem: A Military Novel* (1915) eulogizes the Negro soldier and tells of the relations between a white and a colored family during the second half of the nineteenth century. Colonel Fairfax, a Virginia aristocrat, is the father of a near-white girl, Freda, by Amanda Williams, the mulatto daughter of the caretaker of his estate. A few years later Fairfax moves to Washington and induces his wife to adopt Freda, who is presented as a white girl, as a companion for their son Henry. After receiving a heavy cash settlement upon the death of Fairfax, Freda enriches her education through foreign travel and becomes a belle in Washington society. At the outbreak of the Spanish-American War, Henry, who meanwhile has finished West Point, goes to Cuba as an Army officer; and Freda, whom he admires, follows as a Red Cross nurse. On the island, however, she falls in love with William Henderson, a Negro sergeant who returns her affection but hesitates to wed her because of his race. Henderson and Freda are enabled to marry, however, after Amanda, in a death-bed statement, reveals the facts concerning the girl's parentage.

One of Gilmore's main purposes in *The Problem* is to extol the Negro soldier, and the entire sixth chapter treats the part played by the black man during the Spanish-American War. The romance of Freda and Henderson somewhat recalls the wooing of a Filipino princess by the colored sergeant of "In Love as in War," one of the stories in James E. McGirt's *The Triumphs of Ephraim* (1907).

In the treatment of interbreeding Gilmore shows little originality. The liaison between Colonel Fairfax and Amanda is like that between the parents of the heroine of Ashby's *Redder Blood* and many other such couples in American fiction. Furthermore, in setting the stage for the marriage of Freda and Henderson by revealing that the former is colored, Gilmore employed a threadbare contrivance also used by Micheaux in *The Homesteader.* Probably because of the author's belief that "we are slowly drawing to the place where there is no race, no creed, no color," *The Problem* handles interracial subject matter without rancor or enmity.

### Otis M. Shackelford

Shackelford's *Lillian Simmons, or The Conflict of Sections* (1915) is noteworthy because it treats interracial strife caused by the Negro migration to the North. As the story opens, a fight develops when George Simmons, a colored Chicagoan, nettles Charles Christopher, a newcomer from the South, with remarks such as the following:

> "You Southern niggers come up here and spoil our privileges. . . . There was a time when we could eat in any restaurant in town and now we are barred from all downtown places except Jim Allen's. We used to sit where we pleased in the theatres; we used to be permitted to go to any of the parks, and now that is all over. Just because you Southern people have come up here with your ignorance and roughness."

The clash between the two men is terminated, however, through the intervention of Lillian, Simmons' sister. Later Simmons, becoming envious of Christopher's success as a grocer, burns the Southerner's store but is generously forgiven and accepted as a business partner. At the end of the novel Christopher not only wins Lillian's hand but also converts Chicago Negroes to the advisability of segregated business and social institutions. Of the changed attitude of the Simmons family Shackelford writes:

> They are converted to the idea of Negro enterprise, even if it does invite segregation. They have become convinced that separate schools are not harmful, but are a positive benefit to the race. They furnish employment for the worthy boys and girls of the race and are inducements for them to pursue the higher courses of learning and to strive to excel in them.

By sponsoring business initiative and the social separation of the races, Shackelford shows agreement with the social philosophy of Booker T. Washington. Further concord with the views of the Tuskegee educator is indicated in *Seeking the Best* (1909), a book of autobiography, essays, and poems later bound with *Lillian Simmons*. Reminiscent of Washington, for instance, is Shackelford's contrast of his own racial attitude with that of DuBois:

But, unlike Dr. DuBois, who, in *The Souls of Black Folk*, writes of his early life among children of the other race, and who became shocked and very much grieved on account of the sudden dawning of this awful truth, as he seemed to think it, that there were distinctions on account of color, I always knew of racial differences and conducted myself accordingly, and so was saved from much humiliation along this line.

Also in harmony with Washington's precepts is Shackelford's advocacy of ingratiation as a Negro policy in dealing with Southern white people:

*We must study to please and sympathize with the other race.* And when we have lifted ourselves to such a plane, they cannot oppress us, they cannot resist us; for they are human and can but yield to the laws and promptings which govern in the human breast.

THOMAS H. B. WALKER

Thomas H. B. Walker is the author of two inferior novels, *Bebbly, or The Victorious Preacher* (1910) and *J. Johnson, or The Unknown Man: An Answer to Mr. Thos. Dixon's Sins of the Fathers* (1915). The former is a trivial account of a minister's experiences; while the latter, which at least merits examination, attempts to counteract the propaganda of the author of *The Leopard's Spots* and *The Clansman* by portraying the Negro with favor and esteem. The slight plot of *J. Johnson, or The Unknown Man* deals with the life of a mulatto foundling who is reared and given a college education by an old Negro couple in Georgia. When it is announced that Johnson is the son of a wealthy white Louisianian, he is rejected as a suitor by Susan Smith but is later accepted when it is revealed that the hero's father is of Negro-Creole extraction.

Like other flattering novels of its type, *J. Johnson, or The Unknown Man* gives a positive appraisal of the Negro. For example, in discussing the kindness of the dark-skinned discoverer of the abandoned child, Walker writes:

Now, here was a child, a bright child, an Octoroon; maybe a white child, but somehow she believed it to be of her race. If it had been an Indian of the forest, a Chinese from Hong Kong, or a Saxon of the purest blood, it would have made no difference with Aunt Jane; for in spite of all his shortcomings, in spite of all his faults and sins, the Negro is a good Samaritan; he is hospitable; he will help the needy; yea, he will feed even the slayer of his brother and those who revile, maltreat and abuse him.

Furthermore, as Susan's initial rejection of Johnson's proposal indicates, Walker attributes to the Negro a fervent race pride which renders amalgamation impossible:

"And no Negro woman desires inter-marriage of any kind, legal or illegal, with a white man. To the women of my race, such a thought is odious. . . . In this epistle I voice the sentiment of the mothers of ten million of sable sons and daughters living in America. Like the many other white men of your race, you are my enemy, and I am yours."

Such quotations as the two preceding are sufficient to show that *J. Johnson, or The Unknown Man,* in rebutting the imputations of Thomas Dixon's novels, likewise strayed far from objectivity and social realism.

## Henry F. Downing

Henry F. Downing's *The American Cavalryman: A Liberian Romance* (1917), dedicated to Joel E. and Arthur B. Spingarn of the National Association for the Advancement of Colored People, also treats racial intermixture and presents exemplary Negro characters. After the mysterious disappearance of his young daughter and the death of his grief-stricken wife in West Africa, John Calvert, supposedly a white man, returns to the United States, where he gains political prestige but loses a gubernatorial race because of the opposition of Negro voters. Later informed by Sarah Dale, a middle-aged mulatto, that he and she have the same colored-white parentage, Calvert nevertheless denies that he is a Negro:

"I'm not a Negro. Our father was white and my mother was an octoroon; consequently, if there's any African blood in me, it's only about one-sixteenth of the whole. I'm a white man!"

When Sarah states that her son Paul, a captain in Liberia, is in love with a near-white African girl whose mother, Reesha, "is a Negress pure and simple," Calvert remembers that Reesha is the name of the nurse with whom his child disappeared. A subsequent investigation leads to the recovery of his daughter and the prevention of her marriage to a first cousin. At the close of the novel Paul, having married a member of the Liberian upper class, receives from Calvert a huge grant to be used in the development of the agricultural resources of the West African republic.

Although the major part of *The American Cavalryman* describes the experiences of Calvert's lost daughter in Africa, attention is given to the consequences of miscegenation in the United States. Both Calvert and Sarah are products of interbreeding, and somewhat of a departure from the usual fictional procedure is the former's successful and unabashed refusal to accept the status of a Negro after the revelation of his mixed racial background. The leading characters have high social standing: Paul is a Spingarn medalist and a commissioned officer in the United States Army, his mother maintains a pretentious estate on the Hudson, and his wife is the stepdaughter of the President of Liberia. In its dedication to the Spingarn brothers *The American Cavalryman* suggests the growing influence of the National Association for the Advancement of Colored People upon Negro writers; and, in its manifestation of concern for the welfare of the native population of the West African republic, it is a forerunner of George Schuyler's *Slaves Today* (1931).

### Clayton Adams

Freely admitting his intention to give a favorable portrayal of the Negro in *Ethiopia, the Land of Promise: The Book with a Purpose* (1917), Clayton Adams states that in the writing of the novel he was "actuated both by humanitarian motives and by the desire to place the members of the much-abused Ethiopian race on the stage of human existence as actors in the powerful drama of human life, showing them therein to be men and women endowed with hearts as feeling, with motives as pure, and with aims as high as are those that govern the acts of the children of other races." Insisting that the incidents of the narrative "are unmarred by any touch of exaggeration" and that he has "softened the abhorrence of the reality," he further declares that he has "carefully avoided the portraying of improper relations between the sexes of the white race and the black, except in such cases as go to show that the 'Ethiop' woman is regarded as 'legitimate prey' . . . ." With reference to the purpose of the novel, Adams expresses the hope that through his "bringing certain alarming conditions to the attention of the world, the enlightened members of each of the races will do their best to ameliorate them by diffusing more freely the light of education and culture."

*Ethiopia, the Land of Promise* belies its title by unfolding action that takes place almost entirely in Unionland (the United States). The novel opens in Cargo City (Chicago), where members of the Decemvirate lay preliminary plans for an organization to be known as the Union of Ethiopia, the function of which is "to establish a bank for the handling of funds, the appointment of agents to take census of all the black people of Unionland, the establishment of a publication to be read by all their race, and the levying of an assessment of a stated amount for carrying on the propaganda." After the Chicago conference Allan Dune, the leading character of the narrative, undertakes to organize the Negroes of Savna (Savannah) but is forced to leave the city because he rescues Elsa Mangus, the daughter of one of his colleagues, from two white men who attempt to ravish her. Shortly after his departure, however, Elsa and another Negro are lynched by a bloodthirsty mob. During a Decemvirate mission to Savna a few weeks later, Dune is also lynched because of the false accusation of a white minister's daughter that he attempted to rape her. When a fair-minded white man suggests an impartial investigation in lieu of lynching, one of the callous mobsters replies:

"Wall, I tell yuh, boys, we'll bu'n him fust an' investigate this young fellah's tale afterwards."

Like Sutton E. Griggs's *Imperium in Imperio,* Adams' *Ethiopia, the Land of Promise* presents a vaguely sketched agency designed to safeguard the welfare and interests of American Negro citizens. Despite the author's prefatory promise of objectivity and impartiality, the novel is too much of a polemic to be a work of art.

### SARAH LEE BROWN FLEMING

Likewise an extolment of persecuted but heroic Negro leaders is Sarah Lee Brown Fleming's *Hope's Highway* (1918). Enoch Vance, educated by a liberal master and subsequently given sufficient funds to found Vance Institute for the training of freedmen, becomes widely known as the Leader because of his championship of Negro progress. Much of his work is undone by Joe Vardam, a crafty poor-white politician who sends Tom Brinley, a colored youth aspiring to succeed the Leader, to the chain gang. After escaping and clearing himself, Brinley goes to England, where he finishes his education at Oxford University. During the World War he serves in the French Army and thereafter returns to the United States to complete the work of the Leader. Of his success the author writes:

> Did he raise Vance Institute to its former glory? Yes, nor was that glory all. He did more; for never again in the history of Santa Maria do we hear of the injustice of the whites to the blacks—never again did a Brinley, or an Abbott, or any other member of the Negro race, know the ignominy of working in the chain-gang. For Tom Brinley had turned his people's steps away from the rough road of ignorance into the happy highway of hope.

In *Hope's Highway* the plantation aristocrats are depicted as the benefactors and the poor whites as the enemies of the black man. One of the characters of the book expresses the attitude of the author by saying:

> ". . . And remember, Miss Ennery, the worst enemies of the blacks are not the descendants of their former owners, but a class of poor

whites who have pushed in from the mountains, and who never knew of them, other than that they crowded them out of a livelihood, by having the monopoly of service. This condition, of course, kept them very poor, barely above starvation; hence this is the cause of their intense prejudice. These people prospered after Emancipation, and to-day are the life, politically and commercially, of the South. The Negro, it is true, was caught in a mesh that he is still untangling. It is evident that the only satisfactory solution will be for him to find his own way out."

Written for the purpose of extolling Negro leaders and their sympathizers, *Hope's Highway* has the usual overstatements of novels of its kind.

## *SUMMARY*

During the years between 1890 and World War I, American Negro fiction was, with few exceptions, extremely race-conscious. Chesnutt and Dunbar experimented in the plantation tradition; and Chesnutt, Dunbar, Mrs. Dunbar-Nelson, Durham, and Ellis wrote stories of white people in which the race problem was avoided. A decided majority of writers, however, answered the propaganda of Page and Dixon and sought to give the Negro a more favorable position in national opinion by glorifying him and exposing his oppressors.

In their counterpropaganda Negro fictionists usually portrayed educated and well-mannered colored characters, frequently related by blood to the Southern aristocracy, who often engage in long discussions of racial and political issues and are almost invariably presented as teachers, clergymen, physicians, lawyers, politicians, or journalists. A favorite practice is the depiction of these individuals attending lectures, literary societies, political councils, and institutions of higher education. In order to emphasize the plight of their race, Negro authors described such mistreatment as insult, malicious propaganda, Jim-Crowism, legal injustice, economic exploitation, illicit sexual relationships, peonage, lynching, and rioting, which often bring misery and tragedy not only to Negroes but to whites as well.

In so far as interracial relations are concerned, warmer friendliness is ordinarily manifested for blue-bloods than for poor whites. Sometimes characters venerate parents who are a highborn white gentleman and a colored woman, and generally no condemnation is made of such a relationship if the man is as honorable as Southern mores will permit. Liaisons between white women and Negro men, however, are usually avoided; and though suspense is occasionally stimulated by the suggestion of such affairs, it normally develops that the woman has Negro blood and thus is free to marry her colored lover. An important element in many novels of the period is passing, a subject which attracted Abolitionist authors of both races as well as such post-bellum white writers as Cable, Twain, Tourgee, and Howells. In certain cases Negro novelists—e.g., Mrs. Harper, Chesnutt, Johnson, Ashby, Gilmore, and Downing—used the old line of championing racial justice by sympathetically describing the frustrations and sufferings of the Negro-white hybrid, whom whites ordinarily considered to be superior to blacks because of their possession of Caucasian blood. On the other hand, some Negro authors contended that human beings achieve and excel not because of white paternity but as a result of better parentage and wider opportunities.

American Negro fiction between 1890 and World War I reflects the social and historical trends of the period, especially in so far as they influence the thought and life of colored citizens of the country. Attention is given to repression and disfranchisement from the black man's point of view. The Washington-DuBois controversy receives frequent discussion; and the majority of the writers indicate, either through implication or direct statement, a preference for the militant rather than for the pragmatic and conciliatory school of race leadership.

By praising the merits and palliating the failings of the Negro, most of these early writers proved themselves as guilty of tedium and literary distortion as were Dixon and Page. Their works are usually poor novels, because they are more polemic than fiction, and often poor polemic because they melodramatically plead the case. Nevertheless, these authors told a side of the story that the calumniators of the race did not tell; and four of their number—Chesnutt, Dunbar, Johnson, and DuBois—exerted noticeable influence upon participants in the Negro Renascence of the 1920's.

CHAPTER 3

# The Negro Renascence

## I. *WORLD WAR I*

THE MOST influential force in bringing about the cultural emancipation of the American Negro was World War I. With the beginning of hostilities the influx of European immigrants was suddenly halted, and simultaneously thousands of nationals of the belligerent countries were recalled. American industry, then engaged in making huge profits out of the European war effort, found itself seriously handicapped by a shortage of laborers. In order to meet the pressing demand for workers, Northern industrialists turned to the South and through their agents offered high wages to downtrodden and underpaid Negroes of that section. Attracted chiefly by economic opportunities but also by the promise of better social and educational advantages, black folk began to surge in huge numbers to the great urban centers of the North. Alarmed by the threat to their economic organization of a mass black exodus, Southerners first protested and then resorted to force in an effort to halt the migrants; but the dark tide flowed unceasingly northward, and the ruling class of Dixie learned that Negroes, like any other oppressed group, would not endure deprivation and exploitation if an escape to a better life were possible. As a result of this migration, approximately half a million black folk poured into the North during the World War years, and the total Negro urban population soared from 27.4 per cent to 34.0 per cent between 1910 and 1920. Although the wholesale crowding of Negroes into Northern cities sometimes caused congested housing conditions, sharp residential disputes, tense labor conflicts, and bloody race riots,[1] the gains, as far as black folk were concerned, compensated for the losses. In their new environment, Negroes not only made more money but also obtained better education, fairer treatment in the courts, increased political power, and wider cultural opportunities and developed group action characterized by initiative and self-reliance.

With the entry of the United States into the war in 1917 other developments contributed to the emergence of the so-called "New Negro." During America's brief participation in the crusade "to make the world safe for democracy" black men from the remotest tenant farms of the South mingled with unprejudiced people, realized in the heat of battle their fundamental brotherhood with their white countrymen, and developed an appreciation of the principles of human liberty for which the war was supposedly fought. As a consequence, many black soldiers, upon returning to this country, were no longer characterized by pussyfooting Uncle Tomism but were ready to seek and demand full social and political equality in the democracy for which they had fought and risked their lives. DuBois voiced the sentiments of the "New Negro" when he declared:

> Under similar circumstances we would fight again. But, by the God of Heaven, we are cowards and jackasses if, now that the war is over, we do not marshal every ounce of our brain and brawn to fight a sterner, longer, more unbending battle against the forces of hell in our own land.[2]

## II. *THE GARVEY MOVEMENT*

The proud and assertive racialism stimulated by World War I showed significant blossoming in the Garvey Movement, the initial large-scale organization of the Negro masses in American history. Establishing headquarters in Harlem, Marcus Garvey, the Jamaican leader of the Movement, had a four-fold program: first, to glorify blackness; second, to foster chauvinistic pride in Africa's contributions to civilization; third, to secure the freedom of the Negro in all parts of the world; and, fourth, to establish a black republic in Africa.

In glorifying blackness, Garvey made a passionate appeal to poor, dark-skinned Negroes, a group that had generally received the crumbs from the table in the various parts of the world in which white and black men had been thrown into juxtaposition. The effort was to develop among Negroes a counterpart of the Ku Klux Klan,[3] or what Charles S. Johnson called "a black version of that same 100 per cent mania that now afflicts white America, that emboldens the prophets of a 'Nordic blood renaissance,' that picked up and carried the cry of 'self-determination for all people,' 'India for Indians,' 'A Free Ireland.' "[4] Garvey made blackness the distinguishing mark of his personnel and agencies, and the religion which he devised for his followers included a black God and a black Christ.[5] Closely coupled with this exaltation of blackness was the endeavor to develop pride in the culture and history of the Dark Continent, and to this end Garveyite paraders displayed banners reading "Africa, Mother of Civilization" and "Princes Shall Come Out of Egypt."[6]

The most popular plank of Garvey's platform, however, was the scheme to obtain the freedom of black folk in all parts of the world. Convinced that Negroes could never attain racial equality in the United States, Garvey worked toward an autonomous African state which black folk would control. In preparation for this Negro-administered nation he set up a temporary government called the Provisional Republic of Africa; and to this superstate he attached such agencies as the Universal Negro Improvement Association, the Negro Factories Corporation, the Black Star Line (a steamship company), and *The Negro World* (a weekly publication). Establishing branches of this organization in nations wherein large Negro populations existed, Garvey attracted followers by providing colorful regalia and grandiose titles which succeeded in engendering self-esteem and a strong nationalistic spirit. With a patriotic and race-conscious group supporting him, Garvey voiced his people's desire for freedom and self-government at his international convention in 1921:

"If I can interpret correctly the spirit of the Negro, it is for me to say that Negroes everywhere are determined to be free—determined to be liberated—liberated from mob rule, liberated from segregation, liberated from Jim-Crowism, liberated from injustices of all kinds. Let the world understand that 400,000,000 Negroes are determined to die for their liberty and that if we must die, we shall die nobly, we shall die gallantly, fighting up the battle heights of Africa to plant there the standard which represents liberty. . . ."[7]

The Garvey Movement eventually failed, not so much because of the opposition of prominent Negro intellectuals as because of its leader's financial mismanagement and blundering conceit. Nevertheless, more effectively than any other man of his time, Garvey asserted the Negro's basic dissatisfaction with a subordinate status, enumerated the advantages of international brotherhood among the black folk of the world, and imbued the masses of his race with a passionate desire for the privileges of democracy. It is only natural, therefore, that he should have exerted a profound influence on the writers of the Negro Renascence.

## III. *INTEREST IN AFRICAN ART AND HISTORY*

Although educated Negroes did not collectively board the "Back-to-Africa" bandwagon, they did, concurrently with the Garvey Movement, manifest an increasing interest in the art and history of the Dark Continent. As early as 1915, for example, Carter G. Woodson founded the Association for the Study of Negro Life and History, which, through its quarterly organ, *The Journal of Negro History,* published historical and sociological articles dealing with the Negro in his African and American environment. Another stimulus to the cultural interest of the American Negro in Africa derived from the rediscovery of primitive African painting and sculpture by French artists during the first quarter of the present century. During this period, painters (Picasso, Derain, Matisse, and Vlaminck), composers (Satie, Auric,

Honneger, Milhaud, Poulenc, and Talliaferro), and writers (Guillaume Apollinaire, Jean Cocteau, Max Jacob, Blaise Cendrars, and Reverdy) were inspired by primitive Negro art.[8] Most of these artists were indebted to Paul Guillaume, "who was the first to collect Negro sculpture and allow contemporary artists to study it."[9] It is also noteworthy that Gertrude Stein—author of the *Three Lives* story of "Melanctha," which Cargill has labeled "the first genuinely primitivistic study in American literature"[10]—was likewise a sponsor of the African Art Movement. Further impetus to the dissemination of information concerning the cultural contributions of Africa was given in 1916 by Dr. Franz Boas in *The Mind of Primitive Man.*

*Opportunity,* edited by Charles S. Johnson, one of the nurturers of the Negro Renascence in Harlem, was quick to sense the value of discoveries concerning African art for the American Negro. In May, 1924, *Opportunity* produced an African Art Issue containing Africa-inspired poems by Langston Hughes, Claude McKay, and Lewis Alexander, as well as the following articles: "A Note on African Art" by Alain Locke, "The Temple" by Albert C. Barnes, and "African Art at the Barnes Foundation" by Paul Guillaume. In May, 1926, *Opportunity* ran another Art Number which includes the following authoritative contributions: "The Triumph of Ancient Negro Art" by Paul Guillaume, "Negro Art, Past and Present" by Albert C. Barnes, "Primitive Negro Sculpture" by Thomas Munro, and "The Negro Spirituals and American Art" by Laurence Buermeyer. On March 22, 1928, Barnes spoke on "Primitive Negro Sculpture and Its Influence on Modern Civilization" during the *Opportunity* program over Radio Station WABC. As it may be observed, *Opportunity* had the cooperation of Barnes, Guillaume, and other white authorities in the effort to popularize African art among American black folk. That the attempt did not fail was recognized by Barnes himself:

> The modern Negro's justifiable pride in his race, due largely to universal recognition of his musical accomplishment, has been powerfully

fortified by the rediscovery of ancient Negro sculpture and by the acknowledgment of the most important contemporary artists, of the magnitude of their debt to it.[11]

## IV. *INTEREST IN THE NEGRO BY WHITE WRITERS*

Another development which helped to bring about the Negro Renascence of the 1920's was the increasingly realistic and understanding portrayal of Negro life by white authors after World War I. Admittedly there were scattered outbursts of white-supremacy fiction and occasional resuscitations of the tragic mulatto stereotype. Besides, the mildewed plantation tradition did not pass away, for scattered novels of the period continued to focus with sentimental retrospect upon the civilization of the feudal South. As a matter of fact, the tradition was actually modernized by a group of popular humorists—led by Irvin Cobb, Octavus Roy Cohen, Hugh Wiley, E. K. Means, and Arthur Akers—who rocked America with laughter by portraying Negroes as inferior, unlettered, comical folk chiefly interested in sex, money, horseplay, and imitating white people. The fatuous nonsense propagated by these panderers to the public's love of jokes evades the shameful truths which such writers as Erskine Caldwell and Lillian Smith admit. Just a stone's throw from the humorists who exaggerate Negro drollery and absurdity is Roark Bradford. Bradford's *King David and the Philistine Boys* (1930) and *Ol' Man Adam an' His Chillun* (1928)—the latter is the basis of *The Green Pastures*, a play by Marc Connelly, which is an improvement upon the novel—are ludicrous misrepresentations of Negro religion. *This Side of Jordan* (1929), which falls under the influence of a species of sentimental naturalism, is more plausible but bespeaks the racial preconceptions of the author.

Despite these trends, a steadily increasing number of white authors, including Southerners, showed a disposition to undertake authentic recording of Negro life. The foundations of this inclination were laid in the last quarter of the nineteenth century in the works of such writers as Albion Tourgée, George Washington Cable, and Mark Twain. With the turn of the century, largely in consequence of the increasing popularity of primitivism, which has been defined as "the worship of animalism for its own sake"[12] and as "a kind of Romanticism in which the reader is led to believe that the low-brow is a good fellow and that impulses are more to be trusted than ideas,"[13] and of Freudianism, which has been designated as "the most conspicuous form of the rationalization of sex-primitivism,"[14] the Negro became even more attractive as a subject for literary treatment. Kipling frequently contrasted the white man and the native, often to the advantage of the latter. In 1909 Gertrude Stein, who has already been mentioned as a sponsor of the African art movement in France, suggested in "Melanctha" that instinctive love is best and most satisfying. During the same year Edward Sheldon—who, like Eugene O'Neill, came under the influence of Harvard's Professor G. P. Baker, a firm believer in the dramatic possibilities latent in the Negro—produced *The Nigger*, a play which, in spite of its deficiencies, turned away from the smugly conventional handling of Negro character. In 1914 Vachel Lindsay wrote *The Congo: A Study of the Negro Race*, a poem divided into three parts: "Their Basic Savagery," "Their Irrepressible High Spirits," and "The Hope of Their Religion." O'Neill and Ridgely Torrence followed Sheldon in essaying a realistic treatment of Negro character, the latter writing three Negro plays between 1914 and 1917—*Granny Maumee, The Rider of Dreams,* and *Simon the Cyrenian*. The works of O'Neill, however, are more significant. *Thirst* (1914) includes a West Indian mulatto among three shipwreck victims, and *The Moon of the Caribbees* (1919) is a primitivistic description of the brawls and debauchery of West Indian sluts and British sailors. *The Dreamy Kid* (1919) is a tragedy of Harlem life; while *The Emperor Jones* (1920), one of the most revolutionary plays in the history of the American theater, is an analysis of the fear-inspired disintegration of an ex-Pullman porter who made himself ruler of a West Indian island. *All God's Chillun Got Wings* (1924) describes the failure of the marriage of a neurotic white girl, horrified by African symbols, and a hypersensitive Negro, depressed by race-consciousness.

After World War I, many other writers plunged energetically into the study of black folk; and several produced works which reveal the struggles and persecutions of the Negro. Clement Wood's *Nigger,* Hubert Shands' *White and Black,* and T. S. Stribling's *Birthright,* all published in 1922, exhibit attitudes and subject matter which novelists had generally placed under taboo. *Birthright,* the account of the unsuccessful mission of a mulatto graduate of Harvard to enlighten his people in the South, has been considered noteworthy by Sterling Brown because it "places the Negro at the center of the picture, attempts to show the influence of environment upon character, and attacks injustice."[15] Waldo Frank's *Holiday* (1923), which concludes with a lynching, is the story of the thwarted passion of a white girl and a Negro in a town ironically named Nazareth. In *Dark Laughter* (1925) Sherwood Anderson glorifies the instinctive Negro who, unmindful of moral considerations, is happier because he lives an uninhibited sex life. "When a Negro woman wants to live with another man she does," generalizes Anderson. Perhaps the most popular novel treating the Negro during the 1920's, however, was Carl Van Vechten's *Nigger Heaven* (1926), which will be discussed in the next chapter as a book which made Harlem a national magnet for readers as well as for tourists and downtown New Yorkers, thus clearing the way for fiction by Negroes which followed in its wake. In *Congaree Sketches* (1927) and *Nigger to Nigger* (1928) E. C. L. Adams captures the spontaneity of Negro folk life, but the latter volume also contains trenchant criticism of Southern injustice.

Julia Peterkin, DuBose Heyward, and Howard Odum are not very much concerned with tension and conflict. Simple pictures of the comedy and tragedy of South Carolina plantation life are provided in Miss Peterkin's *Green Thursday* (1924), *Black April* (1927), *Scarlet Sister Mary* (1928), and *Bright Skin* (1932). Convincing depiction of Charleston's Catfish Row is given in Heyward's *Porgy* (1925) and *Mamba's Daughters* (1927). In *Rainbow Round My Shoulder* (1928) and *Wings on My Feet* (1929) Howard W. Odum, who collaborated with Guy B. Johnson in *The Negro and His Songs* (1925) and *Negro Workaday Songs* (1926), recounts the loves, escapades, and wanderings of a colorful folk character named Left Wing Gordon.

This brief account of the most important use of Negro subject matter by white writers before and during the Negro Renascence indicates that strides were made away from caricature, burlesque, and defamation. Although most of these authors, because of a predilection for animalism and fatalism, failed to attain a well-rounded representation of Negro life, their more unbiased approach to racial themes nevertheless inspired colored writers to replace the self-preening provoked by the Dixon-Page libels with a franker self-criticism and self-revelation. The emergence of this new attitude, which made art for art's sake rather than art for race's sake the *summum bonum* of Negro creative effort, was proclaimed in 1926 by Langston Hughes:

> We younger Negro artists who create now intend to express our individual dark-skinned selves without fear or shame. If the white people are pleased, we are glad. If they are not, it doesn't matter. We know we are beautiful, and ugly too. The tom-tom cries and the tom-tom laughs. If colored people are pleased, we are glad. If they are not, their displeasure doesn't matter either. We build our temples for tomorrow, strong as we know them, and we stand on top of the mountain, free within ourselves.[16]

## V. *ASSOCIATION OF COLORED AND WHITE WRITERS*

After World War I, Negro writers, especially those in New York City, fraternized with their white contemporaries. Soon after his arrival in the United States, for example, Claude McKay became friendly with Frank Harris, editor of *Pearson's Magazine,* which published several of McKay's poems. Later McKay became a friend of Crystal and Max Eastman as well as a contributor to *The Liberator,* the successor to *The Masses.* Subsequent to the publication of *Moon Calf* by Floyd Dell, McKay became associate editor of *The Liberator* with the responsibility of handling the sub-editing formerly done by Dell. Of his new position McKay writes:

> I soon became acquainted and friendly with *The Liberator* collaborators and sympathizers: Art Young, Boardman Robinson, Stuart Davis, John Barber, Adolph Dehn, Hugo Gellert, Ivan Opfer, Maurice Becker, Maurice Sterne, Arturo Giovanitti, Roger Baldwin, Louis Untermeyer, Mary Heaton Vorse, Lydia Gibson, Cornelia Barnes, Genevieve Taggard.[17]

After Eastman relinquished the editorship of *The Liberator,* Michael Gold and McKay were appointed executive editors, but their personal and intellectual differences soon resulted in McKay's resignation. James Weldon Johnson was another Negro writer who mingled freely with whites. Annually he, Carl Van Vechten, and young Alfred Knopf had a joint birthday celebration. In *The Big Sea* Langston Hughes writes extensively of uptown and downtown parties in which the Harlem literati hobnobbed with V. F. Calverton, Ernestine Evans, Horace Liveright, Alfred Knopf, Carl Van Vechten, and other figures in the writing and publishing world. These wider contacts—illustrated in the friendships of McKay, Johnson, and Hughes—led to a more active participation of Negro writers in the literary life of the nation.

## VI. *NEGRO AUTHORS AND THEIR PUBLISHERS*

Although the fiction of Chesnutt and Dunbar was handled by major publishing houses between 1898 and 1905, Negro novels and short stories between the latter year and 1923 were almost invariably presented by small firms that were unable to give their authors a national hearing. During these years Johnson's *The Autobiography of an Ex-Coloured Man* and DuBois's *The Quest of the Silver Fleece* were possibly the only novels by Negroes that gained country-wide recognition by readers of both races. After World War I, however, several leading publishers—actuated by many factors, including the popularity of books by white authors about the Negro, the more liberal attitude of white citizens toward the black man during the 1920's, the nation-wide interest in Harlem initiated by Carl Van Vechten in *Nigger Heaven*, the appearance of a talented group of young Negro writers, and the development of a growing number of readers within the colored group—accepted books written by Negro fictionists. It is noteworthy that virtually all the novels of the heyday of the Negro Renascence were published in New York City and that many of them were released by some of the country's outstanding firms. For example, Jean Toomer's *Cane* (1923), Jessie Fauset's *There Is Confusion* (1924), and Eric Walrond's *Tropic Death* (1926) were published by Boni and Liveright; W. E. B. DuBois's *Dark Princess* (1928) and Arna Bontemps' *God Sends Sunday* (1931), by Harcourt, Brace and Company; Walter White's *The Fire in the Flint* (1924) and *Flight* (1926), Nella Larsen's *Quicksand* (1928) and *Passing* (1929), Rudolph Fisher's *The Walls of Jericho* (1928), and Langston Hughes's *Not Without Laughter* (1930), by Alfred A. Knopf; Claude McKay's *Home to Harlem* (1928), *Banjo* (1929), *Gingertown* (1932), and *Banana Bottom* (1933), and Countee Cullen's *One Way to Heaven* (1932), by Harper and Brothers; George Schuyler's *Black No More* (1931) and Wallace Thurman's *The Blacker the Berry* (1929) and *Infants of the Spring* (1932), by the Macaulay Company; Jessie Fauset's *Plum Bun* (1929), *The Chinaberry Tree* (1931), and *Comedy: American Style* (1933), by the Frederick A. Stokes Company; George Schuyler's *Slaves Today* (1931), by Brewer, Warren and Putnam; and Rudolph Fisher's *The Conjure-Man Dies* (1932), by Covici, Friede.

Of equal significance with the wider acceptance of the fiction of colored authors by major publishers was the general tendency to remove the stigma of inferiority from a work simply because it was written by a Negro. After World War I, both publishing houses and national periodicals showed a greater disposition to apply the same yardstick to the productions of Negroes as to the efforts of artists of other races. This more unbiased attitude, much less influenced by racial considerations, was just what the colored literati needed: first, it encouraged them to attain a higher standard of performance than would have been necessary to satisfy the requirements of certain smaller publishing establishments; second, it brought their novels and short stories before the general American reading public; and, third, as an examination of the better anthologies and histories of American literature will reveal, it drew Negro writers, more than ever before, into the main currents of national life and thought. In contemplation of these changes, Charles W. Chesnutt said in 1936: "I have lived to see, after twenty years or more, a marked change in the attitude of publishers and the reading public in regard to the Negro in fiction."[18]

## VII. *HARLEM: MECCA OF THE NEW NEGRO*[19]

After World War I, Harlem—the most densely settled Negro community in the world and the melting pot of dark folk from Africa, the West Indies, Central and South America, and the hinterlands of the United States—became a national vogue. During the Roaring Twenties *Shuffle Along* and *Runnin' Wild* were major box-office attractions; and a Freud-conscious and war-weary country found exhilaration in the recklessness and dynamics of such lyrics as the theme song of *Runnin' Wild:*

> Runnin' wild; lost control
> Runnin' wild; mighty bold,

Feelin' gay and reckless too,
Carefree all the time; never blue
Always goin' I don't know where
Always showin' that I don't care
Don' love nobody, it ain't worth while
All alone; runnin' wild.

Among Negro artists and entertainers who vaulted into the limelight during the decade after the Armistice were Charles Gilpin, Paul Robeson, Roland Hayes, Florence Mills, Rose McClendon, Bessie Smith, Ethel Waters, Louis Armstrong, Josephine Baker, and Bill Robinson.

Attracted by Harlem and its celebrities, white folk began to swarm into the black ghetto. Some came to observe, others to ridicule, still more to laugh, but most came to seek exuberant escape in the so-called exotic primitivism of Negro cabaret life. As Langston Hughes says, "thousands of whites came to Harlem night after night, thinking the Negroes loved to have them there, and firmly believing that all Harlemites left their houses at sundown to sing and dance in cabarets, because most of the whites saw nothing but the cabarets, not the houses."[20] During these "whoopee" years the Cotton Club on Lenox Avenue became one of the most popular night clubs in the country.

For many reasons, most of which have been stated or implied, the Negro literati of the country likewise drifted to New York City. Noting that nearly all the participants in the Renascence were migrants to Gotham, Langston Hughes, himself a native of Missouri, observes that "Jessie Fauset was from Philadelphia, Charles S. Johnson from Virginia, Arna Bontemps from California, Countee Cullen from Kentucky, Aaron Douglas from Kansas, Wallace Thurman from Salt Like City, Rudolph Fisher from Washington, Walter White from Atlanta, Paul Robeson from New Jersey, Ethel Waters from Philadelphia, Richmond Barthe from New Orleans."[21] While some newcomers were interested in successful colored shows on Broadway and Bohemian patronage of Harlem night life, the more serious were attracted by the promise of New York City as a center for the florescence of racial art and literature. Leading publishers were opening their doors, important magazines were giving access to their pages,[22] and white writers were evincing an increasing interest in Negro life and authorship. Furthermore, Harlem was the home of powerful Negro newspapers, of the National Association for the Advancement of Colored People and its mouthpiece, *The Crisis,* and of the National Urban League and its organ, *Opportunity.*

New York City's widely circulated Negro magazines, especially *The Crisis* and *Opportunity*, played a vital part in nurturing the Renascence. "Jessie Fauset at *The Crisis,* Charles Johnson at *Opportunity*, and Alain Locke in Washington," writes Langston Hughes, "were the three people who mid-wifed the so-called New Negro literature into being."[23] Of the role played by *The Crisis* DuBois writes:

> By 1920, we could point out that most of the young writers among American Negroes had made first publication in the columns of *The Crisis.* In the next few years we published work from Claude McKay, Langston Hughes, Jean Toomer, Countee Cullen, Anne Spencer, Abram Harris and Jessie Fauset.[24]

Though irregular and shifting in editorial policy, *The Messenger*—with which A. Phillip Randolph, George S. Schuyler, and Wallace Thurman were connected—also served as a medium for Renascence authors, publishing the first short stories of Langston Hughes. Of brief duration but nevertheless of importance was *Fire*, started in 1926 by Wallace Thurman, Zora Neale Hurston, Aaron Douglas, John P. Davis, Bruce Nugent, Gwendolyn Bennett, and Langston Hughes to "burn up a lot of the old, dead conventional Negro-white ideas of the past, *épater le bourgeois* into a realization of the existence of the younger Negro writers and aritists, and provide us with an outlet for publication not available in the limited pages of the small Negro magazines then existing. . . ."[25] The Spingarn Medal, offered annually for "the highest or noblest achievement by an American Negro during the preceding year or years," and the yearly awards of the Harmon Foundation were instrumental in promoting authorship among Negroes. *The Crisis* and *Opportunity* also gave annual prizes for creative writing.

Thus was the stage set for the flowering of the Negro Renascence in Harlem. National attention was attracted to the black ghetto by the achievements of the race in music and drama as well as by the superficial primitivism of upper Manhattan cabaret life. Colored authors were drawn to New York City by the literary treasure-trove of the black community as well as by the new cordial attitudes of white publishers, editors, and writers. Furthermore, the two major Negro magazines presented the works of Renascence writers, and generous patrons encouraged literary effort by the offer of substantial prizes and awards.

CHAPTER 4

# Fiction of the Negro Renascence

AFTER THE ARMISTICE a war-weary but wealthy nation turned to Harlem for escape and thrills, and the black ghetto suddenly found itself in the role of a magnetic community attracting curious people from all sections of the country. Stimulated by the vogue of the African theme in art, the new interest of white writers in Negro life, the emergence of stellar Negro writers and entertainers, and the captivating appeal of jazz, whites stumbled over one another in a rush to give adulation and recognition to their gifted dark-skinned fellow Americans. While many of these patrons were merely seeking entertainment and exoticism, a few were sincerely interested in the discovery and development of colored talent. For Negroes themselves the Renascence was the period of new opportunities and bright hopes, when their abilities and attainments were at long last receiving attention and reward from the majority group. Under the circumstances it was only natural that Harlem—the center of the Garvey Movement, the African art revival, and the Negro Renascence—should become the cultural capital of black America.

The decade after World War I witnessed many important changes in the themes, attitudes, and backgrounds of fiction by Negroes. Authors began to abandon the apologetic and militant positions usually held in years prior to the war. This does not mean that fiction was no longer employed as a medium of racial defense and protest, because between 1919 and 1924 at least three fictional works written outside Harlem and prior to the peak of Renascence literary activity contain outright propaganda. Herman

Dreer's *The Immediate Jewel of His Soul* (1919), William Pickens' *The Vengeance of the Gods and Three Other Stories of the Real American Color Line* (1922), and Joshua Henry Jones's *By Sanction of Law* (1924) are purpose fiction demanding equality for the Negro. Besides, at least three Renascence novels—Walter White's *Fire in the Flint* (1924), W. E. B. DuBois's *Dark Princess* (1928), and George Schuyler's *Slaves Today* (1931)—are vehicles for racial propaganda. On the whole, however, Renascence fiction does not exhibit the defensive and bitter attitudes which characterized the work of such earlier writers as Griggs, Grant, Downing, and Adams. In most cases Renascence authors demonstrate a better emotional balance and artistic competency as well as a greater inclination to write frankly of themselves and their people. For example, in *Cane* (1923) Jean Toomer dispassionately portrays whites and Negroes in rural Georgia. The Negro bourgeoisie attracted the attention of Jessie Fauset, Walter White, and Nella Larsen, who manifest particular interest in the psychology of caste, passing, and intermarriage rather than in the apotheosis of the mixed-blood. Emphasizing the alleged exoticism and sensualism of Negro life, the Van Vechtenites—Claude McKay, Wallace Thurman, and Arna Bontemps—made a sharp departure from the earlier fiction of protest and apologetics. While the Van Vechten School focused upon primitive aspects of Negro experience, Rudolph Fisher and Countee Cullen wrote novels describing everyday life in black Manhattan and depicting Negroes as distinctive but fundamentally quite like other Americans. What these two writers did for Negroes of the New York scene Langston Hughes did for those of a typical Midwestern small town in *Not Without Laughter* (1936). Eric Walrond and Claude McKay did realistic portraiture of dark folk of the West Indian scene. George Schuyler penned *Black No More* (1931), which mirthfully lampoons both races and thus constitutes another important deviation from the self-preening fiction produced by many race-chauvinists during the first quarter of the century. The following pages of this chapter will provide a more detailed examination of the Renascence fiction introduced in this paragraph.

## I. *EARLY POSTWAR FICTION*

In *The Immediate Jewel of His Soul* (1919) and *By Sanction of Law* (1924) Herman Dreer and Joshua Henry Jones respectively continue the fight against racial oppression by complimenting the educated Negro and exposing the prejudice of the white man. Nevertheless, in these two novels there is a new approach, for the colored heroes, even when pressed to the wall by their adversaries, courageously strike back and prefer injury or even death to submission. While intermarriage is casually approved in the former book, it is supported at length in the latter, which treats the romance of a Southern white girl and a Northern mulatto youth. In *The Vengeance of the Gods and Three Other Stories of the Real American Color Line* (1922) William Pickens, motivated by the desire to offset the conventional black stereotypes of Southern writers, compliments the quick thinking of the Negro and ridicules Nordic superiority. In *Tales of Darkest America* (1920), a volume of short stories written for undistinguished magazines, Fenton Johnson complains of discrimination against Negro authors, which he certainly deserved as a writer of fiction, and also gives one of the first comments in American Negro fiction concerning Bolshevist activities among colored people.

### Herman Dreer

Dreer's *The Immediate Jewel of His Soul* (1919), which the author calls "a story of the earnest Negro, trying to rise into great place," is, as the following prefatory note indicates, another novel written to inspire colored people to emulation and whites to justice:

> To those of the inner circle, I hope these pages will be edification; to those without, I fondly pray that they will be food for thought and a stimulus to unselfishness and fair play.

As the story opens, William Smith, a recent high school graduate in Williamsburg, Virginia, is hailed as a potential successor to Washington and DuBois. After a brief sojourn at a Southern college, located in a city where a lynching is perpetrated, he enters and later graduates from a Northern school "where merit and not color, courage and not color, perseverance and not color, decided the fates of men." Following further study at a theological seminary and a college of agriculture, he accepts the pastorate of a church in Seaton, Virginia.

The novel is built around an address which Smith made before the state convention of his denomination a year after the beginning of his ministerial career. In this speech the emergence of the new Negro, militant in his protest against injustice and insistent upon full equality, is clearly indicated. Endurance and forbearance are shunned as minority-group techniques:

> "Some say, however, that we must have patience, that we must be long-suffering. Great heavens, what do men expect?"

Injury and death are designated as the price the Negro must pay for freedom:

> "Our sin has been not to demand our rights; even if to demand were to die. . . . Even for us there may be no remission of sin without the shedding of blood."

Negroes are urged to avoid clannishness which separates them from the rest of the population:

> "Now when the world is in a death grapple, agonizing to bring men together, shall we by supineness, quiescence, and cowardly submission retard the victory by clannishness, by living unto ourselves, by developing within the land a distinct civilization?"

The race is also admonished to attack segregation in a nation which requires its colored citizens to die for democracy:

> "We must preach the end of segregating movements. When wars are upon us, black and white die together. When peace comes, why can they not live together?
>
> "Think of separate schools for a group of people in a democracy!"

Legal ordinances against intermarriage are assailed:

"If a white man marries a colored woman or a white woman marries a colored man, let us remember that before God there is no difference. Both black and white are His. . . .

"Let our reproach for the marriage between white and black vanish like a mist. Rather reproach the union of unequals, be they white, black, or white and black. . . .

"Do not mistake that I am advocating intermarriage as a group ideal. . . . I am simply indicating the evils which arise by forbidding by law intermarriage."

The National Association for the Advancement of Colored People is commended, and Negroes are reproved for failing to give unanimous support to this organization:

"If our people were alert to their opportunities, why would they permit an organization like the National Association for the Advancement of Colored People to struggle for existence? Why is not every adult black man a contributor to its weal? This society, as it stands for upholding the Constitution of the United States, without equivocation, contending for a democracy not on paper, but in the lives of men, is the most patriotic society in America."

Because of the allegedly radical nature of his address, Smith is forced to give up his church. He then starts an experimental demonstration farm and encourages the co-operation of farmers irrespective of race. Disturbed by the progressive activities of Smith, Robert White, determined to hold Negroes in a subordinate position, calls a conference of the citizens of Seaton. During this meeting Sandy James, in an effort to incite action against Smith, discusses the portrayal of the Negro in Dixon's *The Clansman,* presented on the screen by D. W. Griffith as *The Birth of a Nation:*

All agreed that reflection was necessary. The attempted rape by the lustful, blood-thirsty scoundrel stirred the passionate natures of them all. The suggestion was enough to move to action and produce the effect that several had all the while desired. They seized upon it as the crux of their whole design. Vituperation poured upon vituperation, then many ebullitions of pusillanimity. The lawyer spoke now as if in a political campaign, and used all the tricks of the experienced "fire eater." He recalled the scene in the Southern senate, which Griffith and Dixon have made disgusting and nauseating in the extreme. He followed this with a vivid sketch of the Lieutenant-Governor's effort to force the Governor's daughter to marry him. Then he closed with praise of the Ku Klux Klan, representing it as the savior of the South. He sat down amidst great applause of half the assembly.[1]

Resenting this subtle attempt to arouse prejudice, Ted Nailor, a liberal and fair-minded Southerner, replies:

"This is a new South, and Reverend Smith is the new Negro. The scoundrel shown in The Birth of a Nation, though later than the Uncle Tom type, is also passing. You know as well as I that in the last ten years not a colored man has been lynched in this state for rape. The educated Negro never commits this crime anywhere; the guilty man is the culprit we permit to loaf in the streets."

Determined to punish Smith and to awaken popular sentiment, *The Seaton Gazette* publishes "a biased, sensational article, distorted in the extreme," accusing Smith of being engaged to Nailor's daughter with parental consent and urging white men to rise in demonstration of their disapproval. Ordered to leave town within twenty-four hours, Smith defiantly remains in Seaton and gives the following warning to the mayor:

"No man, Mr. Mayor, has ever been able to run me from what was mine. My reputation and honor cannot go down now. . . . The opportunity has come for me to die not in France, but in America, to help make America safe for democracy. This is the happiest moment of my life. You need not offer me any protection. I have but one request: Tell your friends, I'll kill every man who sets foot on my estate after sundown."

Though the mob assembles and Negroes organize to offer resistance, a riot is averted through intelligent biracial action. At the close of the novel, Smith marries Thelma Haskell, a loyal supporter through all his struggles.

While characterized by the usual exaggerations of race-promoting fiction, *The Immediate Jewel of His Soul* reveals the new militancy of the Negro. Demanding equal rights and full citizenship, the novel lauds the policy of the National Association for the Advancement of Colored People and criticizes Negroes for not giving one hundred per cent support to this agency. The book attacks legal bans against intermarriage, the Negrophobe program of Thomas Dixon, and other evidences of "the brutish malice, the degenerate littleness which is doing its utmost to foster here a separate civilization, separate ideals, separate ambitions, but mutual hates."

### Fenton Johnson

Fenton Johnson, who attained a reasonable measure of success as a poet, is the author of *Tales of Darkest America* (1920), a collection of seven poorly-written narratives. The most useful piece in the volume is the autobiographical "Story of Myself," which traces the writer's struggle to get a college education, to succeed as a teacher in the South, and to gain a foothold as an author and publisher in Chicago and New York City. Johnson refers to the disadvantages of the Negro author:

> It seemed to me like trying to walk the Atlantic Ocean to obtain recognition in the literary world and especially when one was attempting to present the life of the race to which I belong.

One of the earliest references in American Negro literature to Bolshevist activity among Negroes is Johnson's statement that his refusal to co-operate affected the circulation of his periodical, *The Favorite Magazine*:

> I was confronted also by the wave of radicalism that was trying to engulf the race to which I belong, but I refused to sell my soul to the agitators of Bolshevism and brought unpopularity to the magazine among a certain class.

The remaining narratives of *Tales of Darkest America*—"A Very Important Business Man," "A Woman of Good Cheer," "The Sorrows of George Morgan," "Trusting Providence," "The Sorrows of a Stenographer," and "The Carnival"—are magazine stories that demonstrate neither technical ability nor interesting subject matter.

WILLIAM PICKENS

In *The Vengeance of the Gods and Three Other Stories of the Real American Color Line* (1922) William Pickens sets out to vindicate Negro character. In a "Foreword" he declares that "people do not represent another race as beautiful and heroic unless that race is far removed from them in time or space; or unless, as in the case of the white American and the American Indian, the stronger race has killed off the weaker and removed it as a rival." For this reason he contends that if the Negro is to appear in other roles than that of clown, villain, or servant, he must be so presented by the colored author:

> If the Negro wants to be idealized in a world where the Negro is a considerable potential factor, he must idealize himself. . . . It is not simply that the white story teller *will not* do full justice to the humanity of the black race; he *cannot*. A race must present its own case and ennoble its own ideals.

Showing the influence of the Roxana narrative in Mark Twain's *Pudd'nhead Wilson,* the title story, "The Vengeance of the Gods: Blood or Opportunity," essays to show that environment, rather than heredity, exerts the major influence upon human destiny. In the Arkansas delta country a prominent white farmer, John Elliott, has a legitimate son, William, and an illegitimate mulatto offspring, Jim. While Elliott and his wife are in France, Jim is put in William's place by a colored nurse. Brought up as a member of the white race, Jim finishes college and becomes a good citizen; but William, reared as a Negro, is imprisoned and lynched before his identity can be established. This lynching causes the colored nurse to commit suicide, Mrs. Elliott to lose her mind, and Elliott to preach unpopular doctrines of racial equality.

Caucasian superiority is again ridiculed in "The Superior Race," the second story in the volume. Jefferson Davis Jones, Professor of Anthropology at Mobile Institute, suddenly becomes silent on his favorite subject, the natural inferiority of the Negro. It develops that his silence is due to the fact that a Negro proved more stouthearted than he did in a boat which was helplessly adrift in the Gulf of Mexico.

The last two stories of the volume commend the mental alertness of the Negro. In "Passing the Buck" a Negro Pullman passenger, realizing that certain Southerners are about to incriminate him as the attacker of a white woman in her berth, cunningly changes places with a white man and thus causes much embarrassment for those who plotted against him. The final narrative, "Tit for Tat: How Colored Soldiers Defeated the Real Enemy at Grand Villars," presents Negro troops successfully preventing the attempts of their white countrymen to instill prejudice in the French. White Americans make the following disparaging remarks about colored forces:

> "They are not Americans; they are just *niggers*. We only allow them to live in our country because their people were once slaves there. But they are not American citizens and are not even allowed to talk back to white people. And they are very criminal and dishonest; they will steal. They are especially dangerous to women: in our country no white woman dares to go near them unless a white man is with her."

In reply to these charges the Negro soldiers say:

> "Without protest we allow them to live in our country, but they hate us. We are just to them and treat them as men,—as equals before the law; but they are unjust to us and assume an attitude of natural superiority. Many of them are descendants of the German and Austrian, and have much of the old arrogance of their forefathers. Because of their conduct we do not associate with them in our country, and we do not call them Americans: we call them—er—'crackers' and 'pecks'!"

In brief, *The Vengeance of the Gods and Three Other Stories of the Real American Color Line* derides the ethnic superiority of the Caucasian and submits the proposition that opportunity, and not blood, is the more powerful determinant of the course of human life. The book also illustrates that the effects of race prejudice often bring tragedy not only to Negroes but to whites as well. In the last three stories an effort is made to offset "hideous or undesirable or unheroic" black stereotypes through the presentation of manly and circumspect characters.

## Joshua Henry Jones

Joshua Henry Jones's *By Sanction of Law* (1924), which likewise shows the Negro to advantage, is perhaps the only American interracial romance in which the colored wooer of a white woman has no misgivings because of African blood. In this case the lovers are Lida Lauriston, daughter of an aristocratic South Carolina plantation owner and a student at a New England finishing school, and Truman Bennet, a New England near-white of respectable background and a senior at an adjacent men's college. Meeting at a campus reception, Bennet and Lida fall in love and become engaged. When Lida, depressed by the report that her fiancé is a Negro, asks him if he is colored, he replies:

> "Yes, I'm of that race.—There is Negro blood in my veins.—Not slave blood, however—the blood of men is in my veins and of my ancestors and parents.—There's nothing shameworthy in my blood. None of us are responsible for our birth. Our responsibility is the use we make of life. I have been taught that color counts for nothing. It is what we are.—Therefore I forget color. Besides, of what color am I?"

When Lida reproaches him for not telling her of his racial extraction, he says:

> "It never occurred to me that it would make any difference. . . . I loved you and you loved me, of what matter anything else? I gave no thought to ancestry, either yours or mine. When we marry we don't wed ancestry, we wed not tradition, but one another."

Upon hearing of the engagement of Lida and Bennet, Miss Gregory, head of the finishing school, counsels the girl that intermarriage would mean "the sacrifice of home, family, friends, wealth; the causing of bitterness, heartaches on the part of your family and much doubt as to the success of the experiment." When Lida decides to sustain her plighted faith, the principal appeals to Bennet, who answers:

"To rattle the dry bones of ancestry may not be the wisest act for some of us. So far as heritage is concerned, I can boast as much as they, perhaps more. I have as good breeding behind me as the best; my family may not be as wealthy but it certainly has as good training as any in America. I have been as carefully and well reared. So I don't see how the things you mention concern me."

Determined to prevent the marriage, Miss Gregory submits the case to the president of the men's college, who refers it to his faculty for action. During the faculty meeting Donald Armstrong, a Southern professor, recommends the expulsion of the youth:

"The brute! I knew it! I knew it! I always knew it would never do to educate 'niggers.' We must preserve the white race pure. I knew if we allowed them to be educated the next thing they would be wanting to marry our daughters. I wouldn't let him graduate. I'd flunk him. I'd expel him for such uppishness. We know, in the South, how to handle such. We know how to keep them in their places."

After being defended as a gentleman and as a potential husband by the dean of the school, Bennet speaks in his own behalf:

"I want my diploma as a right fully earned; as a matter of justice; as a matter of law. As for the halting of my course; the turning aside from my purpose; repudiating of my pledged word; first halt you the tides; reshape the course of day through night; still the wheels of the universe, yet only death shall rob me of my will to,—right to love the one I love. —Unless it be the lady herself."

When the faculty votes in favor of Bennet, Armstrong resigns.

In the following June the lovers finish their respective courses, and Lida returns to the South to explain the betrothal to her father. After receiving no word from his fiancée for several weeks, Bennet goes to South Carolina, making part of the trip with Dr. Tansey of the college faculty. Meanwhile Lida, having told her father of her engagement, is placed under surveillance and urged to marry John Marley, son of a neighboring plantation owner. When Bennet reaches the Lauriston estate, he is hidden by Lida in a cave where he is later discovered by her brother Elvin, whom he overcomes after a bitter struggle. Successful in making their escape, the pair marry in Orangeburg and leave immediately for Europe. At the end of the book Colonel Lauriston, having lost his mind because of his daughter's elopement, is trampled to death by horses; and Armstrong, convinced of the tragic consequences of interracial strife after Dr. Tansey is killed while seeking to avert a lynching, becomes engaged to Lida's college chum and devotes his life to the improvement of social conditions in the South.

*By Sanction of Law,* undertaking "to show how all can dwell side by side" and "to lay before a fair-minded, love-governed world the only real solution of the many mankind face," is the only American Negro novel that unapologetically proposes intermarriage as an approach to the correction of racial difficulties in this country. Confident that the Negro is "no whit different than any other human being and knowing the fallacy of race prejudice, also the swiftness with which race vanishes when we know one another," Jones presents in Truman Bennet a character who is the embodiment of his attitudes. Unprejudiced, unobsessed by racial complexes, contemptuous of precedence based on color or ancestry rather than on merit, well-bred, and well-educated, Bennet is without the psychological inhibitions usually accorded Negro male participants in interracial romance. Though weakened by idealized characterization, stilted dialogue, and melodramatic action, *By Sanction of Law* provides a fresh approach to the well-worn subject of miscegenation and thus deserves more recognition than it has received.

## II. *SOUTHERN REALISM*

It required many years for white and colored authors of the United States to treat Southern interracial relations, particularly those involving sex, without squeamishness, apology, propaganda, and racial preconceptions. In 1923, however, two friends—Waldo Frank, a Jew, and Jean Toomer, a Negro—handled this subject matter without bias and race-consciousness in *Holiday* and *Cane,* respectively. As a portrayal of Southern life *Cane,* for which Frank wrote a foreword, stands in a class by itself in Negro Renascence fiction.

## Jean Toomer

Toomer's *Cane*—a potpourri of stories, sketches, poetry, and drama—is one of the more significant productions of the Negro Renascence. In this book a colored writer, for possibly the first time in American Negro fiction, handles inflammatory interracial themes without abandonment of the artist's point of view. As Waldo Frank observes:

> For Toomer, the Southland is not a problem to be solved; it is a field of loveliness to be sung: the Georgia Negro is not a downtrodden soul to be uplifted; he is material for gorgeous painting: the segregated self-conscious brown belt of Washington is not a topic to be discussed and exposed; it is a subject of beauty and of drama, worthy of creation in literary form.[2]

*Cane* is divided into three parts. The first, with rural Georgia as a background, sets forth the tragic lives of women of that section. Karintha inevitably becomes a prostitute. Becky, a wanton white woman, bears two colored sons who, after their mother's lonely death, leave their home town bitterly hated by whites and Negroes. Carma is discovered in marital unfaithfulness. Fern unresponsively submits to lustful men who are baffled and ashamed after selfishly satiating their passions. Esther, near-white daughter of a colored merchant, is strangely attracted to a black religious fanatic. Louisa's Negro admirer slashes her white paramour to death and is subsequently lynched.[3] The chief importance of these stories lies in their departure from the traditional treatment of sex by Negro authors. The candor, shamelessness, and objectivity manifested by Toomer in the presentation of these women caused DuBois to designate him as the "writer who first dared to emancipate the colored world from the conventions of sex."[4]

The second part of *Cane* shifts from the folk life of Georgia to the bourgeois Negro society of Washington. Here again Toomer neither debunks nor glorifies but, as Sterling Brown observes, "pictures Washington with the thoroughness of one who knew it from the inside."[5] "Seventh Street," called "a bastard of Prohibition and the War," is a description of a Washington background. "Avey" reflects the trend away from middle-class conventions by revealing the affection of a young man for an orphan woman who is "no better than a whore." "Theater," a study of class-consciousness within the Negro group, unfolds the mutual attraction between a chorus girl and the "dictie, educated, stuck-up" brother of the manager of the show. "Box Seat" recounts an ill-fated middle-class romance. "Bona and Paul," having Chicago as a setting, describes the failure of a white girl and a passing mulatto youth to become lovers because of the boy's own race-consciousness and his associates' suspicion of his swarthy complexion. In the stories of the second part of *Cane,* therefore, Toomer shows the Negro facing the problems of caste, respectability, and prejudice in Washington and Chicago.

The third section, returning to rural Georgia, contains one long and occasionally obscure story, "Kabnis," a character study of a learned but excessively emotional Northern Negro teaching in a small town. Sensitive to white oppression and disgusted by Negro inertia, Kabnis resorts to dissipation and is fired by Hanby, the principal of the school. In his characterization of Hanby, Toomer satirizes the dissimulating Negro administrator who poses as a haughty aristocrat among his own people, as an Uncle Tom among Southern whites, and as a staunch Yankee supporter among Bostonians. Another interesting character is Layman, a soft-pedaling teacher-preacher "who has traveled in almost every nook and corner of the state and hence knows more than would be good for anyone other than a silent man." Layman does not believe in disturbing Southern whites:

"An Mr. Kabnis, kindly remember youre in the land of cotton—hell of a land. Th white folks get th boll; the niggers get th stalk. An dont you dare touch th boll, or even look at it. They'll swing y sho."

Lewis, a purposeful and clear-headed young man, "is what Kabnis might have been," if he had not succumbed to debauchery and despair. Analyzing the character of Kabnis, Lewis says:

"Life has already told him more than he is capable of knowing. It has given him in excess of what he can receive. I have been offered. Stuff in his stomach curdled, and he vomited me."

Evidently Toomer's implication, as Montgomery Gregory suggests, "is that there must be a welding into one great personality of Kabnis and Lewis: the great emotionalism of the race guided and directed by a great purpose and super-intelligence."[6]

*Cane,* being an experimental work in its quest for appropriate literary forms and diction, is debilitated by occasional incoherence, which may have been inspired by Waldo Frank, and undue striving for effect. Munson has noted the architectonic influence of Sherwood Anderson in "Fern" and "Avey" as well as that of Frank in "Theater."[7] All these considerations notwithstanding, *Cane* is noteworthy because of its departure from argumentation and apologetics in the treatment of interracial subject matter as well as because of its prefiguration of Southern realism and Negro self-revelation. As Waldo Frank says:

It is a harbinger of the South's literary maturity: of its emergence from the obsession put upon its minds by the unending racial crisis—an obsession from which writers have made their indirect escape through sentimentalism, exoticism, polemic, "problem" fiction, and moral melodrama. It marks the dawn of direct and unafraid creation.[8]

## III. *COLOR AND CASTE AMONG THE BOURGEOISIE*

Jessie Fauset, Walter White, and Nella Larsen present well-bred, educated, aspiring Negroes who belong mainly to the professional class of the urban North. Among these people economic security and high social standing are in evidence; and within their group, except for minor variations caused by color, they live very much like other respectable middle-class Americans. Attention is focused principally upon attractive and personable mulatto heroines who yearn to "drink life to the lees" but find it difficult to do so because of racial restrictions. When fair enough in color, these women sometimes seek happiness through escape into the white world; but, after the initial thrills of passing are over, they usually long for colored society and come to believe that Negro life, though circumscribed by prejudice and persecution, is not altogether without spiritual and cultural compensations. This point of view, by the way, stands in bold contrast to that expressed in such novels as Vara Caspary's *White Girl* (1929) and Geoffrey Barnes's *Dark Lustre* (1932), in which passing heroines, whose refinement is attributed to Nordic and whose animalism to African extraction, cross the color line because of admiration for white and abhorrence for black people but experience misery because of the "taint" of Negro blood.

### Jessie Fauset

In an introduction to *The Chinaberry Tree* (1931) Zona Gale correctly points out that Miss Fauset's unique contribution has been to present in fiction the lives of contemporary upper-class Negroes:

> It is about these among the American population that Jessie Fauset has chosen to write. She foregoes the color, the richness, the possibility of travesty and comedy and the popular appeal of the uneducated Negro with his dialect and idiom, his limited outlook. And she has turned to

this other field, less spectacular and, to "the General Public" less convincing because so little standardized. She has shown in her novels, men and women of the class to which she herself belongs, with her wide interests and her American and European experiences.[9]

*There Is Confusion* (1924), the trail-blazer among works in which Miss Fauset illustrates that bourgeois Negroes are interesting subjects for literary treatment, is also the first nationally recognized novel by an American colored woman. The action, which is laid chiefly in Philadelphia and New York City during the World War period, is primarily concerned with the Bye and Marshall families and those who are drawn into the tangled skein of their lives. The heroine is Joanna Marshall, a beautiful but snobbish girl whose ambition is to be a singer and dancer. Her aspirations motivate Peter Bye, an impressionable and irresolute youth descended from slaves who had intermixed with Pennsylvania aristocrats, to enter medical school in preparation for a career in surgery. Because Joanna manifests more interest in her profession than in marriage, Bye abruptly withdraws from school, joins an orchestra, and becomes affianced to Maggie Ellersley, who really loves Philip, Joanna's brother. Insulted by a wealthy white woman who had booked his orchestra, Peter returns to medical school and breaks his engagement to Maggie. During World War I Peter joins the American Army and en route to France meets Meriwether Bye, a fatalistic white relative whose liberal racial views lessen Peter's bitterness and give him hope. In France, Philip, also a soldier, becomes reconciled with Maggie, who is serving overseas as a volunteer social worker; and Harley Alexander, a dentist whose inamorata, Vera Manning, is passing in the United States in order to enjoy superior advantages, decides to remain abroad in order to escape the American race problem. After the war Philip dies, but Joanna and Bye settle their differences in well-adjusted family life.

The thesis of *There Is Confusion* is that educated and aspiring Negroes not only must overcome the usual obstacles which other

Americans must transcend but also must undertake a sometimes heart-rending struggle against race prejudice. The difficulty of being a Negro in the United States induces Vera Manning to pass, provokes her lover to practise his profession in France, causes Peter to give up temporarily his studies in medical school, throws innumerable bars before Joanna's progress as a singer and dancer, and frustrates Philip's successful career and marriage. Negroes are pictured as being so relentlessly perplexed by racial considerations that they are unable to make a normal approach to living. Brian Spencer, husband of Joanna's sister Sylvia, probably states the viewpoint of the author when he tells his wife:

> "It [the complex of color] comes to every colored man and every colored woman, too, who has any ambition. . . . But every colored man feels it sooner or later. It gets in the way of his dreams, of his education, of his marriage, of the rearing of his children. The time comes when he thinks, 'I might just as well fall back; there's no use pushing on. A colored man just can't make any headway in this awful country.' Of course, it's a fallacy. And if a fellow sticks it out he finally gets past it, but not before it has worked considerable confusion in his life."

*There Is Confusion,* while not a militantly propagandistic novel, exposes many of the racial disadvantages suffered by Negroes. The consequences of illicit relationships between master and slave are illustrated in the chronicle of the white and black Byes. Legal injustice, peonage, and lynching are not overlooked. The operation of prejudice is revealed in schools, colleges, graduate and professional institutions, stores, restaurants, hospitals, theaters, and even in the world of art. Everywhere in the country the specter of discrimination is shown hovering over the Negro, limiting his sphere of activities, focusing his thinking upon his plight, and obstructing his advancement into a fuller and richer life.

Not all the prejudice in *There Is Confusion,* however, is directed against the Negro by the white group, for there is ample evidence of intraracial caste distinctions among colored Philadelphians. "In Philadelphia," Miss Fauset remarked in discussing the novel, "among colored people, it isn't a question of 'How much have you?' but 'Who are you?'"[10] Therefore Joanna, a typical snob of the Negro elite, tells Maggie, a supposed nobody from the "dump heap," that a girl of her "lowly aims" would only be "a serious hindrance" to Philip. Respectability and lineage, such as that possessed by the Byes and Marshalls, is Maggie's ultimate desideratum. It is cherished so much, as a matter of fact, that Maggie devotes her life to the attainment of it. Through her own diligence she lifts herself and her ex-laundress mother from a blighted slum district to a decent neighborhood. An obsessive desire for a husband of distinction leads her into an unfortunate *mésalliance* with a gambler and into an unhappy engagement to Peter. As friends she wants "impeccable young women with whom she could talk over things, and exchange patterns and recipes, or go to the matinee." At the close of the book, although Philip has died in spite of her loyal nursing, she lives serenely, supported by the unquestioned respectability of the Marshalls.

In brief, *There is Confusion* is one of the important novels of American Negro literature. As Braithwaite has observed, Miss Fauset "has taken a class within the race, given it an established social standing, tradition, and culture, and shown that its predilections are very much like those of any other civilized group of human beings."[11] Because of this achievement, *There Is Confusion* was labeled by Alain Locke as "the novel that the Negro intelligentsia have been clamoring for," as "not merely a race story told from the inside, but a cross-section of the race life higher up the pyramid and farther from the base-line of the peasant and the soil than is usually taken."[12]

Like *There Is Confusion, Plum Bun* (1929) deals with well-bred Negroes in Philadelphia and New York City. Whereas the problem of passing is treated only incidentally in the former novel, it is the principal theme of the latter, which recounts the experiences of Angela Murray as a member of the white group. Leaving her brown-skinned sister Virginia in Philadelphia, Angela crosses the color line in New York City because of her conviction "that the great rewards of life—riches, glamour, pleasure,—are for white-skinned people only." Enrolling as an art student in Cooper Union, she at first exults in her courage to escape the circumscriptions of color and contemplates marriage to Roger Fielding, a member of the American *haut monde*. Fielding, however, accepts her merely as a mistress and discards her as soon as the thrill of conquest is exhausted. Later Angela discovers that she really loves Anthony Cross, a fellow painter who is also passing. In an effort to forget what he considers a hopeless passion for Angela, Cross becomes engaged to Virginia, now a popular and successful Harlemite. Virginia's eventual marriage to Matthew Henson solves the romantic problems of Angela and Cross, who wed and return to the colored group.

*Plum Bun*, like Nella Larsen's *Passing* (1929), mirrors the advantages and handicaps of those who live in the white world after fleeing from the black. Because of the color of her skin, Angela feels justified in entering a sphere of life in which she can find greater ease and freedom:

> "Why should I shut myself off from all the things I want most,—clever people, people who do things, Art,—" her voice spelt it with a capital,—"travel and a lot of things which are in the world for everybody really but which only white people, as far as I can see, get their hands on."

Once among whites, however, she wavers and, like Clare Kendry of *Passing*, sometimes wishes to abandon her hazardous life of pretension. Moreover, just as Clare desires the company of Irene Redfield and dislikes the Negrophobe sentiments of her white husband, so Angela wants the companionship of her brown-skinned sister and recoils from the anti-Negro statements of her aristocratic white lover. In brief, Angela, as Miss Fauset states in discussing *Plum Bun*, "found herself caught up in a network of other factors, loyalty, honor, racial ties, the impulse to side with the weaker even when one perceives with the clearness of long self-denial the advantages of mingling with the stronger."[13] Finally, in spite of her mother's dictum that "life is more important than color," Angela comes to realize, as Miss Fauset again notes, "that her treatment of color is the most important factor in her method of living life."[14] Sheer luck probably saves Angela from a fate as tragic as that of Clare.

In *The Chinaberry Tree* (1931), which is something of a modern analogue to Hawthorne's *The Scarlet Letter,* Miss Fauset turns from an analysis of the problem of passing to a study of the consequences of "the sins of the fathers" in the small town of Red Brook, New Jersey. Two cousins, Laurentine Strange and Melissa Paul, are illegitimate. Laurentine is the mulatto daughter of Aunt Sal, a former Negro housemaid in Alabama, and Colonel Francis Holloway, a Southern blue-blood. Though unable to offer Sal marriage, Holloway had made no secret of his affection and in his will had provided liberally for his mistress and child. On the other hand, Melissa, the unwitting offspring of adultery, is the daughter of Judy, Aunt Sal's sister, and Sylvester Forten, a married Negro. As the novel opens, Aunt Sal, Laurentine, and Melissa are living together in Red Brook, where the townspeople stigmatize the Strange blood as "bad." While Laurentine suffers ostracism caused by bastardy, Melissa enjoys popularity among the colored elite and remains serene in the confidence that her own antecedents had, through wedlock, satisfied respectable conventionalities. Melissa is plunged into despair, however, when her projected marriage to a half-brother, Malory Forten, brings forth the secret of her own extra-marital birth. In the end the two girls transcend the blight of illegitimate birth by becoming the wives of dependable colored men.

In *The Chinaberry Tree* Miss Fauset admittedly seeks to show that the Negro "is not so different from any other American, just distinctive." In illustrating that Negro life may be "complex as well as merely passionate," Miss Fauset, as Burgum notes, is "aided by choosing to treat not of Harlem Negroes but of a small New Jersey community less isolated from the contagion of white example."[15] Burgum also penetratingly observes that "the ideal of respectability which dominates the book is more than an adoption of its stuffy Puritanical survival in the suburban life of bourgeois whites" and that the characters of the novel have "a veneration for chastity which was certainly not caught from white Montclair but from Queen Victoria."[16] DuBois, voicing the opinion of certain Negro intellectuals, hails the book because it shows the American reading public that "prim colored society" exists even in small New Jersey towns, that sexual conduct among Negroes is "not strictly limited to frank prostitution or careless promiscuity," and that "sexual looseness within the race" may "literally blast a household."[17]

*Comedy: American Style* (1933), Jessie Fauset's fourth novel, is the story of a near-white woman's obsessive determination to free herself and her immediate family from the circumscriptions of color in the United States and France. The daughter of a woman who passed for convenience in Massachusetts, Olivia early experienced the crushing indignities inflicted upon those known to be colored and in girlhood vowed to devote her life to guiding her own domestic craft away from reefs of race in America. Marrying Christopher Cary, a light-skinned Philadelphia Negro physician, because of his education and social prestige as well as in consideration of her belief that wedlock with a white man of similar qualifications would be impossible, Olivia becomes the mother of three children—Teresa, Christopher, and Oliver. To Teresa and Christopher, who are light enough to pass, she gives every advantage in culture and education; but before Oliver, the brown-skinned object of her indifference and dislike, she places every possible stumbling block. As a result of this morbid devotion to whiteness, Olivia brings bitter tragedy to her children, her husband, and herself. Teresa, prevented from marrying a young Negro graduate of the Massachusetts Institute of Technology, is forced by her mother into a miserable union with an indifferent, miserly Frenchman. Oliver, the handsome but scorned brown son, is driven to suicide by his mother's statement that the family could live happily in

France "if it just weren't for Oliver" and by the impossibility of visiting his cherished sister Teresa because of her husband's anti-Negro sentiments. The elder Cary, pained by the unhappy marriage of Teresa and the self-inflicted death of Oliver, sinks pathetically into bankruptcy and invalidism. Young Christopher, unknowingly retarded in his wooing of an attractive but obviously colored girl, luckily marries Phebe Grant who, refusing to tolerate Olivia's haughty attitude, helps to bring about Olivia's departure to France and brighter days for the remaining members of the household. At the close of the novel Olivia, ejected by her French son-in-law and supported only by a small allowance which her convalescent husband provides, is wretchedly alone in Paris.

*Comedy: American Style* is the most penetrating study of color mania in American fiction. The success of the book as an analysis of psychopathic Aryanism is due largely to the able characterization of Olivia. Convinced "that God or Nature created only one perfect race—the Caucasians," this woman, endowed with singleness of purpose and relentlessness of action, brings all of the immediate members of her family under her baleful influence. A confirmed adherent of Nordicism, she remains faithful even when receiving the insult and scorn of those whom she worships. So fanatical is she in the quest of white identity for herself and her favored relatives that she shuns the society of Negroes, who painfully remind her of the African blood in her own veins.

The contribution of Jessie Fauset to American fiction can not be gainsaid. In her novels she shows that in the country there are respectable, middle-class colored people whose lives are twisted and distorted because of race prejudice. Like Chesnutt, Miss Fauset is especially interested in bourgeois characters who hover near the color line; but, unlike him, she prefers not a Southern setting but Philadelphia and New York City, with occasional trips to Europe breaking the monotony of background. *The Chinaberry Tree,* an exception to the rule, is laid chiefly in a small New Jersey town; but here again we have decent, educated Negro society. Miss

Fauset's description of the lives and difficulties of Philadelphia's colored elite is one of the major achievements of American Negro fiction.

### Walter White

In addition to treating the problem of passing in the urban North, Walter White's *Flight* (1926) provides a study of the colored bourgeoisie of Atlanta, Georgia. Attracted to Carl Hunter, the irresponsible and mercurial son of a prosperous Atlanta family, Mimi Daquin, a Creole newcomer from New Orleans, submits to his desires and becomes pregnant. Rather than undergo an abortion which her lover recommends, Mimi flees to Philadelphia to give birth to a son, Jean, whom she subsequently places in a Baltimore orphanage. At the request of an aunt, she next goes to Harlem, where she prospers until a visiting Atlanta newsmonger spreads rumors concerning her affair with Hunter. In order to avoid further scandal, Mimi crosses the color line and obtains employment at Francine's, an exclusive Fifth Avenue shop. After rising to an executive position in this establishment, she marries Jimmy Forrester, an affluent white broker. Though comfortably established as a wife, Mimi wonders, after two trips to Harlem during the absence of her husband, "if the sombre, cynical companions she met in her home and in other places were worth the price she was paying for these luxuries." While she is in this state of mind the singing of spirituals by a Negro artist in Carnegie Hall is sufficient to draw her from her husband to "Petit Jean—my own people—and happiness!"

*Flight* affords a vivid commentary on Babbittry and life among Negroes of Atlanta. Through Robertson, Mimi's stepgrandparent, White satirizes Negroes who are preoccupied with the acquisition of wealth. Atlanta's social elite—placing emphasis on light pigmentation and outspoken in their dislike for Catholics, Jews, and black Negroes—are described as "victims of a system which made colour and hair texture and race a fetish." Gossip, slander, bickerings, jealousies, and sartorial competition are listed as the chief activities of bourgeois colored women. The author finds solid worth and genuine strength, however, among poor Negroes who, though deprived and mistreated, can nevertheless sing, laugh, have faith, and find enjoyment in an industrial civilization which often makes the dominant white man unhappy, morbid, and depressed. Describing Mimi's reaction to the ability of these folk to withstand the devitalizing influences of industrialism, White writes:

> She marvelled at their toughness of fibre which seemed to be a racial characteristic, which made them able to live in the midst of a highly mechanized civilization, enjoy its undoubted advantages, and yet keep free that individual and racial distinctiveness which did not permit the surrender of individuality to the machine.
>
> In slavery it had kept them from being crushed and exterminated as oppression had done to the Indian. In freedom it had kept them from becoming mere cogs in an elaborately organized machine.

This power to resist and endure is attributed largely to Negroes' "rare gift of lifting themselves emotionally and spiritually far, far above their material lives and selves."

The Atlanta setting, in which the earlier chapters of the novel are unfolded, is one of interracial tension. Common occurrences are disturbances on street cars, discrimination in stores, political disputes over disfranchisement, misrepresentation in books like *The Clansman*, and inflammatory articles in the public press. These conditions—provocative of suspicion, hostility, and hatred—at length contribute to the outbreak of the Atlanta riot of 1906, a ghastly episode which inspired DuBois's "A Litany at Atlanta," later included in *Darkwater* (1920), and Don Marquis' "Carter" (1921), a short story which also treats the passing of an Atlanta colored man in New York City.

In its latter chapters *Flight* is a study of passing in downtown Manhattan. Race-conscious and anti-Nordic after the Atlanta riot, Mimi leaves her people not because of a deep-seated desire to join the white group but because of the pressure of slander and possible disgrace:

> Thus her passing from the race seemed to Mimi persecution greater than any white people had ever visited upon colored people—the very intolerance of her own people had driven her from them.

In her new environment, however, in spite of the luxuries which her husband provides, she feels that she is "doing a mean and dishonorable thing" and longs for "the spontaneity, the ready laughter, the naturalness" of Negro life.

### Nella Larsen

In *Quicksand* (1928) and *Passing* (1929) Nella Larsen is concerned with the disintegration and maladjustment wrought by miscegenation in the lives of two young colored women. The former novel is primarily a study of the character and experiences of a heroine not white enough to pass but nevertheless not too dark to mingle socially as an exotic personality among fashionable and artistic circles of Copenhagen, while the latter is mainly an analysis of the forces at work in the life of a mulatto beauty who forsakes the Negro group for the white race. In each case the implication is that the Negro-white hybrid frequently fails to attain a satisfactory harmony between his desires and his status in society.

Helga Crane, the heroine of *Quicksand,* is the daughter of a Danish woman and a colored gambler. Scorned after the death of her parents by all members of the American branch of her mother's family except a sympathetic uncle who educates her, she becomes self-conscious concerning her racial background. Deciding to devote her life to the uplift of her father's people, she accepts a teaching position at Naxos, a mammoth Negro educational institution; but the hypocrisy, servility, and snobbishness of the staff provoke her to resign in the middle of the term and break her engagement to a smug and respectable instructor who has adjusted himself to the school environment. At the home of her sympathetic uncle in Chicago, she is rebuffed by his recently acquired wife, who requests that Helga dissociate herself from the family. After many difficulties Helga gets temporary work as the traveling companion and secretary of a Negro woman lecturer, and through her employer later obtains a good position in a New York Negro insurance company as well as desirable lodging quarters at the home of Anne Grey. At first finding contentment and happiness in Harlem, Helga eventually becomes uncomfortable and restless. Especially boring to her are Anne's obsession with the race problem and her ceaseless chatter about the humiliations and injustices suffered by Negroes. Just as her dissatisfaction is developing into anguish, Helga receives a substantial check from her uncle in Chicago and decides to follow his advice by visiting her Aunt Katrina in Copenhagen. In the Danish capital she at first enjoys the luxury of her new surroundings and attracts a host of admirers, including sophisticated Axel Olsen, a famous portrait painter. After two years, however, she again becomes dissatisfied, and her uneasiness increases with the announcement of Anne's coming marriage to Dr. Robert Anderson, a former Naxos principal, who had appealed to Helga since her teaching days. The appearance of Negro enterainers at a Copenhagen vaudeville house further whets her nostalgia for America, and while under the influence of these longings she rejects, for racial reasons, an offer of marriage by Olsen. Realizing that her aching for America is really a homesickness for Negroes, Helga informs her aunt and uncle of her intention to return to the United States. Again in New York, Helga is strongly attracted to Anderson but develops a dislike for him when he refuses the offering of her body. Belittled by the drift of events, Helga wanders out the next night into a rainstorm, takes refuge in a building where a revival is being held, permits herself to be considered converted, and impulsively submits to the physical desires of the pastor. Subsequently marrying the minister, she goes with him to a small Alabama town where she becomes the mother of four children. Though a fifth pregnancy frustrates her immediate plans of retrieving her former social position, Helga nevertheless clings to her dreams of doing so, even in her encompassing and confining motherhood.

*Quicksand,* DuBois commented flatteringly in 1928, is "the best piece of fiction that Negro America has produced since the heyday of Chesnutt, and stands easily with Jessie Fauset's *There Is Confusion* in its subtle comprehension of the curious cross currents that swirl about the black American."[18] While this high evaluation of the novel may be debated, it is hardly deniable that Helga Crane is a convincing portrait of the tragic mulatto. Sensitive because of her questionable background, Helga can not integrate herself into either race. Among Negroes she is bored by Babbittry as well as by interminable discussions of racial oppression, while in the company of whites she is inhibited by convictions concerning intermarriage. In rejecting Olsen's proposal, for example, she declares:

> "You see, I couldn't marry a white man. I simply couldn't. It isn't just you, not just personal, you understand. It's deeper, broader than that. It's racial. Some day maybe you'll be glad. We can't tell, you know; if we were married, you might come to be ashamed of me, to hate me, to hate all dark people. My mother did that."

Helga's attitude toward America is equally confused. On the one hand, she is determined to hold her social freedom in Denmark because of the suffering of black folk in the United States:

> Never could she recall the shames and often the absolute horrors of the black man's existence in America without the quickening of her heart's beating and a sensation of disturbing nausea.

On the other hand, as soon as the novelty of her residence in Copenhagen passes, she longs for Negro communities and for the first time sympathizes with her father for his abandonment of her mother. In brief, racial crosscurrents in the blood of Helga render her an unstable and sometimes paradoxical personality. The aloofness of her American white relatives and the consciousness of her mixed extraction intensify her problems of adjustment.

*Quicksand* also embodies a satire upon large white-supported institutions for the education of Negroes in the South, a glimpse at Harlem during the Renascence period, and a picture of fashionable social life in Copenhagen. Naxos, the school which is ridiculed, is presented as a huge machine accepting no revisions, breaking the wills of enterprising teachers, and creating a wide breach between instructors and students. Insincerity, tyranny, and snobbishness are the main traits of faculty members, most of whom join students in applauding white speakers who advise Negroes to remain in their assigned sphere and to steer clear of independent thought and conduct. In the Harlem scene we find Helga moving among upper-class colored folk whose sophisticated conversation, fastidious dress, well-appointed homes, spirited parties, and militant racial attitudes furnish a radical change from the Naxos way of life. In contrast to the joyousness and glamour of Harlem we observe the stately and formal social life of Copenhagen, where race prejudice is practically nonexistent and Helga enjoys the lavish attention usually accorded an exotic visitor. From these more elevated social planes Helga sinks at the close of the book to the drab and monotonous life of an Alabama small town.

Whereas in *Quicksand* Nella Larsen studies the life of a mulatto girl who never openly relinquishes connection with Negroes, in her second novel, *Passing* (1929), which is dedicated to Carl Van Vechten and Fania Marinoff, she unfolds the experiences of a beautiful woman who severs ties with colored people in order to enter the white group. *Passing,* which probes the psychology of an individual moving from one race to another, is one of the significant studies of its kind in American fiction. The novel is mainly the story of Clare Kendry, the illegitimate daughter of a white wastrel and a colored girl. Rather than accept drudgery in the home of her father's prejudiced aunts, Clare crosses the color line in order to wed John Bellew, a Chicagoan who has acquired considerable wealth in South America. She becomes a mother but is unable to suppress her yearning "to see Negroes, to be with them again, to talk with them, to hear them laugh." In a Chicago hotel she accidentally meets Irene Redfield, a light-skinned girlhood friend who has married a colored physician and moved to New York City. Though at first determined not to serve as a link with Negroes for her passing friend, Irene agrees to come to the Bellew apartment for tea. At this tea Irene meets Gertrude Martin, who has openly married a white sweetheart of her schooldays, and Bellew, who calls Clare "Nig" because of her seemingly darkening complexion and openly expresses his aversion for Negroes. Thus humiliated and insulted by Bellew's disparaging remarks, Irene returns to New York and, supported in her position by her husband, resolves to sever all relations with Clare. Sweeping aside Irene's objections, Clare comes to New York while Bellew is in Florida and, disregarding the inconvenience her presence might occasion, insists upon attending the Negro Welfare League Dance with the Redfields. At first vexed by Clare's wilfulness, Redfield later accepts her company with indulgent pleasure and manifests so much interest in her that Irene becomes suspicious and, distressed by the possibility of broken faith, even considers telling Bellew of his wife's frequent pilgrimages to Harlem. While in this disturbed state of mind Irene, during a downtown shopping tour with a dark friend, accidentally meets Bellew, and, ignoring his genial greeting, continues on her way. His suspicion aroused by Irene's failure to recognize him, Bellew eventually traces Clare to a party at a Negro residence where he, moved by anger and pain, says to his wife: "So you're a nigger, a damned dirty nigger!" Trapped by her husband and embarrassed before friends, Clare falls from a sixth-floor window to her death.

*Passing* provides a study of the life of a young colored woman who repudiates her mother's race in order to escape insult and deprivation. Once comfortably settled in a new environment, however, she can not refrain from seeking the society of Negroes, thus verifying Redfield's observation that passers "always come back." The hazards of passing are illustrated, and chief among these is the possibility that an offspring may have Negroid pigmentation. Clare, usually daring and adventurous, loses courage in contemplation of future motherhood:

"I nearly died of terror the whole nine months before Margery was born for fear that she might be dark. Thank goodness, she turned out all right. But I'll never risk it again. Never! The strain is simply too—too hellish."

Though married to a white man who is aware of her race, Gertrude likewise flinches before the possibility of having dark children. The attitude of Negroes toward passing is succinctly expressed by Irene:

"It's funny about 'passing.' We disapprove of it and at the same time condone it. It excites our contempt and yet we rather admire it. We shy away from it with an odd kind of revulsion, but we protect it."

In brief, *Quicksand* and *Passing* are studies of the warped lives of two attractive young women of biracial parentage, the one too dark to pass but light enough to be accepted socially by unprejudiced Danes, and the other sufficiently fair to mingle freely with white Americans. Racial maladjustment leads Helga to degrading mediocrity in a small Alabama town and Clare to tragic death in New York City.

## IV. *PROPAGANDA*

During the Negro Renascence fictionists did not devote their energies to propaganda so vigorously as they did in the years before World War I. Nevertheless, in this period at least three novels of strongly propagandistic intent were produced by Harlem writers: these were Walter White's *The Fire in the Flint* (1924), W. E. B. DuBois's *Dark Princess* (1928), and George Schuyler's *Slaves Today* (1931). The first attacks oppression and lynching in the Southern small town, the second advocates the international co-operation of darker peoples, and the third exposes the exploitation of native labor in Liberia.

## Walter White

After World War I many factors—including numerous industrial and residential problems caused by the Northward Negro migration, the resentment of the South at being deprived of underpaid black workers, the resurgence of the Ku Klux Klan, and the return of sensitive and militant Negro soldiers—united to make 1919 one of the bitterest years in the history of race relations in the United States. As DuBois observes:

> The facts concerning the year 1919 are almost unbelievable as one looks back upon them today. During that year seventy-seven Negroes were lynched, of whom one was a woman and eleven were soldiers; of these, fourteen were publicly burned, eleven of them being burned alive.
>
> That year there were race riots large and small in twenty-six American cities including thirty-eight killed in a Chicago riot of August; from twenty-five to fifty in Phillips County, Arkansas; and six killed in Washington.[19]

With the outbreak of mob violence in various sections of the country the National Association for the Advancement of colored People organized for determined resistance. In May, 1919, a widely publicized conference on lynching was held in New York City; and the co-operation of the President of the nation, seven governors, and many other influential individuals was obtained. Largely through the efforts of James Weldon Johnson, field secretary of the National Association for the Advancement of Colored People, the Dyer Anti-Lynching Bill was brought before Congress, was passed in the House of Representatives, but was killed in 1924 by a filibuster in the Senate. Equally as aggressive as Johnson in the campaign against mob violence was Walter White, who, after his election as assistant secretary of the National Association in 1918, became prominent as an investigator of lynchings.[20] Between 1918 and 1928 White, who has been previously discussed in this chapter as the author of *Flight*, probed forty-one lynchings and eight race riots. In 1924 he produced *The Fire in the Flint*, one of the most successful exposés of lynching in American fiction; and in 1929, assisted by a Guggenheim fellowship, he wrote *Rope and Faggot: A Biography of Judge Lynch,* a penetrating analysis of the causes, functioning, and cures of mob violence.

*The Fire in the Flint,* in which White uses fiction as the medium for his attack on lynching and the Southern small town, is chiefly the story of Kenneth Harper, a young Negro physician trained in the best universities of America and France. After World War I, Harper returns to Central City, Georgia, where his family resides, to practise medicine and eventually to found a sanatarium for Negroes. Overcoming the handicaps of youth, prejudice, and envious competition, he establishes himself as a successful practitioner and falls in love with Jane Phillips, a capable local girl who teaches in North Carolina. Upon reporting the murder of a colored man by the sheriff's brother and undertaking to organize exploited Negro farmers of the vicinity into co-operatives, Harper incurs the animosity of white citizens. While he is in Atlanta for the purpose of performing an operation and seeking the assistance of liberal whites in the promotion of co-operatives, his young sister Mamie is ravished by a group of white ruffians, and his brother Bob, after wreaking vengeance upon two of her attackers, commits suicide rather than surrender himself to a mob that subsequently riddles his corpse with bullets and burns it in the public square of Central City. Returning to the hate-charged town, Harper, though enbittered and heartbroken because of the fate of his brother and sister, consents to attend Mary Ewing, a white girl whose life he had earlier saved through an operation. On the way to the sick girl's home he is followed by fifteen white men, who hastily conclude that he is consorting with the patient's mother and therefore kill him after he leaves the house.

White's description of Central City is an authentic portrait of a half-rural, half-urban Georgia town. The various sections of the place—the dusty trading district, the respectable residential area, the squalid and filthy Negro ghetto, and the equally dingy and unsanitary cotton mill vicinity in which tubercular and cadaverous poor whites dwell—are convincingly pictured. In this warped environment learning and culture are decadent and effete, but the noxious growth of race prejudice thrives and prospers. Selfish, hypocritical demagogues separate Negroes and poor whites by keeping alive in the latter group a confidence in their own natural superiority and a belief that their safety rests in the subjugation of black people. In every possible way Negroes are made to feel that they are predestined to a subordinate status. They have neither legal redress nor police protection. In business dealings they are the victims of thievery and chicanery. They accept dilapidated schools and underpaid teachers and tolerate the abduction of their women and the lynching of their men. To survive in this Jim-Crow environment they practise dissimulation, evasion, and secretiveness and seek an outlet for their pent-up feelings in emotional religion. Ready to terrorize and punish the black population for infractions of the Southern code, the Ku Klux Klan, having members from all classes of white society, stands dedicated to the maintenance of Nordic supremacy and the perpetuation of the *status quo*. The Klan is especially determined to keep the Negro out of local government so as to sustain such gross violations of right and decency as the sharecropper system. The author describes liberal and sympathetic white Southerners as men "hemmed in, oppressed, afraid to call their souls their own, creatures of the Frankenstein monster their own people had created which seemed about to rise up and destroy its creators." He further points out the failure of Dixie to produce "a martyr to any great moral cause—one who had sufficient courage to oppose, regardless of consequences, any one of the set, dogmatic beliefs of the South."

In training, experience, and racial philosophy Kenneth Harper is similar to his probable archetype, Dr. William Miller of Chesnutt's *The Marrow of Tradition* (1901). Both are products of the best Northern and European schools, both turn their backs on practising above the Mason-Dixon Line in order to devote their efforts to the improvement of the health of the colored people of the South, and both—in spite of all evidence and counsel to the contrary—are optimistic regarding a peaceful settlement of racial difficulties. Much like Miller's are Harper's conciliatory and accommodating views on the Negro's plight:

> His was the more philosophical viewpoint on the race question, that problem so close to him. The proscriptions which he and others of his race were forced to endure were inconvenient, yet they were apparently a part of life, one of its annoyances, a thing which had always been and probably would be for all time to come. Therefore, he reasoned, why bother with it any more than one was forced to by sheer necessity? Better it was for him if he attended to his own individual problems, solved them to the best of his ability and as circumstances would permit, and left to those who chose to do it the agitation for the betterment of things in general. If he solved his problems and every other Negro did the same, he often thought, then the thing we call the race problem will be solved. Besides, he reasoned, the whole thing is too big for one man to tackle it, and if he does attack it, more than likely he will go down to defeat in the attempt. And what would be gained?

Just as Miller, after the slaying of his son in a riot, ministers to the pressing needs of a sick white boy, so Harper, after the loss of his sister and brother, comes to the rescue of a very ill white girl and thus sets the stage for his own destruction. Before his death, however, he reaches the same bitter and rebellious position which Miller finally attains.

Standing in bold contrast to his philosophical and phlegmatic brother, Bob Harper represents Negro combativeness at its zenith. Sensitive and perspicacious, he broods over prejudice and is easily stirred to resentment and anger. Upon his brother's advice he gives up his earlier plans to live in the North and decides to prepare himself for a legal career as champion of his people in the courts of the South. All these hopes are frustrated when he takes revenge for his sister's ravishment into his own hands.

More than any other novel of the Negro Renascence, *Fire in the Flint* probes the precarious position of Negroes in a small Southern town. As a living argument against prejudice and brutality, the author presents a refined, intelligent, and prosperous family that suffers insults, injuries, and deaths because of superficial distinctions based on color and caste. The difficulties of the Negro professional man are set forth, and attention is called to his troubles with dominant whites as well as with Negroes whose slavery-conditioned minds make them reluctant to trust trained members of their own race. Also revealed is the success of the Southern ruling class in pitting poor whites against Negroes by nurturing concepts of Nordic superiority.

### W. E. B. DuBois

After World War I, Negroes in the United States manifested a greater interest than ever before in the colored peoples of other nations and realized that the problem of race is universal rather than national or provincial in scope. Upon being sent to France immediately after the Armistice by the National Association for the Advancement of Colored People in order to study the treatment and the record of American Negro soldiers, DuBois determined to take advantage of the opportunity to call a Pan-African Congress to voice the sentiments of the Negroes of the world before the Peace Congress at Versailles. Through the intercession of Blaise Diagne, a Senegalese member of the French Chamber of Deputies, DuBois was able to get "the consent of Clemenceau to hold in February, 1919, at the Grand Hotel in Paris, a Pan-African Congress of fifty-seven delegates including sixteen American Negroes, twenty West Indians, and twelve Africans."[21] Though the work of this conference was not significant, DuBois was convinced that a Pan-African Congress was needed to promote "not race war and opposition, but broader co-operation with the white rulers of the world, and a chance for peaceful and accelerated development of black folk."[22] Accordingly, in 1921 the Second Pan-African Congress met in London, Paris, and Brussels, attracting world-wide attention and drawing 113 accredited delegates. The third Congress was held in London, Paris, and Lisbon in 1923, and the fourth in New York City in 1927. A fifth was planned for Tunis, Africa, in 1929, but was blocked by the French government; and a belated effort to transfer the meeting to the West Indies was not successful. "No further efforts have been made," said DuBois in 1940 concerning attempts to hold other sessions of the Congress, "yet the idea is not entirely dead."[23]

*Dark Princess* (1928), which follows *The Quest of the Silver Fleece* (1911) to become DuBois's second published novel, reflects the thinking of its author on the advisability of the international collaboration of darker races.[24] The leading characters of the book are Matthew Towns, a brilliant young Negro who bolted from medical school in New York City because he was not permitted to do obstetrical work in a white hospital, and Kautilya, a beautiful and cultured princess of Bwodpur, India. Towns meets Kautilya in Berlin, where he falls in love with her. She invites him to represent the American Negro in a meeting of the subcommittee of the Great Council of Darker Peoples. During this meeting—despite the objections of Japanese, Chinese, Egyptian, Indian, and Arabian members—Kautilya contends that black folk should be considered for representation in the general organization and dispatches Towns to the United States to make recommendations on the incorporation of a militant group led by Miguel Perigua, a bitter and fiery West Indian living in Harlem. Finding that terrorism and revolt constitute Perigua's program, Towns reports that the West Indian's organization is not deserving of support but that in the movement for racial justice Negroes of the United States "are a tremendous social force, an economic entity of high importance." Perigua seeks to wreck a special train carrying officers and members of the Ku Klux Klan to Chicago, but Towns exposes the plot after discovering that Kautilya is also a passenger. Although the princess tries to take the blame for the intended wreck, Towns receives a ten-year prison sentence. Freed through the intervention of Sara Andrews, secretary of a Negro shyster of Chicago, Towns rises rapidly in corrupt Illinois politics, gains a seat in the state legislature, and is nominated for the House of Representatives. After Kautilya urges Towns not to become a pawn of moneyed interests, he gives up his political career, deserts Sara, whom he had married in a loveless match, and obtains a divorce which enables him to become the husband of the princess and the father of Madhu, Maharajah of Bwodpur and "Messenger and Messiah to all the Darker Worlds."

*Dark Princess* is significant because it is the only novel by an American Negro which makes an exhaustive study of the place of black folk among the darker races of the earth. As a framework for his interracial and international ideology, DuBois invents the Great Council of Darker Peoples to represent colored races who suffer under the injustice and oppression of the white group. At first the majority of the Council believe that African and American Negroes are unworthy in ability and qualifications to participate in the movement toward the uplift and emancipation of darker folk. Towns, however, argues that American democracy proves the cultural possibilities of the average man, regardless of race, when given adequate opportunities:

"America is teaching the world one thing and only one thing of real value, and that is, that ability and capacity for culture is not the hereditary monopoly of a few, but the widespread possibility for the majority of mankind if they only have a decent chance in life."

In the end, therefore, black folk are accepted into full membership in the Council; and Kautilya sends Towns the following report:

"The Great Central Committee of Yellow, Brown, and Black is finally to meet. You are a member. The High Command is to be chosen. Ten years of preparation are set. Ten more years of final planning, and then five years of intensive struggle. In 1952, the Dark World goes free—whether in Peace and fostering Friendship with all men, or in Blood and Storm—it is for them—the Pale Masters of today—to say."

*Dark Princess* is important not only because it is the first novel by an American Negro to take a cosmopolitan view of the plight of darker races; it is also noteworthy because it offers a more detailed satire of contemporary Negro political organization than any other work of fiction by a colored writer of this country. In order to expose nefarious political activities among American Negroes, DuBois selects Chicago as his setting and directs attention to Sammy Scott, a Negro political boss, and to Sara Andrews, his crafty and acquisitive secretary. Towns learns very early that money is the guiding and controlling force in American politics:

> He had no illusions as to American democracy. He had learned as a porter and in jail how America was ruled. He knew the power of organized crime, of self-indulgence, of industry, business, corporations, finance, commerce. They all paid for what they wanted the government to do for them—for their immunity, their appetites; for their incomes, for justice and the police. This trading of permission, license, monopoly, and immunity in return for money was engineered by politicians; and through their hands the pay went to voters for their votes. Sometimes the pay was in cash, sometimes in jobs, sometimes in "influence," sometimes in better streets, houses, or schools.

With this knowledge it was not hard for Towns to become a vital cog in Scott's machine. DuBois directs the spotlight upon bribery in the city administration and police protection of gamblers, bootleggers, prostitutes, and petty thieves; upon adroit techniques for winning the support of the clergy through large contributions and the co-operation of women through the formation of powerful clubs; upon unavailing petitions of reformers for social justice; upon insincere tactics for appeasing and compromising with powerful opposing groups; and upon undercover bargains and agreements with white political organizations. DuBois's exposure of greed and graft in Chicago's South Side is one of the best revelations of its kind in contemporary American fiction.

Besides providing an analysis of South Chicago politics, *Dark Princess* directs attention to other phases of Negro life in the United States. We follow Kautilya through employment as servant, tobacco hand, maid, factory worker, and labor agitator in her effort to get first-hand knowledge of the American Negro masses; and we see Towns employed as scullion, Pullman porter, and subway digger. Race prejudice is manifested in the discriminatory practices of medical schools, the colorphobia of the Ku Klux Klan, and the lynching of an innocent Pullman porter. Fleeting glimpses are given of respectable Negro society in Atlanta and Chicago. In the main, however, DuBois is more of a propagandist than a realistic painter of folk and the social scene.

### George Schuyler

Although George Schuyler is jocular and flippant in *Black No More* (1931), which will be treated later in this chapter, he is serious and propagandistic in *Slaves Today: A Story of Liberia* (1931), which exposes the persecution of Liberian natives by the Americo-Liberian ruling class. Basing his story upon a three-month visit to the African West Coast in 1931, and admittedly taking characters from real life, the author hopes that his book will lessen the exploitation of native groups by supposedly civilized peoples:

> If this novel can help arouse enlightened world opinion against this brutalizing of the native population in a Negro republic, perhaps the conscience of civilized people will stop similar atrocities in native lands ruled by proud white nations that boast of their superior culture.

The propaganda of *Slaves Today* is constructed around the love of Zo, a handsome young man of Takama, and Pameta, the youngest and favorite daughter of Chief Bongomo. When Bongomo, who has failed to send his monthly requisition of rice and palm oil to Boloba, seeks vengeance after a humiliating public whipping ordered by Commissioner David Jackson, he is shot to death. Subsequently Pameta, who has just married Zo, attracts the fancy of the lustful federal agent and is kidnapped. Determining to recover his bride, Zo follows Jackson's company to Boloba, where he is apprehended and lashed. Forcefully assigned to a group of men transporting rice and palm oil to Monrovia, Zo is eventually carried to a Spanish cocoa plantation in Fernando Po, where he spends two years as a virtual slave. Upon returning to Monrovia at the close of his term, Zo finds Pameta dying of a venereal disease contracted from Jackson. Infuriated by the fate of his wife as well as by his own sufferings, Zo murders Jackson before being killed by a guard.

*Slaves Today* exposes the exploitation of Liberian natives both in their homeland and in Fernando Po by the Americo-Liberian ruling class, whose freed ancestors had come from Maryland to Africa a century earlier to start a place of refuge for downtrodden Negroes. Of this dominating group Schuyler writes:

> Their forefathers had come here to this expanse of jungle to found a haven for the oppressed of the black race but their descendants were now guilty of the same cruelties from which they had fled. The Americo-Liberians were to rule; the natives to obey.

The tyrannical upper class extracts food, labor, and money from the native population by force and treaty. In a conversation with the truckling Bishop of Liberia, for example, Tom Saunders, the leader of the progressive group opposing and challenging the forces of ruin and destruction, reveals the extent of the profiteering operations of the public officials:

> "Do you realize, Bishop, that hundreds of men have been sent into virtual slavery this year; that their homes have been broken up and family life destroyed? Do you know that scores of towns have been overtaxed and dozens of chiefs humiliated by public whippings? Do you know that soldiers go about the country doing as they please, destroying huts and violating women?"

Economic parasitism is not the only failing of the rulers, however, for Schuyler points out that they live openly in immorality and debauchery. Concubinage, gluttony, and drunkenness join graft, fraud, and slave traffic in contributing to the undermining and ruination of the little republic. If conditions in Liberia are bad, those in Fernando Po are worse. On the vast cocoa plantations of this Spanish possession Liberians are compelled to work for a mere pittance under revolting conditions. Subjected to long hours, frequent lashings, and extended incarceration, the men have slight chance for escape and waste their meager earnings on diseased prostitutes. Public health is at low ebb, largely because yellow fever, elephantiasis, and venereal infection flourish among the conscripted laborers.

*Slaves Today* is a noteworthy American novel calling attention to the sufferings and hardships of black folk on the Dark Continent. The main public officials are thinly disguised: Tom Saunders, for example, may be easily identified as T. J. R. Faulkner, a prominent Liberian liberal who worked tirelessly for supervised elections and other reforms in the small African republic. Dewey R. Jones writes as follows concerning the crusade of Schuyler and Faulkner for justice and fair play in Liberia:

> It is here [in *Slaves Today*] that Mr. Schuyler, with considerable skill, lets his readers into the picture of slavery as it is being carried on today. It is practically the same picture drawn by Mr. Faulkner in his appeal to America and Europe two years ago—the appeal which resulted in the resignation of the President of Liberia. Prof. Charles S. Johnson . . . who represented the United States on an international investigation commission which went into Liberia at the request of Mr. Faulkner last year, has reported a story very similar in content to *Slaves Today,* if not like it in form. And Mr. Schuyler himself prepares the American reader for the facts in his book by a series of articles on Liberia and her slave traffic which was published in the leading American dailies and copied in one or two of our weeklies.[25]

In brief, *Slaves Today,* a well-documented attack on an iniquitous system of oppression, ranks as another manifestation of the growing concern of the American Negro for the welfare of colored people in other parts of the world.

## V. *THE VAN VECHTEN VOGUE*

> I am fully aware of the reasons why Negroes are sensitive in regard to fiction which attempts to picture the lower strata of the race. The point is that this is an attitude completely inimical to art. It has caused, sometimes quite unconsciously, more than one Negro of my acquaintance to refrain from using valuable material. . . .

The squalor of Negro life, the vice of Negro life, offer a wealth of material to the artist. On the other hand, there is very little difference if any between the life of a cultured and wealthy Negro and that of a white man of the same class. The question is: Are Negro writers going to write about this exotic material while it is still fresh or will they continue to make a free gift of it to white authors who will exploit it until not a drop of vitality remains?[26]

In the above words Carl Van Vechten, over six months before the publication of *Nigger Heaven,* expressed the attitude governing his writing of a novel that affected the work of Negro fictionists more than any other book in the history of American literature. Capitalizing on the alleged animalism and exoticism of Harlem life, *Nigger Heaven* was the first and most popular novel dealing with life in the black ghetto during the Roaring Twenties. Appearing at the proper time, when the Negro was emerging as a stellar performer in music and in the theater as well as when white America was curious about picturesque and exciting facets of Harlem life, the book enjoyed immediate popularity and became a sort of guidebook for visitors who went uptown seeking a re-creation of the primitive African jungle in the heart of New York City. The songs and blues selections by Langston Hughes not only augmented the appeal of the book but also drew widespread attention to the rising literati of Harlem.

Van Vechten builds his representation of Harlem around a slender plot tracing the romance of Mary Love, a respectable librarian, and Byron Kasson, an unstable and race-conscious young Philadelphian who comes to New York City to seek success as a writer. The lovers are moderately happy until Lasca Sartoris, "a gorgeous brown Messalina of Seventh Avenue," bewitches the would-be author and then deserts him for Randolph Pettijohn, the Bolito King. Rendered insanely vengeful by being jilted, Byron impulsively fires two bullets into the prostrate body of Pettijohn, who has previously been fatally wounded by a pimp called the Scarlet Creeper, and thereafter helplessly surrenders to police.

On the crowded canvas of his book Van Vechten presents

many colorful aspects of Harlem life. He gives an account of a lavish week-end party at the Long Island estate of Adora Boniface, an ex-music hall diva who also maintains a luxurious residence in Strivers' Row on West 139th Street. He essays to delineate bourgeois respectability in the life of Mary Love, who associates with young writers and other professional men, frequents dinner and bridge parties, attends plays and musical entertainments, reads reputable books (including Gertrude Stein's *Three Lives,* which made a deeper impression than any of the others), and appreciates primitive African sculpture. He describes the picturesque Charity Ball, a huge paid dance given annually by a group of socially prominent colored women, and sets forth views of Negroes concerning passing, miscegenation, inter- and intra-racial color prejudice, and many other matters.

Van Vechten paints Harlem cabaret life with obvious gusto. He is fascinated by the barbaric rhythms of Negro jazz, the tom-tom beat of the drum in the band, and the melting bodies of intoxicated dancers swaying to sensuous music. Contemplating the cabaret, Van Vechten surmises that Negroes are primitive and atavistic. In the singing of spirituals and jazz, black folk are described as "recognizing, no doubt, in some dim, biological way, the beat of the African rhythm." Even Mary Love, in spite of her respectability and horror of promiscuity, is convinced that her race is essentially savage:

> Savages! Savages at heart! And she had lost or forfeited her birthright, this primitive birthright which was so valuable and important an asset, a birthright that all the civilized races were struggling to get back to—this fact explained the art of a Picasso or a Stravinsky. To be sure, she, too, felt this African beat—it completely aroused her emotionally—but she was conscious of feeling it. This love of drums, of exciting rhythms, this naive delight in glowing colour—the colour that exists only in cloudless, tropical climes—this warm, sexual emotion, all these were hers only through a mental understanding. . . .
>
> We are all savages, she repeated to herself, all apparently, but me!

Of a two-day love orgy of Byron and Lasca, Van Vechten writes:

There were rages, succeeded by tumultuous passions; there were peaceful interludes; there were hours devoted to satisfying capricious desires, rhythmical amours to music, cruel and painful pastimes.

In describing a scene at the Black Venus cabaret, Van Vechten rhapsodizes:

The music shivered and broke, cracked and smashed. Jungle land. Hottentots and Bantus swaying under the amber moon. Love, sex, passion . . . hate.

Ever the painter of the exotic and fantastic, Van Vechten undeniably took particular delight in emphasizing—even in exaggerating and distorting—the primitive aspects of Harlem. To him the cabaret was a transplanted jungle, and Negroes were creatures of impulse and emotion, yearning for animalistic exhibitions of Africa. This stress upon the Negro as a child of nature did at least three things: first, it increased the influx of white visitors to upper Manhattan; second, it created a furious controversy among Negro intellectuals; and, third, it made American publishers and readers ready and eager for works with a similar emphasis by colored writers.

In the metropolitan dailies *Nigger Heaven* usually received favorable reviews—e.g., that of Carl Van Doren in *The New York Herald Tribune* for August 22, 1926, and that of Harry Hansen in *The New York World* for August 28, 1926—which stimulated a wide reading of the novel and a hegira of white folk to Harlem. In "The Ebony Flute," a monthly column in *Opportunity,* Gwendolyn Bennett records the power of *Nigger Heaven* in attracting outsiders to the black ghetto. Placed on the stands in August, the book was so popular by October, as Miss Bennett notes, that sightseers, visitors, and other strangers were "said to be 'van vechtening' around."[27] Intrigued by the primitivistic portrayal of the Negro in the book, whites from downtown and elsewhere temporarily neglected Greenwich Village to explore Harlem and enjoy the Negro.

While *Nigger Heaven* was generally received with favor by

white critics and readers, it aroused a storm of controversy among Negro intellectuals. Commendatory reviews were given by Wallace Thurman in *The Messenger* for September, 1926; by Charles S. Johnson in a letter to Carl Van Vechten published in *The Pittsburgh Courier* for September 4, 1926; by James Weldon Johnson in *Opportunity* for October, 1926; and by George Schuyler in *The Pittsburgh Courier* for November 6, 1926. Unfavorable reactions were expressed by Hubert Harrison in *The Amsterdam News* for October 9, 1926; by Floyd Calvin in *The Pittsburgh Courier* for November 6, 1926; by Dewey R. Jones in *The Chicago Defender* for November 24, 1926; by Henry Bibb in *The Chicago Whip* for November 24, 1926; and by W. E. B. DuBois in *The Crisis* for December, 1926. Voicing nearly all dissenting reactions to the novel, DuBois argues that *Nigger Heaven* is "a blow in the face," "an affront to the hospitality of black folk and to the intelligence of white," "a caricature," "a mass of half-truths," and "an astonishing and wearisome hodgepodge of laboriously stated facts, quotations and expressions, illuminated here and there with something that comes near to being nothing but cheap melodrama."[28] Reflecting the sentiments of Negroes who liked the novel, James Weldon Johnson insists that *Nigger Heaven* is "an absorbing story," "comprehends nearly every phase of life in the Negro metropolis," "draws on the components of that life from the dregs to the froth," and ranks as "the most revealing, significant and powerful novel based exclusively on Negro life yet written." Johnson holds that the book "is all reality" and "does not stoop to burlesque or caricature." In his opinion, Van Vechten is "the first white novelist of note to undertake a portrayal of modern American Negro life under metropolitan conditions" and "the only white novelist who has not viewed the Negro as a type, who has not treated the race as a unit, either good or bad."[29]

To the present-day critic, viewing *Nigger Heaven* over twenty years after it was published, it appears that the proper evaluation of the novel is at a point somewhere between the appraisal of

DuBois and that of Johnson. In stylizing the primitivism of the Negro and the jungle atmosphere of the Harlem cabaret, Van Vechten was doing no more than Langston Hughes had done in *The Weary Blues* (1925).[30] Van Vechten knows, or should know, that the Negro is no more primitivistic and atavistic than any other racial group that has been transplanted to America. He was merely a literary faddist capitalizing upon a current vogue and a popular demand. He did not deserve the vitriolic criticism of DuBois, for he frankly set out to exploit the exotic and the animalistic elements in Harlem life. At the same time, moreover, he did not merit the high praise of Johnson. There were significant facets of Harlem life which Van Vechten did not know and therefore could not describe; and surely Gertrude Stein, T. S. Stribling, Waldo Frank, and several other white predecessors of Van Vechten in the use of Negro subject matter made departures from the stereotyped presentation of colored characters.

All these considerations notwithstanding, the Van Vechten Vogue exerted profound influence upon American Negro literature. Two years after he had published *Color* (the featured poem, "Heritage," begins thus: "What is Africa to me?") Countee Cullen produced *Copper Sun* (1927), which shows the imprint of the Dark Continent in its title. Partly in awareness of "the traditional jazz connotations,"[31] James Weldon Johnson called his versified sermons *God's Trombones* (1927). Wallace Thurman collaborated with William Jordan Rapp in 1929 to produce *Harlem,* a play dealing with life in the black ghetto. But the emphasis upon jazz, sex, atavism, and primitivism, whether inspired by *Nigger Heaven* or not, is much more obvious in novels and short stories than in poetry and drama. Fictional works that stress these elements are Claude McKay's *Home to Harlem* (1928), *Banjo* (1929), and *Gingertown* (1932), Wallace Thurman's *The Blacker the Berry* (1929) and *Infants of the Spring* (1932), and Arna Bontemps' *God Sends Sunday* (1931). Excepting *Banjo* and *God Sends Sunday,* the scene of these narratives is laid principally in New York

City; and even in these two variant novels there is the same preoccupation with sensual pleasures and instinctive living. Like *Nigger Heaven,* the Harlem-centered works ordinarily depict cabaret scenes, interracial social gatherings, and the Negro literati. The low-life characters of these books are primarily concerned with pleasures of the hour—food, intoxicants, and sex. They unapologetically follow natural impulses and have no such moral codes as those of the respectable colored bourgeoisie. Moreover, unlike the propagandists, they have little desire to flay prejudice or effect racial reforms.

## Claude McKay

Claude MaKay denies the influence of *Nigger Heaven* upon his first work of fiction, *Home to Harlem* (1928),[32] which had greater popularity than any other novel of the Negro Renascence; but the fact remains that *Home to Harlem* capitalizes upon sex, the cabaret, atavism, and other selling points of the Van Vechten Vogue. The central character is Jake Brown, who deserts the American Army in Brest because he has to work in labor battalions rather than fight the enemy. Returning to the United States via London, he goes directly to Harlem, where he discovers sexual bliss in the arms of Felice, a beautiful brown girl. Losing her address and failing to locate her thereafter, Jake plunges into the fast life of Harlem, maintaining himself as a longshoreman and as a dining-car cook. We follow him to cabarets, pool rooms, chitterling joints, gambling dives, speakeasies, amusement basements, buffet flats, dance halls, prostitution houses, dining cars, and waiters' quarters. During this tour we observe streetwalkers, show girls, alcoholics, sweet men, scabs, loafers, loan sharks, and other characters of Harlem's underworld. Eventually Jake finds Felice and, in order to escape arrest as a military deserter, flees with her to Chicago.

Immediately after publication, *Home to Harlem* was censured by certain Negro intellectuals because it supposedly outstripped

*Nigger Heaven* in magnifying licentious and promiscuous aspects of life in upper Manhattan. For example, Dewey R. Jones, writing in *The Chicago Defender* for March 17, 1928, complains:

> *Home to Harlem* is *Nigger Heaven* in a larger and more violent dose. Where Mr. Van Vechten hesitated to delve too deeply into the morass of filth with which we know all Harlem abounds, Mr. McKay comes "full steam ahead" and "shoots the works."

While admitting certain merits of the novel, DuBois decries McKay's catering to "that prurient demand on the part of white folk for a portrayal in Negroes of that utter licentiousness which conventional civilization holds white folk back from enjoying" and protests that the book "for the most part nauseates me, and after the dirtier parts of its filth I feel distinctly like taking a bath."[33] It must be admitted that there is some basis for DuBois's objection to McKay's novel. Though rooted firmly in the author's experience,[34] *Home to Harlem* is painted in exaggerated colors and saturated with libertinism. In his preoccupation with muck and sensual excesses McKay, like Van Vechten, fails to give a well-rounded picture of Negro life. This faddistic emphasis upon overpainting and overliving, this lack of balance, inevitably spelled the doom of the Van Vechten Vogue.

It would be unjust, however, to say that *Home to Harlem* is entirely a riot of exotic color and orgiastic indulgences. In the character of Ray, Jake's Haitian friend and the probable counterpart of the author, McKay portrays a sensitive, intelligent Negro who has a distaste and sometimes an aversion for his low-life environment. His dream is to be a writer. Upset in his thinking by World War I and the Russian Revolution, he stands as a confused black man in a social order dominated by whites. In his wide reading, which ranges from Sappho to Sherwood Anderson, he discovers no solution to his dilemma. He shrinks from marriage because he does not want to "become one of the contented hogs in the pigpen of Harlem, getting ready to litter little black piggies." Finding slight meaning in human existence, he cynically considers himself "a misfit" and sometimes wonders if he can abandon his education and lose himself "in some savage culture in the jungles of Africa." The obvious implication of *Home to Harlem*, then, is that a *carpe diem* philosophy gives unlettered Jake happiness, while knowledge of books brings thoughtful Ray disillusionment and despair.

Ray is the chief connecting link between *Home to Harlem* and McKay's second novel, *Banjo* (1929), an impressionistic kodaking of life among the colored boys of the Marseilles breakwater. A decided change, however, has taken place in Ray's outlook on life. In spite of poverty and introspection, he has made headway as a writer and is determined to tell his story regardless of the color prejudice of readers:

> "If I am a real story-teller, I won't worry about the differences in complexion of those who listen and those who don't. I'll just identify myself with those who are really listening and tell my story."

Ray is still conscious of the oppressive impact of Occidental civilization upon the cultivated Negro mind:

> Oh, it was hell to be a man of color, intellectually and naturally human in the white world. Except for a superman, almost impossible.

Nevertheless he is determined not to let Anglo-Saxon standards rob him of independence and happiness:

> But of one thing he was resolved: civilization would not take the love of color, joy, beauty, vitality, and nobility out of *his* life and make him like one of the poor mass of its pale creatures. . . . Rather than lose his soul, let intellect go to hell and live instinct!

The main character of McKay's second novel is not Ray, however, but his friend Banjo, an irrepressible and irresponsible vagabond who—picking up odd jobs as seaman, longshoreman, farm hand, and factory worker—has wandered over much of North America and Western Europe. With Banjo and his companions we frequent bistros, bars, cabarets, eating sheds, and hovels of the Ditch, Marseilles's seaside slum district, and hear folk tales and racial discussions by colored men from all parts of the world. We note the evidence of first-hand knowledge in McKay's portraiture of tramps, seamen, soldiers, pimps, peddlers, gamblers, beachcombers, and prostitutes of the Mediterranean port; and we follow Banjo's casual and unashamed liaisons with Latnah, a mixed-breed girl from Aden, and Chère Blanche, a French prostitute of the Ditch. Late in the novel Jake of *Home to Harlem* meets Ray and the beach boys at a Marseilles bar. During a happy reunion Jake describes several years of family life with Felice in Chicago, the birth of a son named for Ray, a year in Harlem, a weariness of domesticity, employment as a seaman, and a current resolution to settle down to marriage upon his return to New York. At the close of the novel, the beach gang having dissolved, Ray zestfully sets forth on a vagabonding expedition with Banjo.

*Banjo*, like *Home to Harlem,* springs directly from the experience of its author. McKay had lived in Marseilles, mingling with black men from Africa, the United States, and the West Indies.[35] Dwelling in the Vieux Port, he had observed the life there and had participated in it. He confessedly was inspired to undertake *Banjo* because Senghor, an African nationalist, wished he "would write the truth about the Negroes in Marseilles."[36] To McKay's credit, *Banjo* is a fairly authentic depiction of life among those who dwell between the old port and the breakwater in the motley metropolis of Southern France. Though showing occasional proclivities for trumped-up exoticism and debauchery, the novel has social perspective, a quality lacking in *Home to Harlem,* and offers a well-rounded picture of the society with which it deals. Of documentary value are discussions of the Negro problem by individuals from various countries of the world. In *Banjo,* as DuBois has noted, "McKay has become an international Negro. He is a direct descendant from Africa. He knows the West Indies; he knows Harlem; he knows Europe; and he philosophizes about the whole thing."[37]

In six of the twelve stories of *Gingertown* (1932), his third volume of fiction, Claude McKay returns to the Harlem setting. A considerable part of the action takes place in cabarets, casinos, tonsorial parlors, and speakeasies; and once again cabaret entertainers, pimps, longshoremen, railroad men, bellhops, and chambermaids are leading characters. In contrast to *Home to Harlem,* however, the New York tales of *Gingertown* are largely concerned with intra- and inter-racial prejudice. "Brownskin Blues" and "Mattie and Her Sweetman" are stories of the love of dark women for yellow men. In the former Bessie, a cabaret singer hopelessly in love with a "sweet man" who has deserted her for a mulatto girl, has this creed: "When the light-skinned mens they go with the dark gals they think they is Gawd and gotta be worshiped, and it's the same with the yaller gals going with dark mens." Nevertheless, she submits to a faithful yellow lover. In the latter Mattie is not so fortunate and ousts her lover because he scornfully refers to her ebony hue. McKay points out that "there is no greater insult than calling a black person black." "Near-White," like Jessie Fauset's *Plum Bun* and Nella Larsen's *Passing,* treats life across the color line in Manhattan. Discontented with the circumscribed experience of a Harlem Negro, Angie Dove thinks that she is entitled to a place in white society "by right of feeling, of birth, and by right of color." As a passer, however, she leaves her white lover because he states he would "sooner love a toad" than a quadroon or octoroon. "Highball" deals with the pitfalls of intermarriage. Nation Roe, a celebrated entertainer who has divorced his colored wife in order to marry a white woman, is depressed by the apparently changed attitude of his friends of both races. Extremely color-conscious, he ejects his wife because her friends laughingly call him "a prune." The two remaining Harlem stories are not concerned primarily with problems of color and race. "The Prince of Porto Rico" shows how a bellhop traps his unfaithful wife and murders her lover, while "Truant" presents a railroad pantryman who deserts his spouse because of her preoccupation with "social position."

Since McKay wrote *Home to Harlem, Banjo,* and *Gingertown*

while abroad, he was not considered by a few critics as a participant in the Negro Renascence in New York.[38] Nevertheless, *Home to Harlem* emphasized those aspects of Harlem low-life earlier stressed in *Nigger Heaven*. The Van Vechten approach is also evident in *Banjo* and *Gingertown*, but these two volumes are more faithful renderings of their milieus. Sex is a powerful motivating influence in most of McKay's work. The heroes of *Home to Harlem* and *Banjo* are spontaneously amoral in their sexual conquests; and Ray, the intellectual who is at first restrained by conventional rules and taboos, finally decides that the instinctive is preferable to the rational life.

### Wallace Thurman

*The Blacker the Berry* (1929), Wallace Thurman's first novel, is a study of intraracial color prejudice operating upon Emma Lou Morgan, black daughter of a light-skinned mother whose family motto was "whiter and whiter every generation" until their "grandchildren could easily go over into the white race and become assimilated so that problems of race would plague them no more." From the first Emma Lou feels the burden of blackness, her color having alienated her parents and contributed to the estrangement of her mother from a second husband. Leaving her provincial home city of Boise, Idaho, to attend the University of Southern California, Emma Lou is depressed by the assembly-line methods of this huge educational institution as well as by the snobbishness of her colored schoolmates. After three years of college life she goes to Harlem, where darkness of skin frustrates her ambition to obtain employment as a stenographer in a Negro real estate firm. Gaining work as the maid of a white theatrical star, Emma Lou becomes infatuated with Alva, a New Yorker of mulatto-Filipino extraction. Her hypersensitiveness about color, however, results in Alva's abrupt departure. Unhappy without her lover, Emma Lou nevertheless finishes City College, passes the school board examination, and attracts the serious attentions of an unappealing but respectable mulatto. Upon hearing of Alva being left prostrate from alcoholism and stranded with his idiot child, she goes to nurse him. When he regains strength, however, he recommences his dissolute way of life and handles her as if she were a hired servant. Disgusted with this treatment, Emma Lou leaves.

The thesis of *The Blacker the Berry* is that a black woman—unless unusually talented, attractive, or wealthy—faces insurmountable social barriers within her race in the United States. A dark skin handicaps Emma Lou, who is distinctly an ordinary character, in adjusting herself in a metropolitan university, acquiring desirable social contacts, obtaining white-collar employment, and holding the affection of men she would have liked to marry.

*The Blacker the Berry* imitates *Nigger Heaven* in its treatment of Harlem. The usual pictures are painted of cabaret life, speakeasies, rent parties, midnight vaudeville shows, and ballroom dances. Two "sugar daddies," Alva and Braxton, are among the principal characters. Emma Lou shows incontinent tendencies in a group largely obsessed with sex, drinking, dancing, and gambling. At a rent party she meets such Renascence satellites as Tony Crews (Langston Hughes?) and Cora Thurston (Zora Neale Hurston?), and hears biting explanations of color snobbishness within the Negro group by Truman Walter (the author?). Late in the novel Emma Lou gets employment as personal maid to the wife of Campbell Kitchen, who, "along with Carl Van Vechten, was one of the leading spirits in this 'Explore Harlem; Know the Negro' crusade." Kitchen, who is likely Thurman's version of Van Vechten himself, receives the following encomium:

> He, unlike many others, was quite sincere in his desire to exploit those things in Negro life which he presumed would eventually win for the Negro a more comfortable position in American life. It was he who first began the agitation in the higher places of journalism which gave impetus to the spiritual craze. It was he who ferreted out and gave publicity to many unknown blues singers. It was he who sponsored most of the

younger Negro writers, personally carrying their work to publishers and editors.

In his second novel, *Infants of the Spring* (1932), Thurman castigates the younger debauchees among the Harlem intelligentsia and satirizes participants in the Negro Renascence. The focal point of the action is Niggeratti Manor, a spacious residence converted into studios for Negro artists and writers by Euphoria Blake, who believes that artistic achievement can bring her people greater freedom. In operation, however, the Manor becomes, to borrow Euphoria's words, "a miscegenated bawdy house" inhabited by comparatively unproductive artists and their mistresses, parasites, and white associates, most of whom are engrossed in drunkenness and venery. The leading members of this decadent clique are Raymond Taylor, a talented writer handicapped by confused thinking and disturbing race-consciousness; Samuel Carter, a militant white man ineffectively championing the cause of the American Negro in order to satisfy a martyr complex; Paul Arbian, a gifted painter, irresponsible poseur, confessed homosexualist, and devout admirer of Oscar Wilde; Eustace Savoy, an elegant tenor ashamed of the spirituals because of their slave origin but unable to make headway as a singer of classics in the white world; Pelham Gaylord, an obsequious and hopelessly inept painter and versifier; and Stephen Jorgenson, a Scandinavian neurotic fascinated by Harlem and colored women. At the close of the book, Euphoria having closed Niggeratti Manor because of the immorality of the tenants, Taylor faces an uncertain future, Carter is estranged from the set as a result of his duplicity, Arbian is a pathetic suicide, Savoy is disillusioned and dying in a city hospital, Gaylord is serving a jail sentence on a charge of rape, and Jorgenson is teaching in Westchester County in order to avoid a psychopathic revulsion for Negroes.

Perhaps the most interesting sections of *Infants of the Spring* are those containing satirical comments on the Negro Renascence. Though the so-called "New Negro" was acclaimed and patronized throughout the United States as a phenomenon in art, Thurman observes that very little "was being done to substantiate the current fad, to make it the foundation for something truly epochal." Through Taylor he protests "that the average Negro intellectual and artist has no goal, no standards, no elasticity, no pregnant germ plasm." Again using Taylor as a medium, he contends that Jean Toomer is the "only one Negro who has the elements of greatness" and that the others are without genuine ability:

"The rest of us are mere journeymen, planting seed for someone else to harvest. We all get sidetracked sooner or later. The older ones become warped by propaganda. We younger ones are mired in decadence. None of us seem able to rise above our environment."

Taylor attributes the emphasis upon abnormality in the literature of the Negro Renascence to the vogue of Faulkner and Hemingway. To make his satire of the Negro Renascence more personal, Thurman assembles the leading writers—Sweetie Mae Carr (Zora Neale Hurston?), Tony Crews (Langston Hughes?), DeWitt Clinton (Countee Cullen?), Cedric Williams (Eric Walrond?), Dr. Manfred Trout (Rudolph Fisher?), and others—at Niggeratti Manor upon the request of Dr. Parkes (Alain Locke?) to establish a salon and a concerted artistic movement. The purpose of the meeting is lost, however, in a heated debate concerning whether the "New Negro" should cultivate his African heritage, espouse full rights of citizenship, join the proletariat in an effort to overthrow capitalism, or strive for individual self-expression. Through Taylor, Thurman recommends the last-named course:

"Individuality is what we should strive for. Let each seek his own salvation. To me, a wholesale flight back to Africa or a wholesale allegiance to Communism or a wholesale adherence to an antiquated and for the most part ridiculous propagandistic program are all equally futile and unintelligent."

In *Infants of the Spring* Thurman had an unusual opportunity to produce a competent satire upon the young libertines of upper

Manhattan and the participants in the Negro Renascence. He himself was a member of the Harlem literary coterie, and his home was a favorite meeting place for certain bohemians of black Manhattan and Greenwich Village. In practice, however, Thurman showed himself unable to master this rich literary material. *Infants of the Spring* reveals an author morbid in outlook, diffuse in thinking, and destructive in purpose. Nowhere do we find the spontaneous humor which characterizes George Schuyler's *Black No More.* Every indication suggests that Thurman had not settled in his own mind the many issues that he introduces helter-skelter in the book. More than any other novel, therefore, *Infants of the Spring* illustrates the decadence of the Van Vechten Vogue which, like the Elizabethan tragedy and the Restoration heroic play, spent itself in excesses and exaggerations.

### Arna Bontemps

A writer of poetry and juvenile stories,[39] Arna Bontemps prior to 1940 had written three major works of fiction, including two historical novels. His first, *God Sends Sunday* (1931), shows the imprint of the Van Vechten Vogue, although it does introduce, as Sterling Brown observes, "a new character and a new milieu, both colorful, and both authentic parts to fill out the saga of Negro life."[40] In other words, *God Sends Sunday* follows *Nigger Heaven* in its emphasis upon sex and fast living, but differs in its introduction of a main character who is a celebrated jockey and a prodigal libertine in the racing centers of the Mississippi Valley. Born on a Red River plantation, Little Augie, being too frail for hard work, becomes an expert rider. Going to New Orleans on a steamboat, he eventually becomes a famous jockey wearing the colors of Horace Church-Woodbine, an aristocratic horse-fancier, and the lover of Florence Dessau, a voluptuous mulatto beauty. Though a satellite in drinking, gambling, and sporting circles, Augie is unhappy because of a secret passion for his employer's mistress. In an effort to forget her, he goes to St. Louis in quest of "a new world of fancy yellow women" and meets Della Green, a seductive prostitute who temporarily satisfies him. Some time later he returns to New Orleans and wins Florence, who soon deserts him because of his repeated failures in racing and gambling. Hoboing to a California town where his sister lives, Augie rapidly disintegrates, becoming a pitiable drunkard, a pathetic wooer of fickle young girls, a nostalgic dreamer of earlier triumphs, and finally a penniless murderer fleeing to Tia Juana.

In its abandonment of the Harlem background, *God Sends Sunday* exemplifies a new trend in fiction showing the influence of *Nigger Heaven*. Besides, more than any other novel in the Van Vechten tradition, it avoids race consciousness. This impartial treatment evoked the following comment from Laurence Stallings:

> It is without any resentment of color distinctions, being unique in that the disadvantages of being black in this country are not lamented. I cannot detect in any sentence either irony or pity.[41]

On this same point Gwendolyn Bennett remarks:

> I am happy that not even the most belligerent reader will be able to accuse this Negro writer of propaganda. There is no slightest hint of the race problem between its covers. Mr. Bontemps piles on color, not in order to make a brief for his people, but rather to make a portrait of them.[42]

This new realistic and dispassionate handling of racial subject matter represents a departure from the conventional use of such material by Negro writers before World War I.

## VI. *HARLEM REALISM*

While the Van Vechtenites were primarily interested in exploiting exotic and animalistic aspects of Negro life, Rudolph Fisher and Countee Cullen were concerned with providing a more representative picture of Harlem. Fisher's *The Walls of Jericho* (1928) and *The Conjure-Man Dies* (1932) and Cullen's *One*

*Way to Heaven* (1932) show that sex and the cabaret are not the major diversions of all Harlemites, and that in the black ghetto there is some regard for cerebration, respectability, and morality.

### RUDOLPH FISHER

In his treatment of Harlem in *The Walls of Jericho* (1928) Rudolph Fisher, concentrating upon the everyday life of the Negro metropolis, describes the relations of representative Harlemites with each other as well as with their white associates. The main thread of the story recounts the wooing of Linda Young, a respectable housemaid, by Joshua "Shine" Jones, a piano mover. After Linda relinquishes her job at the home of Miss Agatha Cramp, a professional benefactor of suffering races, to become a domestic in the home of Fred Merrit, a militant colored attorney who, in defiance of threats, has moved into an exclusive white neighborhood, "Shine" angrily expresses his contempt for high-toned Negroes by saying: ". . . Dickties is evil—don' never trust no dickty." When Linda is assaulted, "Shine" concludes that the attacker was Merrit. Bent upon vengeance, he seeks the lawyer and finds him grieving over the charred picture of his mother in the ruins of his home which had been maliciously burned by unknown parties. Unable to strike a man in the throes of loss and suffering, "Shine" departs and later discovers that Linda's assailant and the destroyer of Merrit's residence was Henry Patmore, a suave billiard hall proprietor against whom the attorney had earlier gained a court decision. After giving Patmore a sound thrashing, "Shine" becomes reconciled to Merrit, who finances him in a transfer business which enables him to expedite his quest of Linda's heart.

*The Walls of Jericho* successfully interweaves life in at least three separate levels of Harlem society. One of the social strata is that represented at Patmore's Pool Parlor, a drinking and gambling center where lower classes vent their spleen for "dickties." Patmore is a flashily dressed ladies' man. Among his patrons are "Shine," "Jinx" Jenkins, and "Bubber" Brown, all three of whom are furniture movers by vocation. Referring to the habitat of these characters, Fisher writes:

A city jungle this, if ever there was one, peopled largely by untamed creatures that live and die for the moment only. Accordingly, here strides melodrama, naked and unashamed.

In striking contrast to the group at Patmore's place is the respectable domestic class, exemplified by Linda and Merrit's housekeeper, Arabella Fuller. Linda does not easily submit to male conquest, avoiding the blandishments of Patmore and not yielding to "Shine" until sure of his honorable intentions. The third Harlem group portrayed in *The Walls of Jericho* is the sophisticated coterie that mingles freely with white people. The leader of this set, "superiorly self-named the Litter Rats," is J. Pennington Potter, a proud, loquacious, and pompous person who believes that amalgamation is the only key to interracial harmony. On the other hand, Merrit, also a member of the set, is vigorously anti-Nordic and has this comment to make concerning his intention to move into a white neighborhood:

"All of you know where I stand on things racial—I'm downright rabid. And even though, as Tod suggests, I'd enjoy this house, if they let me alone, purely as an individual, just the same I'm entering it as a Negro. I hate fays. Always have. Always will. Chief joy in life is making them uncomfortable. And if this doesn't do it—I'll quit the bar."

Merrit's bitterness springs from a knowledge of his mother's exploitation by white men and of his own illegitimate birth:

She had always seemed to him a symbol of sexual martyrdom, a bearer of the cross, as he put it, which fair manhood universally placed on dark womanhood's shoulders.

Fisher's descriptions of the general social life of Harlem are realistic. We catch glimpses of church life, the Sunday promenade on Seventh Avenue, the coarse fun of pool room patrons, and the General Improvement Association Annual Costume Ball at Manhattan Casino. At the last-named affair all Harlem society, "from the rattiest rat to the dicktiest dickty," rub elbows, as the profits are to be devoted to Negro advancement. The white patrons of the ball, according to Fisher, are of three kinds:

> The first coming to enjoy not the Negroes but themselves, hence perfectly at ease; the second coming to raise up the darker brother, hence sweetly beaming and benevolent; the third coming to see the niggers, hence tortured with smothered comment and stifled expression.

During the ball Miss Agatha Cramp, misled by Merrit's fair complexion, expresses her views on Negro inferiority to the amused attorney and thereafter, upon learning of his racial identity, is extremely disconcerted. Miss Cramp is represented as a professional benefactor of the downtrodden. Having assisted destitute Frenchmen, starving Poles, and poverty-stricken Russians, she suddenly becomes interested, through a conversation with Linda, in the Negro uplift work of the General Improvement Association.

In his treatment of the General Improvement Association Fisher satirizes the National Association for the Advancement of Colored People. J. Pennington Potter, for example, wisecracks that Negro agencies seek to furnish "delineation, history and prophecy in a single title." Again, Linda, in a conversation with Miss Cramp, gives the following unwittingly derogatory account of the work of the organization:

> "Well, they collect a dollar a year from everybody that joins, and whenever there's a lynching down South they take the dollar and send somebody to go look at it."

In one of his few personal expressions on the race problem, Fisher suggests that Negroes and whites can reach a better mutual understanding by overlooking ethnological considerations:

> Here is the hedonistic paradox if anywhere, that one best learns the facts of a race by ignoring the fact of race. If Nordic and Negro wish truly to know each other, let them discuss not Negroes and Nordics; let them discuss Greek lyric poets of the fourth century, B.C.

*The Walls of Jericho,* resorting neither to debunking nor to glorification, handles racial issues with independence and objectivity. This novel reveals the first Negro author skilled in comic realism and able to use irony and satire not only upon whites but also upon various classes of his own people. Fisher's preoccupation with humanity, rather than with race, enables him to tell a dispassionate story. *The Walls of Jericho,* in brief, shows that Fisher has an intimate understanding of the Harlem scene as well as the ability to treat this setting with frankness and detachment. Much of Fisher's success in depicting the Negro in New York City is traceable to his mastery of Harlem speech, an asset which moved John Chamberlain to say:

> His ear is remarkable; he can catch all the gradations of slang; and in a different field he is the peer of Ring Lardner as a manipulator of native idiom.[43]

Further evidence of Fisher's knowledge of Harlem and its inhabitants is revealed in his short stories and in his second novel, *The Conjure-Man Dies* (1932). Three of his stories—"Blades of Steel," "The City of Refuge," and "The Promised Land"—appeared in *The Atlantic Monthly,* while "High Yaller" was released in *The Crisis. The Conjure-Man Dies,* in which all of the characters are colored, is the first full-length detective novel written by an American Negro. Turning from controversial racial issues, the book is a refreshing creation that compares favorably with other works of its type. In establishing the guilt of a paranoiac murderer, Fisher not only makes use of his own medical and psychiatric training but also introduces interesting sidelights on the Harlem policy racket and African sex ritual. "Jinx" Jenkins and "Bubber" Brown, brought over from *The Walls of Jericho,* furnish spicy comic relief; and Dr. John Archer, who has the leading male role in the novel, deserves a place in the gallery with Van Dine's Philo Vance and other well-delineated heroes of detective fiction. The most original creation in the book, however, is N'Gana Frimbo, an African prince educated at Harvard and practising as a psychiatrist in Harlem.

## Countee Cullen

In his contribution to "The Negro in Art: How Shall He Be Portrayed," a symposium which appeared in *The Crisis* for August, 1926, Countee Cullen had this to say about the treatment of the Negro in American fiction:

> There can be no doubt that there is a fictional type of Negro, an ignorant, burly, bestial person, changing somewhat today, though not for the better, to the sensual habitue of dives and loose living, who represents to the mass of white readers the be-all and end-all of what constitutes a Negro. . . . For Negro artists to raise a hue and cry against such misrepresentations without attempting, through their artists, to reconstruct the situation seems futile as well as foolish. . . . We must create types that are truly representative of us as a people, nor do I feel that such a move is necessarily a genuflexion away from true art.[44]

It is quite likely that Cullen had the foregoing opinions as he wrote *One Way to Heaven* (1932), for this novel takes a different view of Harlem from that of Carl Van Vechten in *Nigger Heaven* and that of McKay in *Home to Harlem*. While Van Vechten and McKay are chiefly concerned with hot spots and hot living in dark Manhattan, Cullen is principally interested in the sophisticated intelligentsia and the respectable church-going common folk of the black ghetto.

Less successfully than Fisher's *The Walls of Jericho*, *One Way to Heaven* interweaves a low-life and an upper-class plot. The hero is "black and handsome" Sam Lucas, a one-armed card trickster and professional religionist. Lucas attends the watch-night testimonial services of the largest church in Harlem and, in order to gain the financial assistance of the parishioners, drops a greasy deck of cards and a highly polished razor on the floor as he answers the call of an evangelist. Deeply moved by Lucas' seeming conversion, Mattie Johnson, a comely member who is "black, not dull like pitch, but bright like jet," invites the trafficking proselyte, who likes "black women best," to a New Year's Day dinner at her home. Eventually Lucas marries Mattie because she, refusing to be enjoyed and then discarded like the other women in his life, insists upon "a preacher, witnesses, a license to be framed, and a true husband." At the invitation of Constancia Brandon, Mattie's wealthy mulatto employer, the wedding is held before a select gathering of colored socialites and their white friends. As time passes Lucas drifts from Mattie and, after the stillbirth of their child, takes up with Emma May, a Harlem slut. While living with Emma May, Lucas suddenly contracts double pneumonia, but before dying, in order to satisfy his wife concerning the redemption of his soul, he successfully simulates a vision of his salvation.

*One Way to Heaven* is an authentic portrayal of church life in Harlem. Having known his material first-hand from boyhood, Cullen gives convincing description of watch-night meeting, communion, and other services of the African Methodist Episcopal Church. Realistic portraiture is done in the painting of the Reverend Clarence Johnson, the famous singing evangelist from Texas, and Aunt Mandy, "a pillar of the church, giving of her earthly substance to a degree that was truly sacrificial, and of her time to an extent which made her ignorant of nearly all else save church ritual." Not altogether free from superstition, Aunt Mandy sometimes attempts, "by reading tea leaves and coffee dregs, and by consulting her cards, to speed the blessings of Heaven or to ward off, if possible, some celestial chastisement."

Less genuine is Cullen's description of upper-class life in Harlem, for the author here forsakes realism for satire. Keen pleasure is taken in ridiculing the Harlem social register, the "New Negro" coterie, colored reactionaries to whom all Negro literature after Dunbar and Chesnutt is anathema, narrow-minded bigots of the biracial Booklovers' Society, inquisitive white writers mingling with colored people in order to get material for their books, scholarly white researchers on Negro life and culture, advocates of the Back-to-Africa Movement, and pseudo-scholars who deprecate darker folk as "indolent, untrustworthy, unintelligent, unclean, immoral, and cursed of heaven." The magnetic personality drawing the representatives of these divergent groups together is Constancia Brandon, a facetious and smooth-tongued exhibitionist who derives much pleasure from the interracial circle of which she is the center. She states her personal views on race as follows:

"It isn't being colored that annoys me. I could go white if I wanted to, but I am too much of a hedonist; I enjoy life too much, and enjoyment isn't across the line. Money is there, and privilege, and the sort of power which comes with numbers; but as for enjoyment, they don't know what it is. . . . So long as I have my happiness to consider, I'll not go to the mountain. If the mountain wants me, let it come to me. It knows where I am."

*One Way to Heaven*, though not so successful as *The Walls of Jericho* in interlacing the lower-class and upper-class threads of action, stands with Fisher's novels in offsetting the emphases of the Van Vechten Vogue. The book shows respectability in dark Manhattan, gives convincing description of Negro church life in New York City, and directs satiric thrusts at Harlem socialites and their white acquaintances.

## VII. *WEST INDIAN REALISM*

It was to be expected that Eric Walrond and Claude McKay, two of the significant writers of the Negro Renascence, would turn to their native West Indies for fictional material. Walrond is the author of *Tropic Death* (1926), which contains ten naturalistic studies of Negro life in the Caribbean area. McKay, who has been previously discussed in this chapter in connection with the Van Vechten Vogue, is the writer of *Gingertown* (1932) and *Banana Bottom* (1933), both of which treat life in his Jamaican homeland.

## Eric Walrond

In *Tropic Death* (1926) we see West Indian islands parching under a pitiless sun or flourishing during the rainy season, observe lustful and drunken thugs on ships plying between coastal cities, note the degradation and exploitation of dusky peons laboring in quarries or at the Panama Canal, find prostitution and miscegenation in urban and rural communities, and hear of the baleful workings of obeahism, a form of sorcery and magic practised by natives of the region. The ten pieces of the volume are related in that each is concerned with human death, and that each reflects the naturalistic theory that man is a helpless animal impelled primarily by instinct and controlled mainly by capricious forces.

In *Tropic Death* Walrond never openly arraigns social corruption; he does not protest the sordid existence of those who dwell in cabins, tenements, labor camps, and brothels below the Gulf Stream. Raising no issues and reaching no conclusions, he is content to picture objectively the economic and social disorganization of Negro life in the region. Several stories divulge the mistreatment of colored workers, particularly those in the Canal Zone. For example, in "Panama Gold" Poyer, a British subject who has lost a leg while working at the Panama Canal, relates that at first the Americans did not want to compensate him but that he was eventually successful in getting indemnification:

> "I let dem understand quick enough dat I wuz a Englishman and not a bleddy American nigger!"

In "Subjection" a Negro worker at Colon is killed by a United States marine for defending a weak fellow laborer. Walrond makes the following ironical comment on this homicide:

> In the Canal Record, the Q. M. at Toro Point took occasion to extol the virtues of the Department which kept the number of casualties in the recent labor uprising down to one.

In the Caribbean area, racial oppression is accompanied by buckra sexual conquests which produce a mixed-breed population. Interracial liaisons are mentioned in "The Vampire Bat," wherein Bellon Prout, the leading white character, thus muses upon discovering a deserted colored infant:

> Another of the colony's lurking evils, the desertion—often the murder of illegitimate Negro babes.
>
> O God—another of the island's depraved nigger curses!

Within the colored group, light-skinned individuals lament their African blood and adopt a superior attitude toward blacks. In "Palm Porch," for example, Miss Buckner, hostess of a prostitution house in which her daughters cater exclusively to white men, "would have liked to be white; but alas! she was only a mulatto." She is offended because one of her girls, who is as "white as a white woman," elopes with a black man, and because another marries a mulatto who "was not, alas! white." In this color-conscious environment, where whiteness is socially advantageous, blacks sometimes hate lighter colored folk. In "The Yellow One," for instance, a ship's cook's ebony-hued mate detests a Cuban because the latter's appearance enables him to mingle as a social equal with white people.

Sterling Brown has noted that the approach in *Tropic Death* is "unapologetically naturalistic,"[45] and Rebecca Chalmers Barton has observed that the atmosphere is one "in which individuals struggle not only against each other but against ominous natural and supernatural forces."[46] Both of these comments are substantiated in the book, for in the sun-smitten setting of *Tropic Death* men not only victimize one another but also fall before drought, heat, fire, storms, sharks, poison, disease, and obeah. Life is lived recklessly in this environment where death is lurking.

Perhaps the chief significance of *Tropic Death* lies in its dispassionate and realistic treatment of the life of colored people outside the United States. This manifestation of interest in the welfare of exploited racial groups in other countries reveals the Negro novelist awakening to the realization that the campaign for social justice will not be fully won until a victory is gained not only in the United States but in other lands as well.

### Claude McKay

McKay's third novel, *Banana Bottom* (1933), like four of the twelve stories of his *Gingertown* (1932), is a commentary on folk life in the author's native Jamaica. The plot is unfolded against an authentic background which presents clearly drawn characters and such community activities as tea-meetings, picnics, barbecue dances, house parties, yam-digging, pimento-picking contests, revivals, obeah rites, and interracial labor disturbances. The heroine of the story is Bita Plant, a dark girl who, after being seduced at the age of twelve by an idiot, is adopted by Malcolm Craig and his wife Priscilla, white missionaries in rural Jamaica. Experimenting in the Christianization of a native, the Craigs educate Bita in England and subsequently accept her as a member of their own household. The respectability of the mission becomes so monotonous and tiresome, however, that Bita intractably defies her guardians in order to enjoy the company of Hopping Dick, a shiftless but personable gambler. Becoming contemptuous of her education, religion, and social position, and refusing to conform to the rigid discipline prescribed by her benefactors, Bita returns to secular life. Because irresponsible Hopping Dick shrinks from matrimony, she marries Jubban, a black peasant with whom she finds contentment, and makes the following quotation from Pascal's *Pensées* the guiding principle of her life: ". . . la vraie morale se moque de la morale; la morale du jugement se moque de la morale de l'esprit." (". . . true morality laughs at morality; the morality of the judgment laughs at the morality of the mind.")

Depicting folk life and social stratification in Jamaica, *Banana Bottom* is fundamentally a dramatization of what Alain Locke has called "a provincial duel between peasant paganism and middle class Puritanism."[47] McKay's thesis is that missionary discipline, even when administered by such a zealous and strong-willed crusader as Priscilla Craig, can not invariably curb and smother instinctive and hedonistic urges of the common folk. Craig privately surmises that Bita would be happier among her own primitive people:

Perhaps she would realize a completer life in a different sphere. Who knows but that many of those natives whom they were seeking to advise as mentors and ministers might prefer their own particular patterns of life and living and do better in their simple way perhaps than many of their guardians and teachers?

McKay evidently looks with favor upon Squire Gensir, an unprejudiced old folklorist who manifests no missionary inclinations in his relations with the native peasantry:

How different his life had been from the life of the other whites. They had come to conquer and explore, govern, trade, preach and educate to their liking, exploit men and material. But this man was the first to enter into the simple life of the island Negroes and proclaim significance and beauty in their transplanted African folk tales and in the words and music of their native dialect songs.

## VIII. *THE MID-WESTERN SMALL TOWN*

During the Renascence period Negro writers explored many new milieux, including Europe and the West Indies, but Harlem and the rural South remained the favorite settings. It is noteworthy that Langston Hughes, who writes extensively of dark Manhattan in his poetry, deserts the black ghetto in *Not Without Laughter,* his only published novel, to study the position of the Negro in the Mid-Western small town, where persecution and prejudice are not extreme but are nevertheless prevalent.

### Langston Hughes

In an article in *The Amsterdam News* for July 9, 1930, Langston Hughes is quoted as having made the following statement concerning his objectives in *Not Without Laughter* (1930):

> In this book I have attempted to depict what I believe to be more or less typical small-town life in any town outside of the South. I am interested primarily in life, not local color, so I have chosen as a setting for this first novel of mine not what have become practically conventional life backgrounds for Negro tales, that is Harlem and the South, but rather what I feel is more truly American—the average, small Main Street town.[48]

Largely deriving its plot and characters from the personal experiences of its author,[49] *Not Without Laughter* tells of a poor Negro family living in Stanton, Kansas. Aunt Hager Williams, an elderly laundress and a devout Christian, has three daughters —Tempy, Annjee, and Harriett. Tempy, having married a railway mail clerk, joins the Episcopal church and adopts a supercilious attitude toward her relatives. Annjee is the wife of Jimboy Rodgers, a guitar-plunking vagabond. Harriett is an attractive girl wincing under the prejudice of white Stantonians and yearning for a richer life than the small town affords. The remaining member of the family is Sandy, son of Annjee and Jimboy, whose early life constitutes the main action of the novel. We follow Sandy through grade school; see him employed successively at a barber shop, a hotel, and a printing establishment; observe his growing understanding of sex and race prejudice; and finally watch him go to Chicago, where Harriett, who rises from prostitution to become a celebrated blues singer, rescues him from the seemingly interminable up-and-down routine of an elevator operator and undertakes to finance his further education with the hope that he may fulfil his grandmother's dreams by uplifting the black race.

In *Not Without Laughter* we are introduced to carnivals, public dances, church activities, lodge demonstrations, and other popular diversions. We are shown immoral and corrupting influences at work in Negro barber shops, billiard halls, and red-light districts as well as in white hotels where colored men serve in menial capacities. Everywhere, even in public schools, we witness the destructive and warping influence of prejudice and segregation upon the Negro mind. Though Aunt Hager patiently and unprotestingly accepts suffering and privation as her unfortunate lot, her daughters and grandson chafe under the reins of white oppression. Especially bitter and rebellious is Harriett, whose rancor and enmity began in early childhood and rapidly developed because of insult, Jim-Crowism, and unequal opportunities. In a family conversation she expresses her racial attitudes as follows:

"They wouldn't have a single one of us around if they could help it. It don't matter to them if we're shut out of a job. It don't matter to them if niggers have only the back row at the movies. It don't matter to them when they hurt our feelings without caring and treat us like slaves down South and like beggars up North. No, it don't matter to them.... White folks run the world, and the only thing colored folks are expected to do is work and grin and take off their hats as though it don't matter. O, I hate 'em! I hate white folks! You can pray for 'em if you want to, mama, but I hate 'em! . . . I hate white folks! . . . I hate 'em all!"

Also scornful of her mother's religion, Harriett acrimoniously comments that Jesus is "white and stiff and don't like niggers!" On the other hand, Tempy, a bourgeois Negro, believes that imitation of the dominant whites is the way to racial adjustment:

Colored people certainly needed to come up in the world, Tempy thought, up to the level of white people—dress like white people, talk like white people, think like white people—and then they would no longer be called "niggers."

At the same time, however, Tempy declares allegiance to the militant rather than to the conciliatory school of Negro leadership:

"Teaching Negroes to be servants, that's all Washington did! DuBois wants our rights. He wants us to be real men and women. He believes in social equality. But Washington—huh! Don't talk to me about Washington. Take DuBois for your model, not some white folks' nigger."

In Stanton there is also ample evidence of intraracial discord arising from color and class distinctions. Aunt Hager distrusts Jimboy on the basis of pigmentation:

"Who ever heard of a nigger named Jimboy, anyhow? Next place, I ain't never seen a yaller dude yet that meant a dark woman no good— an' Annjee is dark!"

Furthermore, Tempy and the respectable middle-class which she represents are the targets of irony and ridicule. Harriett, for example, does not "want to be respectable if I have to be stuck up and dicty like Tempy is." She prefers her own life of laughter and revelry to Tempy's world of make-believe.

Cargill considers *Not Without Laughter* "one of the best fictional treatments of the Negro in American letters."[50] The leading characters in the book are ably delineated. Aunt Hager is a well-drawn carry-over from the plantation tradition, and Harriett represents the new militant Negro. The chief merit of the novel, however, is its detached but sympathetic story of the life of a colored youth. Hughes would have done well to treat Sandy at greater length as James T. Farrell handled "Studs" Lonigan, and Alain Locke presumably had this in mind when he wrote:

> If this book were a trilogy, and carried its young hero, Sandy, through a typical black boy's journey from the cradle to the grave, we might perhaps have the all-too-long-prayed-for Negro novel.[51]

## IX. *SATIRE*

American Negro writers have generally been defensive, apologetic, or commendatory in the treatment of their own people, but bitter, critical, and militant in their attitudes toward their white oppressors. They have usually handled racial issues with painful seriousness and, in calling attention to social abuses, have almost invariably failed to appreciate the value of rollicking satire as a vehicle for the exposure of injustice and hypocrisy. In *Black No More* (1931), however, George Schuyler, who has already been considered in this chapter as the author of *Slaves Today,* breaks from the past and employs satire to make fun of both races indiscriminately.

GEORGE SCHUYLER

George Schuyler has attracted attention through his editorials in *The Messenger,* his contributions to *The American Mercury,* and his weekly column in *The Pittsburgh Courier.* Strongly influenced by Henry L. Mencken, Schuyler delights in ridiculing smugness and hypocrisy. Successful as a hack-writer and as a columnist, he turned to the novel in *Black No More* (1931), which is dedicated "to all Caucasians in the great republic who can trace their ancestry back ten generations and confidently assert that there are no black leaves, twigs, limbs or branches on their family trees."

The plot of *Black No More,* though fantastic, is not altogether unconvincing if one accepts the major premise. Dr. Junius Crookman, a Negro physician who assumes that the elimination of dark-complexioned people will solve the race problem, discovers Black-No-More, a glandular treatment which will turn Negroes white. The first of thousands of New Yorkers to receive this treatment is Max Disher, whose ambition is to win the love of an alluring Southern blonde who rebuffed him in a Harlem cabaret. Going to Atlanta in search of this girl, Disher finds the Knights of Nordica (the Ku Klux Klan), led by the Reverend Henry Givens, much disturbed by Crookman's discovery. Posing as a member of the New York Anthropological Society, Disher becomes Grand Exalted Giraw of the Knights of Nordica and joins Givens in an elaborate scheme to use the threat to Caucasian racial purity involved in Black-No-More as a means of extracting a fortune from the white people of the South. Finding that the object of his quest is Givens' daughter, Disher woos and marries her. Meanwhile Black-No-More is creating a sensation among Negroes: colored leaders vainly strive to stem the stampede to Crookman's sanitariums, the masses withdraw their support from racial businesses and uplift organizations, and Negro politicians lose power and influence. Moreover, radical changes take place in the social structure of the South: black folk unite in a hegira to the North to seek Crookman's treatment, millions of dollars are lost because of the abandonment of Jim-Crow facilities, taxes soar from salaries paid according to white standards, colored babies are born to outwardly white couples, and the Republican Party challenges Democratic supremacy in the hitherto Solid South. In the Presidential race the Republicans nominate Goosie and Gump for re-election to oppose Givens (the Imperial Grand Wizard of the Knights of Nordica) and Arthur Snobbcraft (President of the Anglo-Saxon Association of America) and, after a vitriolic campaign, sweep to a landslide victory. About the same time Dr. Samuel Buggerie, a scientist engaged by the Democrats of the South, makes the startling disclosure that almost fifty million Americans—including himself, Givens, Snobbcraft, and many other distinguished Southerners—have Negro blood. While the nation seeks to recover from the shock caused by the announcement of the possession of African blood by many white citizens, Disher's wife gives birth to a dark son but feels consoled after her husband admits Negro descent. To avoid mob action, Disher and Givens take their families and closest friends by plane to Mexico; but later Buggerie and Snobbcraft, likewise seeking to escape the wrath of Southern whites, are trapped and lynched in Mississippi. At the close of the novel, as a result of Dr. Crookman's announcement that genuine Caucasians are several shades darker than counterfeit ones, Americans place a premium upon swarthiness and, in an effort to avoid extreme whiteness, submit themselves to sun baths and skin stains.

In *Black No More* Schuyler lays bare the pusillanimity, stupidity, selfishness, opportunism, and materialism of Americans, white as well as black. He shows how the Southern ruling class fosters hatred between poor whites and Negroes in order to acquire wealth and maintain supremacy. Once an official of the Knights of Nordica, for example, Disher exploits the prejudice of poor whites for the purpose of filling the coffers of his organization:

For an hour Matthew told them at the top of his voice what they believed: i.e., that a white skin was a sure indication of the possession of superior intellectual and moral qualities; that all Negroes were inferior to them; that God had intended for the United States to be a white man's country and that with His help they could keep it so; that their sons and brothers might inadvertently marry Negresses, or, worse, their sisters and daughters might marry Negroes, if Black-No-More, Incorporated, was permitted to continue its dangerous activities.

Schuyler also divulges the hypocrisy and venality of clergymen who are more concerned with personal gain than with moral living. Moreover, he blasts the pretensions of the Southern aristocracy and unveils the anti-Negro, anti-Semitic, and anti-Catholic activities of this class. Negroes are likewise ridiculed with gusto. The leaders of the National Social Equality League (the National Association for the Advancement of Colored People), the Negro Data League (the National Urban League), and the Back-to-Africa Society (the Garvey Movement) are lampooned as self-seekers primarily interested in the exploitation of their followers. Adultery, graft, and debauchery are listed as failings of men of high position in both races; and the implication of the book is that human beings, regardless of pigmentation, are fundamentally the same under the skin.

Though frequently lapsing into farce and burlesque, *Black No More* is a bantering indictment of the racial attitudes of white and black Americans. Taking a broad view of the color problem of the country, the book is refreshing because of its raillery at both races. As Alain Locke observes, *Black No More* "is evidence of the novelty and the potential power of the satirical attack on the race problem in fiction."[52]

## X. *THE CLOSE OF THE NEGRO RENASCENCE*

During the Negro Renascence substantial progress was made. Many of the old stereotypes were destroyed, new milieus were explored, and for the first time white publishers and readers were generally receptive to self-revelation by Negro authors. Throughout the 1920's, nevertheless, there were at work internal and external forces which were destined to bring Renascence fervor to a close.

In the first place, the Renascence could not long survive because it was primarily a fad and, as such, was subject to fall before the first violent shock or the first new rage. In 1928, the peak year of Renascence enthusiasm, Alain Locke shrewdly realized that the movement was short-lived:

> The year 1928 represents probably the flood-tide of the present Negrophile movement. More books have been published about Negro life by both white and Negro authors than was the normal output of more than a decade in the past. More aspects of Negro life have been treated than were ever dreamed of. The proportions show the typical curve of a major American fad, and to a certain extent, this indeed it is. We shall not fully realize it until the inevitable reaction comes; when the popular interest flags, the movement will lose thousands of supporters who are now under its spell, but who tomorrow would be equally hypnotized by the next craze.[53]

The drift of events proved that Locke was right, for "the inevitable reaction" came in the following year in the form of the Wall Street débâcle which, as Langston Hughes wittily remarks, "sent Negroes, white folks and all rolling down the hill toward the Works Progress Administration."[54] After the financial crash, as Hughes further notes, "the white people had much less money to spend on themselves, and practically none to spend on Negroes, for the depression brought everybody down a peg or two."[55] It did not take long for hard times to affect the Negro artist adversely, as the following observation by Hughes indicates:

> That spring for me (and, I guess, all of us) was the end of the Harlem Renaissance. Sophisticated New Yorkers turned to Noel Coward. Colored actors began to go hungry, publishers politely rejected new manuscripts, and patrons found other uses for their money. The cycle that had charlestoned into being on the dancing heels of *Shuffle Along* now ended in *Green Pastures* with De Lawd.
>
> The generous 1920's were over.[56]

The stock market collapse drew the veil from most of the superficialities and weaknesses of the Negro Renascence. At once it became evident that the movement was too largely sponsored by whites, for, when their support was withdrawn, enthusiasm and vitality lapsed. The Renascence was not a racial literary revolution, nor was it an activity stemming indigenously from the people. Moreover, it did not have stimulation similar to that which motivated modern literary revivals in Russia and Ireland. "The ordinary Negroes," writes Hughes, "hadn't heard of the Negro Renaissance."[57] The movement was thus doomed to short-lived tenure because it did not have the support of the group which it undertook to express.[58]

Besides suffering from too much reliance upon white support—this suffering was practically inevitable in view of the fact that Negroes had not become a considerable part of the American reading public—the Renascence was further debilitated by an excessive interest in Harlem, particularly in its exotic and pseudo-barbaric aspects. This preoccupation, which was partly stimulated by the fascination of the black ghetto for Americans of the Jazz Age, resulted in more than one-half of the fictional works discussed in this chapter having their main setting in New York City. Benjamin Brawley, conservative critic and arch foe of the Van Vechtenites, early complained that for the Renascence writers "Harlem has been an obsession."[59] James Weldon Johnson also pointed out that Renascence writers, in their all-engrossing attention to the Van Vechten Vogue, neglected phases of Harlem life that have universal literary value and appeal:

> But there is the real and overshadowing Harlem. The commonplace, work-a-day Harlem. The Harlem of doubly handicapped black masses engaged in the grim daily struggle for existence in the midst of this whirlpool of white civilization. There are dramatic values in that Harlem, too; but they have hardly been touched. Writers of fiction, white and black, have limited their stories to Harlem as a playground, and have ignored or not recognized the fundamental, relentless forces at work and the efforts to cope with them. This is, of course, understand-

able; picturesque and exotic phases of life offer the easier and more alluring task for the fictionist. But the sterner aspects of life in Harlem offer a unique and teeming field for the writer capable of working it. Under these aspects lie real comedy and real tragedy, real triumphs and real defeats.[60]

Another factor which contributed to the decline of the Negro Renascence was an emphasis upon social commingling rather than upon solid literary progress. In the preceding chapter mention was made of the numerous uptown and downtown parties which the Negro literati attended. Hughes states that "in those pre-crash days there were parties and parties."[61] Hughes also says that Wallace Thurman was pessimistic about the future of race literature because he believed that "the Negro vogue had made all of us too conscious of ourselves, had flattered and spoiled us, and had provided too many easy opportunities for some of us to drink gin and more gin, on which he thought we would always be drunk."[62] According to Claude McKay, there were some who were interested in the Negro literary revival mainly because it afforded excellent opportunities for social climbing. "I was surprised," he comments, "when I discovered that many of the talented Negroes regarded their renaissance more as an uplift organization and a vehicle to accelerate the pace and progress of smart Negro society."[63]

## XI. *SUMMARY*

"The decade 1919-1929," writes Carl Van Doren, "was the liveliest in the history of American fiction."[64] Certainly, in so far as Negro fiction is concerned, this observation is correct, for the works of colored writers were produced in greater numbers and with much more publicity than ever before.

In the early post-war works of Herman Dreer, William Pickens, and Joshua Henry Jones, the death knell of Uncle Tom and Uncle Remus is sounded, and the emergence of a new Negro—

disdainful of supplication, uninhibited by defeatism, unapologetic in protest, and assertive in demands for justice—is signalized.

The hub of the Negro literary revival was New York City, which during this period, as Van Doren notes, "was more distinctly the literary capital than ever before."[65] To the black belt of this metropolis—which was also the American center of the Garvey Movement, the African art revival, and the Negro literary world—flocked a group of colored writers who gained a country-wide hearing and helped to make Harlem a national magnet.

For the Negro fictionist the Renascence was a period of bursting bonds and expanding horizons. There was a general tendency to avoid the idealized characterization and pompous utterance of the anti-repressionists, and more and more writers ceased making their works vehicles for lectures on the race problem and took greater cognizance of universal esthetic values.

The subject matter, attitudes, and backgrounds of the fiction of the Renascence were more varied than those of the years before World War I. Toomer wrote of Southern interracial relations with objectivity and detachment that betray no ethnological preconceptions. Giving particular attention to the passing of maladjusted heroines in New York City, Miss Fauset, White, and Miss Larsen described the lives of cultured, educated, and progressive colored people in the urban North. In novels of propagandistic intent White, DuBois, and Schuyler, respectively, attacked lynching, the universal exploitation of darker races, and the mistreatment of Liberian natives. McKay, Thurman, and Bontemps succeeded Van Vechten in dramatizing sex and the cabaret. Veering somewhat from the faddistic emphasis and bacchanalian revelries of the Van Vechtenites, Fisher and Cullen sought to show that Harlemites had more respectable diversions than wine, women, and song. Turning from Harlem in his only novel, Hughes studied the position of the Negro in the Mid-Western small town. Likewise deserting the Harlem setting, Walrond and McKay painted authentic pictures of folk life in their native West

Indies. In one of the most frolicsome satires in American literature Schuyler produced a fresh approach to the color problem by making a laughingstock of both races.

The Harlem awakening was thus foreordained to a short life for several reasons. First, the support of the Negro reading public was not strong enough to sustain the movement through the depression after the withdrawal of white patronage beginning about 1929. Second, to a great extent the Renascence spirit manifested itself in ways not conducive to the cultivation of art having universal appeal and permanent value. And, lastly, the portrayal of Harlem in most of the novels of the period was produced in answer to faddistic demands and hence was doomed to neglect after the passing of the Negro vogue. The great failure of the Renascence, therefore, was to make a fetish of the cabaret and not to produce consummate studies of Harlem life. As Sterling Brown points out:

> Focusing upon carefree abandon, the Harlem school, like the plantation tradition, neglected the servitude. Except for brief glimpses, the drama of the workaday life, the struggles, the conflicts, are missing. And such definite features of Harlem life as the lines of the unemployed, the overcrowded schools, the delinquent children headed straight to petty crime, the surly resentment—all of these seeds that bore such bitter fruit in the Harlem riot—are conspicuously absent.[66]

Although the above-mentioned conditions predestined the Renascence to brief duration, American Negro literature gained rather than lost as a result of the Negro vogue of the 1920's. During the Renascence period, colored writers broke away from many of the pre-World War I taboos and stereotypes, made self-revelation and self-criticism more important considerations in their art, produced a varied body of literature, and demonstrated to publishers and readers in the United States that the Negro author is an important factor in the country's artistic life. When the froth of the Harlem craze was cleared away, there remained rich substance which became a firm foundation for the literary labors of later years.

CHAPTER 5

# The Depression Decade

## I. *THE DEPRESSION*

THE STOCK MARKET CRASH of October, 1929, wrought sweeping changes in American life. Huge fortunes vanished like mist. Machines and men became idle. Relief agencies and breadlines multiplied. Traditionally the last to be hired and the first to be fired, Negroes felt economic dislocation perhaps more acutely than any other group in the country. Bereft of employment and bearing the double burden of color and caste, they endured disadvantage and privation in all sections of the United States. In the South they winced under a vicious sharecropper and tenant-farmer system; and in the North, where they had prospered during the boom period, they fell into the clutch of overcrowding, poverty, crime, and disease.

## II. *PROLETARIANISM*

The depression accelerated the extension of proletarian ideology in the United States. Left-wing propagandists—arguing that competitive and monopolistic capitalism inevitably usurps advantage and produces a working class subject to exploitation, unemployment, poverty, disease, war, and degradation, and that this group must organize to achieve the classless society of tomorrow—had been active in the country since the early 1920's. It was not until the organization of *The New Masses* in 1926,[1] however, that a vigorous and concentrated appeal was made to the workers themselves. Members of the staff of *The New Masses* were James Rorty, Joseph Freeman, Edmont Arens, and Michael Gold, the last-named soon becoming the dominant spirit in the magazine, which aggressively undertook to encourage social protest from the proletarian viewpoint. Chiefly through the efforts of *The New Masses* in the creative field and of *The Modern Quarterly* in criticism, the Marxist point of view was disseminated throughout the country during the depression years.

"The decade 1929-39," as Van Doren has noted, "saw a widespread and searching revision of the picture of American life which American fiction had been drawing since the earliest days."[2] This observation is doubtless correct, for the depression decade witnessed a rapid expansion of the proletarian tradition in American letters. In the left-wing movement literature was expected to serve as partisan polemic contributing to the destruction of private property and the establishment of social control of the instruments of production. Joseph Freeman voiced the conventional revolutionary concept when he said that "art, an instrument in the class struggle, must be developed by the proletariat as one of its weapons."[3] As a result of this theory there developed an oft-repeated proletarian novel pattern which Carl Van Doren has described as follows:

> The action was likely to come to its head in a strike, and it took for granted an essential class conflict between the owners and the landless, propertyless workers. The heroes, in a time of unprecedented unemployment, were men desperately looking for work or trying to keep their jobs. The strongest virtue celebrated in the novels was proletarian solidarity. The future, the novelists insisted, lay with the proletariat, which must and would develop a working-class culture.[4]

Left-wing fiction stressed interracial action. In Scott Nearing's ironically titled *Free-Born* (1932), which Sterling Brown labels "the first revolutionary novel of Negro life,"[5] the hero, whose parents have been lynched and whose sweetheart has been ravished and killed, joins the proletariat in the crusade for "a free world under working class control." Though snubbed by labor leaders and imprisoned, he tenaciously struggles for the liberation of those "who never were freed. . .who keep your high and mighty world a-goin'." Myra Page endorses the co-operation of white and black workers in *Gathering Storm* (1932), while in *A Sign for Cain* (1935) Grace Lumpkin relates the experiences of a young organizer who undertakes to bring together toilers of both races. In *Jordanstown* (1937) Josephine Johnson, whose *Now in November* (1934) and *Winter Orchard* (1935) depict the misery of the Negro masses, presents a colored woman who advocates workers' solidarity: "She sits in those evenings with her gaunt hands in her great lap, staring at nothing, the hard thoughts marching through her mind, considering not *My* people or *My* race, but *Us*." Proletarian fiction was re-enforced by other literary forms, particularly by such plays as Frederick Schlick's *Bloodstream* (1932), John Wexley's *They Shall Not Die* (1934), and Paul Peters and George Sklar's *Stevedore* (1934).

The chief influence of the depression and proletarianism upon the Negro was to guide his thinking from racial to class channels. Immediately after World War I the Negro took pride in his color and in his African background. The Garvey Movement extolled blackness and the Dark Continent, and colored intellectuals enthusiastically pointed to the excellencies of primitive African art. Negro writers strove above all else to be racial and, generally speaking, their protest was likewise racial. After 1929, however, economic conditions in the nation forced the Negro to think in terms of class. Although continuing to feel the heaviest impact of the economic blow, he found that white toilers showed increasing willingness to join him in the campaign for higher wages and union recognition. During the depression strikers and demonstrators of both races banded together to demand relief and jobs. Even in such states as Arkansas and Mississippi black and white tenants and sharecroppers, kept apart in earlier years by race-baiting demagogues, sometimes collaborated in spite of threats, violence, and accusations of "Red Russianism." In December, 1930, three thousand workers, two-thirds of whom were Negroes, demanded employment or relief in Birmingham; and during the same month interracial hunger marches were staged in Toledo, Charlotte, and Denver. In numerous cities Negro consumers refused to spend where they could not get work and, with white assistance in certain instances, obtained jobs at firms which had previously drawn racial lines in giving employment. The Herndon and Scottsboro cases drew national attention.

The interracial plank of the Communist Party found a degree of support among prominent Negroes. James W. Ford, having joined the Communist Party in 1926, became its candidate for the vice-presidency of the United States in 1932 and 1936 on a platform which included "equal rights for Negroes." Richard Wright and Langston Hughes, two of the leading Negro creative writers of the time, sympathized with the left-wing movement. Also manifesting the proletarian outlook, Paul Robeson, one of America's foremost actors and singers, made the following comment after his shift from the fashionable West End stage to the Workers' Unity Theatre in London:

> "When I sing 'Let My People Go,' I want it in the future to mean more than it has before. It must express the need for freedom not only of my own race. That's only part of the bigger thing. But of all the working class—here, in America, all over. I was born of them. They are my people. They will know what I mean."[6]

## III. *LIBERALISM*

Although the depression and proletarian ideology caused the Negro to think increasingly in terms of class, only a small proportion of the colored population of the country actively participated in the left-wing movement. Outside the ranks of the revolutionaries, however, there were increasing numbers of liberals who were not leftists but who nevertheless espoused full participation of the Negro in American democracy. Accepting the theory that the government should be the servant of all the people and should afford justice, freedom, and the opportunity for maximum personal growth for every citizen, these liberals set themselves against reactionary forces and attacked economic, social, and political inequities. As a result of their activities, the depression decade witnessed a further breaking down of racial barriers. In spite of the dissent of repressionists like Bilbo, "Cotton Ed" Smith, and Talmadge, the leaders of the major political parties gave the black man a better deal. Accepted as political confreres, Negroes sought and gained a number of important local, state, and national posts, including a seat in the House of Representatives. As members of the C. I. O. and the A. F. of L., black men exerted increasing influence in the world of unionism. Administered by an interracial body, the National Association for the Advancement of Colored People continued to wage a fight for the full citizenship of the Negro. Numerous other organizations fought distinctions made on the basis of race and color. Ethnologists disproved theories of racial purity and superiority, and in the field of scholarship several noteworthy studies were produced jointly by Negro and white authors. Father Divine opened the doors of "heaven" to "angels" of both races. In brief, although prejudice and persecution still persisted, the depression saw a gradual lowering of racial bars and an increasing tendency to accept the Negro as a full-fledged American.

## IV. *TREATMENT OF THE NEGRO BY WHITE WRITERS*

In this chapter mention has already been made of the place accorded Negro characters in proletarian fiction by white authors. This does not mean that the plantation tradition was altogether silenced. As a matter of fact, the sentimental paternalism of the old school was continued in such books as Stark Young's *So Red the Rose* (1934), Margaret Mitchell's *Gone With the Wind* (1936), Archibald Rutledge's *It Will Be Daybreak Soon* (1939), and Frances Gaither's *Follow the Drinking Gourd* (1940). Furthermore, regional novelists continued to exploit the naive, picturesque, and primitive qualities of the dark folk of their respective districts with emphasis neither upon racial issues nor upon economic and social disadvantages. In the thirties, for example, Julia Peterkin and DuBose Heyward maintained their places as the leading writers of this school. Following in the Peterkin tradition, Mrs. L. M. Alexander in 1934 won a $10,000 award with *Candy*, a story of Negro life at Mimosa Hill Plantation.

For the most part, however, white fictionists of the economic crisis avoided the plantation tradition and pagan quaintness, and tended to treat the Negro with understanding and objectivity. "There was," as Carl Van Doren observes, "less romance than realism in the New South."[7] This more enlightened approach to the representation of Negro character was due largely to the work of T. S. Stribling, Erskine Caldwell, and William Faulkner. During the depression period Stribling, whose *Birthright* gave a fresh interpretation of Negro life in 1922, wrote his trilogy of Southern life—*The Forge* (1931), *The Store* (1932), the winner of the Pulitzer prize for that year, and *Unfinished Cathedral* (1934). Though casting the spotlight upon the Vaiden family, this series treats unflinchingly almost every phase of the Southern color problem from slavery down to the present day. Stribling exposes the injustice and selfishness underlying prejudice and persecution, and his analysis reveals the effects of racial discord upon white and black alike.

Focusing upon proletarian types and treating them with ironical humor, Caldwell shows that poor whites and Negroes are victims of a crushing economic and social system in his native Southland. In *American Earth* (1931), his first book of short stories, "Saturday Afternoon" unfolds the lynching of a Negro farmer, while "Savannah River Payday" recounts the fiendish mutilation of the corpse of a black man killed in a sawmill accident. In *Tobacco Road* (1932) Jeeter Lester rationalizes as follows after Dude recklessly runs down a Negro pedestrian: "Wal, niggers will get kilt." Despite the remarkable characterization of Simeon Dye, "it is the suffering of the Negroes," Cargill has noted, "that we retain from *Journeyman*."[8] *Kneel to the Rising Sun* (1935), another volume of short stories, continues the crusade for social justice. The title piece—relating the betrayal of Clem, a Negro sharecropper, by his white friend, Lonnie—is considered important by Sterling Brown because it discovers the Negro "as part of the working class."[9] Caldwell's outstanding attack upon racial persecution, however, is *Trouble in July* (1940), a diagnosis of the canalized and unreasoning mob psychology which results in the lynching of a Negro youth named Sonny Clark. "If conditions are ever better in the South," Cargill observes, "if the treatment of the colored man is ever more humane, we are going to owe a very great debt to Erskine Caldwell."[10]

Though yielding at times to the contradictions and deceptions of the plantation tradition, William Faulkner is generally a naturalist keenly aware of the many problems of caste and race in the South. Usually he views Southern society with a steady eye, portraying both races without the traditional preconceptions; but his interpretations, whether stated or implied, are mostly pessimistic. *The Sound and the Fury* (1929) presents minor but convincing Negro characters. *These Thirteen* (1931) contains "Dry September" and "That Evening Sun," stories that deal with Negro life. The former is the account of a lynching, and the latter of the exploitation of a colored woman by a white man. The reaction of the woman's husband reveals Faulkner's understanding of the Negro:

> "I can't hang around white man's kitchen. But white man can hang around mine. White man can come in my house, but I can't stop him. When white man wants to come in my house, I ain't got no house. I can't stop him, but he can't kick me outen it. He can't do that."

It is in *Light in August* (1932), however, that Faulkner delves most deeply into Southern problems of caste and race. The leading male character is Joe Christmas, the son of a white woman and a colored man. Reared by his fanatical Negrophobe grandfather, Christmas is accepted as a white person until the circumstances of his birth are disclosed. Developing self-abhorrence because of his Negro blood and seeking compensation through the exploitation of white women, he eventually falls into a liaison with Miss Burden, a descendant of Yankees. After murdering his mistress largely because of hatred for her race, Christmas is lynched. *Light in August* is a bold indictment of the hypocrisy and prejudice which make the South blind to its own delinquencies. The arraignment continues in *Absalom, Absalom!* (1936), with emphasis upon the theme of incest. "Of all Southern writers," Beach maintains, "Faulkner is the one who has been least restrained by regard for convention or for the sensibilities of his own people."[11]

The works of Stribling, Caldwell, and Faulkner show that miscegenation was still popular as a literary theme during the 1930's. Not all writers, however, could depart from traditional taboos. In *The No-Nation Girl* (1929) and *Love Fetish* (1933) Evans Wall repeats time-worn generalities about the mulatto. Précieuse, heroine of the former volume, supposedly inherits emotionalism from her Negro mother and civilized restraint from her white father:

> The girl's half-heritage of savagery rose in a flood that washed away all trace of her father's people except the supersensitiveness imparted by her taut nerves. She must dance or scream to relieve the rising torrent of response to the wild, monotonous rhythm.

In Fannie Hurst's *Imitation of Life* (1933) Peola, who finally marries across the color line, insists: "I won't be a nigger! I won't be a nigger!" The heroine of Marie Stanley's *Gulf Stream* (1936) is a color-conscious Creole who bears a child for a white man but subsequently discovers that one "can't hide from God and Affaca." In *Children of Strangers* (1937) Lyle Saxon depicts an attractive octoroon who, after having a child by a white outlaw, finally gives herself to a "shut-mouth nigger—studying to himself all the time, wanting to learn to read letters." There were other books, however, which broke many of the precedents of miscegenation fiction. Roy Flannagan's *Amber Satyr* (1932) sets forth the love of a white farmer's wife for a colored worker and the killing of the latter by the woman's two brothers, one of whom was the father of an illegitimate child by the victim's daughter. In *Naked Foot* (1934) Emily Hahn places her setting in Africa and recounts the liaisons of a native woman with several white men. Clement Wood's *Deep River* (1934) treats the married life of a Southern white woman with a Negro concert singer. Willa Cather's *Sapphira and the Slave Girl* (1940) probes the jealousy of a white wife for a mulatto slave whom she suspects of being her husband's mistress.

Possibly stimulated by the work of Stribling in *Birthright* and *Unfinished Cathedral,* several novelists offered varying interpretations of the educated Negro. In *Dark Surrender* (1933) Ronald Kirkbride presents Tom Lee, a Negro who leaves his recent bride on a South Carolina plantation and goes to Harvard, where he graduates with distinction, and to Europe, where he receives acclaim as a scholar and poet. Eventually viewing the progress of educated Negroes as imitations "of the accomplishments of the white man," Lee makes his way back to the South, where he reclaims his wife and tells the Boss that dark folk "who have aspirations, who yearn to be great" are not "true negroes," and that a Negro must choose between two paths: "either to live in the happy continuance of life, enjoying from day to day what the simplicity of his race can supply, or to pursue knowledge, awaken false senses, false ambitions, and become a wanderer in another man's world." In *Portrait of Eden* (1934) Margaret Sperry shows how Samuel Lyman, a millionaire who undertakes to enlighten a Southern town, meets a pathetic death, and how his Negro coworker, Dr. Burt MacIntyre, is ruthlessly murdered. William March's *Come In at the Door* (1934) ably describes the intimate intellectual bond between a white boy and his colored tutor. Though Hallie F. Dickerman compliments the talented mulatto hero of *Stephen Kent* (1935), she utilizes the old formula of racial atavism. Hamilton Basso's *Courthouse Square* (1936) shows how the efforts of liberal whites to assist a Negro physician in erecting a sanatorium for his people are thwarted by race hatred and mob violence. In the opinion of the leading white character of James Saxon Childers' *A Novel About a White Man and a Black Man in the Deep South* (1936), the Negro "has long ago walked out of his blackness and is only a man," but the action of the book clearly demonstrates that the majority of Southerners are not of the same mind. In a Northern college white Gordon Nicholson and black Dave Parker become friends and, upon meeting years later in Birmingham, continue their relationship as social equals. Because of community pressure Nicholson is ostracized, and his sister Anne loses her fiancé and commits suicide. Though the author does not succumb to defeatism, the friends finally bow to Southern mores and follow divergent paths.

While not writing fiction that may be construed as protest, certain authors gave a more faithful and representative portrayal of everyday Negro life than did the Peterkin school. Borrowing characters from her drama, *Roseanne,* Nan Bagby Stephens convincingly depicts colored folk of a small Georgia town in *Glory* (1932). In *Death Is a Little Man* (1936) Minnie Hite Moody sympathetically renders the trials and tribulations of an industrious Negro woman dwelling in the slums of Atlanta. Julian R. Meade's *The Back Door* (1938) likewise deals authentically with the experiences of a Negro woman worker. Alain Locke called Mary Lou Payton, the heroine of this novel, "the most fully characterized Negro servant in all the tedious range of Negro servitors in American fiction."[12] In *The Heart Is a Lonely Hunter* (1940) Carson McCullers dispassionately handles Negro and white characters living in a small Southern town.

There were other novelists, however, who followed Caldwell, Stribling, and the revolutionary fictionists by writing protest realism. Welbourn Kelley's *Inchin' Along* (1932) presents a progressive Negro sharecropper who narrowly escapes mob violence.

John L. Spivak's *Georgia Nigger* (1932), a thesis novel based upon actual conditions, attacks peonage and the chain gang through the experiences of David Jackson, a young Negro who falls into the tentacles of the vicious Southern convict-lease system. In Robert Rylee's *Deep Dark River* (1935) a Negro sharecropper, having aroused antagonism by objecting to his wife's affair with a white plantation manager, succeeds in slaying his would-be assassin and in obtaining the counsel of an able white woman lawyer but receives a sentence of life imprisonment. Theodore Pratt's *Big Blow* (1936) has an interesting Negro character who is the sturdy protector of a poor white girl living by herself. Don Tracy's *How Sleeps the Beast* (1938) is a forceful indictment of lynching. In "Runagate Nigger" and "The Funeral," stories in William March's *Some Like Them Short* (1939), protest is made against the plight of the Negro in the South. The former tale presents a Southern landlord who, because of the intercession of a Northern newspaper woman, is brought before a federal court on the charge of fleecing his Negro tenants and blocking their escape to the North. The latter narrative directs attention to a cook's young girl who, having been whipped for secretly watching a white girl's funeral, hangs herself with the hope that in death she, too, will receive eulogistic comments and an elaborate ceremony.

## V. *EFFECT OF PROLETARIANISM AND LIBERALISM UPON NEGRO LITERATURE*

As a result of the class-consciousness, liberalism, and humanitarianism of the depression years, Negro writers increasingly tended to examine the life of their people from a universal rather than an ethnocentric point of view. To authors primarily concerned with human values both racial exhibitionism, such as the jungle pose of certain writers of the Renascence, and assertive Negrophile propaganda, such as that of most Negro fictionists before World War I, were anathema. The devotion to research which characterized the period stimulated literature dealing with the racial past, while an increased interest in the life of the masses encouraged works about folk on the farms and in the factories. Although most colored writers continued to use their own race as subjects, their ideology, as the following chapter will show, was not entirely race-motivated. This broadening of literary outlook from a restrictively racial to a broadly human point of view is the tendency which chiefly distinguishes Negro writing of the 1930's from that of earlier years. "The stock market crash of October, 1929," as Benjamin Brawley pointed out in discussing the transition from the Renascence to the depression decade, "was as important to literature as to economics."[13]

CHAPTER 6

# Negro Fiction of the Depression

THE 1930'S SAW sweeping changes in the authorship of American Negro fiction. Of all the writers discussed in some detail in Chapter IV, only Arna Bontemps and Langston Hughes held on and produced volumes of fiction during the decade from 1933 to 1942. Bontemps deserted the Harlem Jazz School to write historical novels, while Hughes moved toward proletarian analysis and protest. Although Zora Neale Hurston was a participant in the Renascence, her first book of fiction did not appear until 1934, when the fervor of the gay 'twenties had disappeared. Chief among Negro novelists who made their debut during the 1930's were Miss Hurston, George Wylie Henderson, George W. Lee, Waters Edward Turpin, Richard Wright, and William Attaway. Other new fiction writers of the period were Mercedes Gilbert, John H. Paynter, Victor Daly, John H. Hill, and O'Wendell Shaw.

When the depression struck in 1929, the fad of adulating and patronizing things Negro began to subside. No longer buttressed by white devotees of the heyday of the Renascence, Negro writers turned more and more to materials which genuinely interested them rather than to sensuous and bizarre themes which delighted American readers during the boom years. In general, the fiction of the depression period may be regarded neither as propagandistic nor exhibitionist. In the main, the important novels and short stories of the decade avoided stereotypes and drew characters from real life. Self-preening and assertive racialism is conspicuous by its absence. Increasingly the Negro was considered as a member, rather than as an outcast, of the American family, and his difficulties as merely a special phase of general social maladjustment. Not a single novel by a Negro between 1933 and 1942 is devoted to the theme of passing, and more interest is shown in the problems of the masses than in the culture of the bourgeoisie. The death knell was sounded for the Harlem vogue. As early as 1931 Alain Locke perceived that the much exploited Harlem literary revival "was after all a product of the expansive period we are now willing to call the period of inflation and overproduction,"[1] and from a long-range view in 1939 he recognized that the participants were writers who "went cosmopolite when they were advised to go racial, who went exhibitionist instead of going documentarian, who got jazz-mad and cabaret-crazy instead of getting folk-wise and sociologically sober."[2]

Important departures were made from Renascence paths in the fictional output of the period. John H. Paynter, John H. Hill, and Arna Bontemps, reflecting the growing interest in the historical background of dark folk, wrote novels treating phases of the Negro past. Bontemps' *Black Thunder* (1936) and *Drums at Dusk* (1939) won rating as good historical fiction. Specializing in family chronicle, Waters Edward Turpin produced *These Low Grounds* (1937) and *O Canaan!* (1939), the first giving pictures of life along Maryland's Eastern Shore and the latter of South Side Chicago during depression years. In *Not Only War* (1932) Victor Daly described racial tensions in a Southern community and in the armed forces, both in the United States and in Europe, during World War I. In *Greater Need Below* (1936) O'Wendell Shaw delivered a scathing indictment of the administration of a tax-supported college for Negroes in a Southern state. White politicians and Negro school officials bear the burden of Shaw's bitter attack. Langston Hughes and Richard Wright, the two best-known Negro writers of the decade, used fiction as a vehicle for proletarian propaganda, with the latter's *Native Son* (1940) enjoying unprecedented popularity and influence among novels written by Negroes in this country. Zora Neale Hurston, George Wylie Henderson, George W. Lee, and Mercedes Gilbert drew intimate pictures of black folk in the rural South. In *Let Me Breathe Thunder* (1939) William Attaway, shaking himself free of racial thematic limitations, relates the experiences of young migrant workers in the Far West.

## I. *HISTORICAL FICTION*

In spite of the magnetism of Harlem for the American reading public, it is almost incredible, in view of the race pride engendered among Negroes by the Garvey Movement and the African art revival, that a historical novel did not appear during the flood-tide of the Renascence. Conditions in the 1930's, however, virtually assured the appearance of historical fiction by Negroes. The Association for the Study of Negro Life and History exerted powerful influence, establishing *The Journal of Negro History* on a sound basis, starting *The Negro History Bulletin* for a popular audience in 1937, bringing about the national observance of Negro History Week, and helping to effect the introduction of a course in Negro history at most Negro schools. The three major Negro universities—Atlanta, Fisk, and Howard—promoted extensive research in the racial past. Important libraries, such as the Schomburg Collection of the New York Public Library, systematically gathered literary materials concerning the history and culture of black folk. Colored playwrights explored the dramatic possibilities of episodes from Negro history in Africa and America in *Negro History in Thirteen Plays* (1935). At the same time, white writers turned enthusiastically to the story of the black man. As Sterling Brown says:

> The African slave-trade, the antebellum and the reconstruction South are popular hunting grounds. Some novelists continue the plantation tradition, some, the anti-slavery tradition, and many others, in the spirit of regionalism, seek the truth of their sectional pasts, without apology and without indictment.[3]

As historical treatments of the Negro, Hildegarde Swift's *Railroad to Freedom* (1932), which recounts the life of Harriet Tubman, and Leonard Ehrlich's *God's Angry Man* (1933), which tells the story of John Brown but also includes sympathetic portraiture of such colored Abolitionists as Frederick Douglass and Harriet Tubman, are particularly significant.

The first genuine historical novel by an American Negro after World War I was John H. Paynter's *Fugitives of the Pearl* (1930), an amateurishly executed account of the attempted flight of a group of slaves from Washington to Philadelphia in 1848. This work was followed by John H. Hill's *Princess Malah* (1933), a belated and anachronistic tribute to the slaveholding aristocracy of Virginia during the years before the Revolutionary War. Arna Bontemps' *Black Thunder* (1936), a treatment of the slave insurrection under Gabriel Prosser in Virginia in 1800, and *Drums at Dusk* (1939), a story of the Negro uprising which resulted in Haitian independence and the ascendancy of Toussaint L'Ouverture, are historical novels that indicate the rich possibilities of future work in this field. In general, Negro historical novelists manifest a preference for episodes revealing black folk in heroic roles.

### John H. Paynter

John H. Paynter's *Fugitives of the Pearl* (1930), a pioneering experiment by a Negro writer in the use of racial history as material for fiction, describes the attempted escape of seventy-seven slaves from Washington to Philadelphia on the *Pearl,* a schooner captained by an Abolitionist. The flight, undertaken in 1848, when the nation was celebrating the overthrow of despotism in France, would have been successful if a servile Negro free-dealer had not betrayed the plot. After describing the seizure of the runaways, the author relates the various experiences of a liberty-loving family on slave ships, in New Orleans, in Washington, and in Baltimore, and shows how each member gains freedom, either through manumission or escape.

Though unconvincing in local color, characterization, and

dialogue, *Fugitives of the Pearl* nevertheless manages to expand an historical incident and to illustrate the dissatisfaction of ante-bellum Negroes with bondage. A fairly competent job is done in depicting the surprise, disappointment, and vexation of Washington citizens at the flight of the Negroes. Tribute is paid to such eminent Abolitionists as Garrison, Phillips, Lovejoy, Tappan, Douglass, Lucretia Mott, Purvis, Ward, Pennington, Garnet, and Still. In the final analysis, however, *Fugitives of the Pearl* is more successful as a laudatory chronicle of Negro slaves than as an accomplishment in historical fiction.

### John H. Hill

Likewise complimentary to the ante-bellum Negro is John H. Hill's *Princess Malah* (1933), a historic romance covering the brief period from the capture of Fort Duquesne to the fall of Quebec and recounting the activities of Malah, a noble woman of white, Indian, and Negro extraction. The legal daughter of George Washington's brother Lawrence and a woman of the Tuscarora tribe, Malah holds high rank both at Mount Vernon and among the Indians. Espousing the cause of the British against the French, she had earlier contributed to George Washington's successful campaign against Fort Duquesne, had enlisted the aid of the Confederacy and other tribes for General Braddock, and because of her efforts was elected princess and queen by the Five Nations and their associates. After obtaining overwhelming Indian assistance for General Johnson in the final drive against the French, Malah marries Chief Coldfoot, sachem of the Miami Confederacy.

Hill admittedly wrote *Princess Malah* in order "to depict the relationship existing between master and slave in the period of our history just prior to the Revolutionary War." The picture that he paints is exaggeratedly pleasant. The first families of Virginia once more parade as the genial guardians of contented slaves. In this instance, however, the bondmen, seldom lapsing into dialect or indecorous conduct, match the polished gallantry of their owners.

Social realism is hinted but not realized. Aristocrats, domestics of mixed blood, black manual laborers, white overseers, poor whites, and Indians are listed as the main social groups of the time; and occasional references are made to their interplay. The dislike of poor whites for Negroes and wealthy landowners is mentioned but not developed. The unfavorable aspects of miscegenation are skimmed over, as sympathetic masters and mistresses publicly recognize their colored relatives and often accord them positions of honor. Considerable attention is given to balls, banquets, wedding feasts, and other elaborate social events. The author is too engrossed in painting a flattering picture of the blue bloods and black servitors of Mount Vernon, White House (the Custis mansion in New Kent County), and Williamsburg to give a realistic presentation of the period which he essays to re-create.

### Arna Bontemps

Arna Bontemps, who was discussed in Chapter IV as the author of *God Sends Sunday,* a novel in the Van Vechten tradition, here appears as the writer of *Black Thunder* (1936) and *Drums at Dusk* (1939), two important experiments in historical fiction. The former treats the abortive slave insurrection under Gabriel Prosser in Virginia in 1800, the immediate cause of which is the fatal whipping of Bundy, an old serf who had long yearned for freedom and had received inspiration from the rise of Toussaint L'Ouverture. Bundy's devotion to liberty strikes a sympathetic chord in the heart of Gabriel, who determines to seek deliverance for himself and his fellow bondmen. Immediately instituting plans for a mass onslaught upon Richmond, Gabriel and his co-workers are heartened not only by the success of black rebels in San Domingo but also by the doctrines of Les Amis des Noirs. The audacious plans of the conspirators are balked by a severe tempest which prevents united effort as well as by the betraying confessions of two Negroes. In the subsequent confusion, terror-stricken authorities hang numerous innocent slaves before capturing Gabriel and other leaders of the revolution.

The underlying thesis of *Black Thunder,* like that of Paynter's *Fugitives of the Pearl*, is that Negro slaves, with the exception of a small number bound in mind as well as in body, had an obsessive love of freedom. Mention has been made of the Abolitionist sentiments of Bundy, Gabriel, and their associates. But hatred of slavery was not limited to those who wore shackles. Among free Negroes there was a deep desire for general emancipation; and Mingo, one of this class, remarks to Gabriel: ". . . I'm free now, but it ain't no good being free when all yo' people's slaves, yo' wife and chilluns and all." Furthermore, there were opponents of bondage among whites, particularly in a small group of French liberals living in Richmond. Accepting the French Revolution ideals of liberty, equality, and fraternity, and inspired by the philosophy of Rousseau and Voltaire, these individuals opposed rich planters and sought to abolish caste distinctions which operated to the disadvantage of poor whites and Negroes. Though marked as Jacobins and revolutionaries, they agitated to elevate the American proletariat and to accelerate the triumph of social justice for abused groups throughout the world.

*Black Thunder* is written with restraint and detachment. Bontemps portrays slaves, freedmen, planters, and French radicals with impartiality, showing no disposition to glorify pro-Negro nor to traduce anti-Negro characters in the book. Miscegenation on the Southern scene is not blinked. Furthermore, Bontemps succeeds in weaving Gabriel's uprising into the web of state and national life. We observe the Virginia legislature considering the sectional segregation of Negroes as an approach to the solution of racial difficulties and note the Federalist press, while championing a second term for John Quincy Adams, citing Gabriel's insurrection as an offshoot of the radicalism of Thomas Jefferson and his adherents. Although *Black Thunder* is not without blemish,

A. B. Spingarn is quite correct in his observation that the book is "the best historical novel written by an American Negro."[4]

Also a record of the Negro's quest for freedom is Bontemps' second historical novel, *Drums at Dusk,* an account of the black insurrection which resulted in the independence of Haiti and the emergence of Toussaint L'Ouverture. Making but few revisions in the generally accepted versions of the early stages of the revolution,[5] Bontemps builds the historical narrative around the romance of Celeste Juvet, a girl of French parentage, and Diron de Sautels, a young French aristocrat who is a member of Les Amis des Noirs, an antislavery worker, and an ardent reader of such thinkers as LaRochefoucauld, Lafayette, Danton, Robespierre, Brissot, Gregoire, and Raynal. Celeste lives with her grandmother on the large Breda plantation superintended by M. Bayou de Libertas, a benevolent overseer employed by a French nobleman whose profligate cousin, Count Armand de Sacy, uses the vast colonial estate as a dumping ground for discarded mistresses. De Sacy's inhuman treatment of sick bondmen and the subsequent mass suicide of twenty-four Gold Coast slaves serve to hasten the peasant uprising which results in the overthrow of the aristocracy and the ascendance of Toussaint L'Ouverture. In the bloody holocaust which accompanies the insurrection de Sacy meets a horrible death, and a terrific toll of life is taken on both sides.

The blow which the blacks strike for freedom is partly inspired by the liberal ideology of the French Revolution and the propagandistic endeavors of Les Amis des Noirs. Two years had passed since the storming of the Bastille, and the doctrines of the "rights of man" had been carried to the colonies and had taken particularly deep root in Haiti. Young de Sautels, for example, had spread liberal ideas among abused blacks, and—in spite of the friction among landed gentlemen, petits blancs, and mulattoes—his sympathies were with the downtrodden masses:

> Diron was not sure just where his allegiance belonged, and he cared much less. For how important was the quarrel between ten thousand

aristocrats, thirty thousand low-class whites, and forty thousand mulattoes in Saint Domingue when there were five hundred thousand—half a million—slaves on the island still in the chains of unspeakable bondage! Nature was being thwarted and opposed by perverse and corrupt man. The whole creation cried against the infamy of man's vile institutions. All the woes of the human family were easily traceable to the same point: denial of the natural, elemental rights of man.

Bontemps paints a vivid picture of social upheaval and class prejudice in tropical San Domingo. Struggling for control are the wealthy elite, the low-class whites, and the free mulattoes. The aristocrats, dominating slaves who outnumber all other inhabitants by nearly ten to one, keep their positions secure by intimidating the blacks and playing them against the mulattoes. The patricians live in luxury, diverting themselves with expensive banquets and dazzling apparel. Miscegenation is rampant, as lecherous aristocrats frequently manifest a preference for "chocolate" and openly flaunt their yellow mistresses. In handling black workers, however, the wealthy class is not so tender. Revolting conditions prevail in slave ships, where diseased natives are packed spoon-fashion, and on many plantations. This cruel treatment accelerates the extension of liberal views and the meteoric rise of such leaders as Brisson, Boukman, and L'Ouverture. In brief, *Drums at Dusk*, a worthy successor to *Black Thunder*, is another vivid illustration of the richness of the Negro's past as a source for historical fiction.

## II. *FICTION OF WORLD WAR I*

"The critical decade which followed the World War saw, in the United States as in other countries," as Carl Van Doren notes, "many novelists bent on showing how unheroic the conflict had been, how cruel, wasteful, stupid."[6] Among the major works of American fiction which appeared during these years were John Dos Passos' *Three Soldiers* (1921), E. E. Cummings' *The Enormous Room* (1922), and Ernest Hemingway's *A Farewell to Arms* (1929). During this period, however, Negro fiction writers failed to exploit the World War I theme, and it was not until the appearance of Victor Daly's *Not Only War* in 1932 that a colored author undertook a novel with this mammoth conflict as a background.

### VICTOR DALY

Written by a first lieutenant in the Thirty-Seventh New York Infantry, Victor Daly's *Not Only War* (1932) is the first novel by a Negro to study at length the psychology and experiences of the colored American soldier in World War I. Dedicated "to the army of the disillusioned," the book sets out to show that for the Negro the great conflict was not only the physical hell that Sherman knew but was also an inferno of the spirit:

> William Tecumseh Sherman branded War for all time when he called it Hell. There is yet another gaping, abysmal Hell into which some of us are actually born or unconsciously sucked. The Hell that Sherman knew was a physical one—of rapine, destruction and death. This other, is a purgatory for the mind, for the spirit, for the soul of men. Not only War is Hell.

The main characters are Montgomery Jason and Miriam Pinckney, both colored college students, and Bob Casper, a military school graduate and son of a South Carolina colonel. En route to Spartanburg, Casper meets Miriam and, disregarding his belief "in the Baptist Church, the supremacy of the white race and the righteousness of the Democratic Party," becomes her paramour. After being discovered in a clandestine meeting with her lover, Miriam leaves town. Later Casper and Jason join the Army and go to France, where the former instigates the demotion of the latter because the Negro happens to be quartered in the home of a beautiful French girl. Subsequently, during a major drive against the Germans, Jason finds Casper wounded and, though tempted to pass him by, finally tries to rescue him. Before the pair can reach a place of safety, however, both are killed by enemy fire and are found "the next morning, face downward, their arms about each other, side by side."

"It is certainly to be marvelled," observed Alain Locke soon after the issuance of *Not Only War,* "that with all of the fiction of the war, the paradoxical story of the American Negro fighting a spiritual battle within a physical battle has just now been attempted."[7] Race prejudice in the United States, however, is more important to the author than the position of the Negro soldier in the international struggle in Europe. With reference to the possibility of justice for the Negro in America, the implications are pessimistic. In reply to Jason's contention that the government would reward the Negro for loyalty in time of war, Roscoe Simms, one of his friends, says:

"I read somewhere that the loyalty of a slave to his master is a vice. No amount of sacrifice on your part or my part, will ever soften the hearts of these crackers towards us. You're just condemned to ride in a Jim Crow car for the rest of your life. Your children will attend Jim Crow schools—war or no war—fight or no fight. You'll live in a segregated neighborhood for the remainder of your days—and they'll lynch you whenever they get ready."

Converted to Simms's views after his demotion, Jason muses:

"Maybe Roscoe Simms was right after all. It was a white man's war. It would take more than war, and bullets, and death to wipe out race prejudice. . . . Fellows like Casper would never change. They just hated black people, and that was all there was to it. It was a creed with them."

On the whole, *Not Only War* is too preoccupied with race prejudice to be a successful war novel, for South Carolina receives more consideration than France. Furthermore, the plot depends heavily upon accidental occurrences, the characters are not fully realized, and the setting is not convincingly described. The book is noteworthy, nevertheless, because it is a path-breaking effort in a fertile field.

## III. *PROLETARIAN FICTION*

After the stock market debacle of 1929 the proletarian note in American Negro fiction sounded with ever-increasing volume. Around 1930 Langston Hughes manifested leftist inclinations and later expressed his ideology in *Scottsboro Limited: Four Poems and a Play in Verse* (1932), *Don't You Want to Be Free?* (1938), and *A New Song* (1938). *The Ways of White Folks* (1934), the only volume of fiction which Hughes has released since *Not Without Laughter,* contains one story that shows radical sympathies. The chief proletarian spokesman among Negro writers, however, was Richard Wright, whose *Uncle Tom's Children* (1938) and *Native Son* (1940) rank among the more important works of contemporary American fiction.

### Langston Hughes

After the publication of *Not Without Laughter* in 1930 Langston Hughes aligned himself with the proletarian school of American writers. The transition is heralded in the writing of a poem called "Advertisement for the Waldorf-Astoria," a work of social protest which caused a rift between the poet and a patron who wanted him to be the incarnation of the primitive. *Scottsboro Limited: Four Poems and a Play in Verse* (1932) contains straightforward proletarian propaganda. Hughes was also a left-wing spokesman in his prose contribution to Jacob Burck's *Hunger and Revolt: Cartoons* (1935), in an experimental poetic play entitled *Don't You Want to Be Free* (1938), and in *A New Song* (1938), a booklet of verse.

The only one of the fourteen stories of *The Ways of White Folks* (1934) which aggressively voices proletarian ideology is "Father and Son," wherein Hughes states:

Crucible of the South, find the right powder and you'll never be the same again—the cotton will blaze and the cabins will burn and the chains will be broken and men, all of a sudden, will shake hands, black men and white men, like steel meeting steel!

The remainder of the stories expose hypocrisy and oppression in various strata of white society. Interracial sex relations are the theme of several pieces. In "Little Dog" a respectable middle-class spinster relinquishes her apartment to escape the physical magnetism of a Negro janitor. "Mother and Son" describes the Negrophobia aroused among the white populace of an Ohio town by the birth of a colored child to the wife of a prosperous farmer. "A Good Job Gone" shows how a wealthy New York debauchee disintegrates and loses his mind after being jilted by a fascinating woman from Harlem. "Red-Headed Baby" describes the irresponsible attitude of a white seaman toward his child by a mulatto girl living near the Florida coast. Written in epistolary form, "Passing" contains an apology to a Negro mother by her son who, having crossed the color line in Chicago, snubs her while in the company of his white fiancée. "Father and Son," which embodies the plot of the drama *Mulatto* (1935), relates how the hatred of a proud Georgia planter for his defiant mulatto son results in the murder of the former and the lynching of the latter. This narrative affords a convincing picture of the bold cohabitation of white master and colored concubine in the rural South, sets forth the superior advantages and resentful attitudes of certain offspring of such liaisons, and skirts difficulties inherent in the sharecropper system. Southern contempt for the educated Negro, a factor treated in "Father and Son," stimulates in "Home" the lynching of a young colored violinist who innocently becomes too friendly with a white music teacher of a Missouri town.

In several stories Hughes satirizes condescending and patronizing members of the white group. In "Slave on the Block" Michael and Anne Caraway, who at first think Negroes are "too charming and naive and lovely for words," later discover that their two colored servants dislike being considered primitive and inferior. "Poor Little Black Fellow" recounts how the Negro protégé of an aristocratic New England family shocks his guardians by marrying a Roumanian girl during a European tour. In "The Blues I'm Playing" a gifted Harlem pianist incurs the disfavor of a patron by marrying a Negro physician and preferring the blues to the classics. "Rejuvenation through Joy" caricatures a New York cult which offers happiness to bored plutocrats by instructing them in the supposed spontaneity and primitivism of Negro life. In "Cora Unashamed" a mulatto maid disgraces her respectable employers by revealing that their daughter's death was caused by an enforced abortion.

Two stories set forth the hard lot of the Negro worker. In "One Christmas Eve" Arcie can neither spend Christmas Eve with her son nor purchase Yuletide gifts for him because her employers are shopping and spending so freely that it is necessary to cut her small salary. "Berry" tells the story of a colored boy who, hired at a much lower salary than that of his white predecessor in a children's sanatorium operated by a swindling physician, gains the affection of the inmates but loses his job because of a trivial and unavoidable accident. The title of the book is taken from the following observation of Berry:

> "Besides, the ways of white folks, I mean some white folks, is too much for me. I reckon they must be a few good ones, but most of 'em ain't good—leastwise they don't treat me good. And Lawd knows, I ain't never done nothin' to 'em, nothin' a-tall."

In spite of the author's prefatory explanation that he really means "some white folks," *The Ways of White Folks* is the outstanding indictment of Nordicism in modern American fiction. The target of attack is American racism at all levels—lower-class, bourgeois, and capitalist—and in representative sections—Southern, Northeastern, and Mid-Western. Because of its preoccupation with race prejudice, *The Ways of White Folks* suggests that Hughes is as much disturbed by color as by caste distinctions. Nevertheless, the volume signalizes the emergence of proletarianism in American Negro literature and thus opens the way for the fiction of Richard Wright.

RICHARD WRIGHT

During the past ten years Richard Wright, who is preparing a novel "about the status of women in modern American society,"[8] has gained nation-wide prominence as a literary diagnostician of racial and economic ills, particularly as they affect Negroes of the United States. In 1936 his short story "Big Boy Leaves Home," later included in *Uncle Tom's Children*, was heralded as one of the noteworthy contributions to *The New Caravan*. In the following year "The Ethics of Living Jim Crow: An Autobiographical Sketch" was acclaimed as one of the best pieces in *American Stuff*, anthology of the Federal Writers' Project. Appearing in 1938, *Uncle Tom's Children*—selection of Lewis Gannett, Harry Scherman, and Sinclair Lewis as winner of the $500 first prize in a contest conducted by *Story* among men and women in the Federal Writers' Project—received commendation as the best fiction of Southern Negro life by a colored author since Jean Toomer's *Cane* (1923) and as a work worthy to rank with the regional realism of T. S. Stribling, William Faulkner, and Erskine Caldwell. "Bright and Morning Star," which originally appeared in *New Masses*, was selected by the late Edward J. O'Brien as one of the two best stories of 1939 and as one of the fifty best stories written since 1915. Wright's most significant fiction to date, however, is *Native Son* (1940), a best seller and Book-of-the-Month Club selection, the genesis and development of which are traced in "How 'Bigger' Was Born," an article by the author in *The Saturday Review of Literature* for June 1, 1940. Converted into a drama through the collaboration of Wright and Paul Green of the University of North Carolina, and subsequently staged under the direction of Orson Welles, *Native Son* lasted fourteen weeks on Broadway before closing with a short run at the Apollo Theatre in Harlem.

As a successful and influential author, Wright focuses attention upon the warping and stunting effect of racial discrimination and economic oppression upon the downtrodden and underprivileged classes of the United States, and blames brutal and prejudiced whites as well as complacent and cowardly blacks for much Negro crime and delinquency. His special forte in depicting the circumscribed life of the Negro was early shown in his revolutionary verse[9] and in "The Ethics of Living Jim Crow: An Autobiographical Sketch." In the latter piece, which is divided into nine thumbnail parts, Wright relates how he learned through first-hand experience to conform to the standards of conduct prescribed by the Southern white man for the Negro. Among the lessons that he received were that a Negro should never fight a white person, should always stay in his place, should unfailingly add *sir* to a *yes* or a *no* addressed to white adults, should not expect equal protection under the law, should never undertake to defend Negro women imposed upon by white men, should unresistingly indulge the exploitation of Negro women by white men, should be oblivious to the physical charms of white women, should anticipate severe punishment if discovered consorting with white women, and should avoid the following topics in discussions with white people:

> American white women; the Ku Klux Klan; France, and how Negro soldiers fared while there; French women; Jack Johnson; the entire northern part of the United States; the Civil War; Abraham Lincoln; U. S. Grant; General Sherman; Catholics; the Pope; Jews; the Republican Party; slavery; social equality; Communism; Socialism; the 13th and 14th Amendments to the Constitution; or any topic calling for positive knowledge or manly self-assertion on the part of the Negro.

The occurrences described in "The Ethics of Living Jim Crow: An Autobiographical Sketch" take place in the Mid-South: the first eight incidents deal chiefly with experiences of the author in Jackson, Mississippi, while the ninth and last sets forth his activities as an optical shop employee in Memphis, Tennessee, where his Jim-Crow education "was no longer brutally cruel, but subtly cruel."

Reverting to agricultural and small-town scenes, Wright continues his indictment of the South in *Uncle Tom's Children: Four Novellas* (1938), whose preliminary note announces the passing of the traditional Uncle Tom and the emergence of the militant new Negro:

> The post Civil War household word among Negroes—"He's an Uncle Tom!"—which denoted reluctant toleration for the cringing type who knew his place before white folk, has been supplanted by a new word from another generation which says:— "Uncle Tom is dead!"

"Big Boy Leaves Home," the first of these novellas and one of the most authentic pictures of a boys' gang in American fiction, deals with the tragedy resulting from the prankish decision of four Negro boys to go swimming in a pond where Negro bathers are not allowed. Once in the water, the naked youngsters become frightened at the approach of a white woman who walks near their clothes under a tree. When the youths rush to regain their garments, the terrified woman screams for her escort, who appears with a gun and kills two of the youngsters before meeting his own death at the hands of Big Boy, the leader of the gang. Through the aid of Negro citizens Big Boy escapes to Chicago in an express truck, but his remaining companion is caught by irate white citizens and lynched. "Big Boy Leaves Home" shows that crime inevitably springs from the denial of adequate recreational facilities, and the series of murders in the story may be traced to the meaningful comment of one of the boys: "The white folks got plenty swimmin pools n we ain got none." The narrative also sets forth the fear and hatred engendered by the Southern way of life, for Big Boy justifies the murder of the woman's escort on the ground that "yuh never can tell erbout white folks" and dreams of the possible glory of killing a dozen or even a score of white men before meeting his own death. After its release in *The New Caravan* (1936) "Big Boy Leaves Home" was hailed by Alain Locke as "the strongest note yet struck by one of our writers in the staccato protest realism of the rising school of proletarian fiction."[10]

The second novella, "Down by the Riverside," treats the heightened interracial tension of a Mississippi Valley flood disaster. Mann, a Negro farmer, uses a boat stolen by a relative to row his wife, who is in child labor, to a Red Cross hospital. Encountering the stranded owner of the boat and killing him in self-defense, Mann proceeds through turbulent waters to the nearest town, where, after a levee break, he heroically saves many lives, including those of the wife and children of the man he murdered. Identified by those he rescued and arrested by military police, Mann is later fatally wounded while making a hopeless attempt to escape. "Down by the Riverside" discloses various aspects of racial oppression during the 1927 Mississippi flood catastrophe. Negroes, conscripted to pile sand and cement bags on the levee, are slain for trying to escape. Medical attention, given bluntly, is provided in unsatisfactory and segregated quarters; and martial law, administered harshly, is conducted with bias and intimidation.

"Long Black Song" mirrors the exploitation of unprotected Negro women by white men and the insecurity of the independent Negro landowner. Sarah, left with her child on the farm while her husband Silas goes to town to sell cotton and purchase supplies, is seduced by a white traveling salesman. Returning home, Silas finds incontrovertible evidence of his wife's unfaithfulness and punishes her severely. Embittered by his persecution, Silas sardonically declares:

> "The white folks ain never gimme a chance! They ain never give no black man a chance! There ain nothin in yo whole life yuh kin keep from em! They take yo lan! They take yo freedom! They take yo women! N then they take yo life! . . . Ahm gonna be hard like they is! So hep me, Gawd. Ah'm gonna be *hard*. When they come fer me Ah'm gonna *be* here! N when they git me outta here theys gonna *know* Ahm gone! Ef Gawd lets me live Ahm gonna make em *feel* it!"

When the salesman returns the next morning the abused husband murders him. The partner of the slain man escapes, however, and assembles a mob which, after losing two of its members before Silas' gunfire, ignites his barricaded house and watches it burn with the helpless victim inside. Remorseful after her seduction, Sarah is conscious of the senselessness of interracial strife:

White men killed the black and black men killed the white. White men killed black men because they could, and black men killed white men to keep from being killed.

"Fire and Cloud," the fourth and final novella of the volume, employs a theme not previously used in fiction by Negroes. Negroes and poor whites of a small Southern city are in the grip of starvation and unemployment; and wealthy citizens, though able to alleviate the misery, are hoarding food and money. Because of the acute suffering, Dan Taylor, a Negro minister who has earlier served as a mediating agent between his race and the ruling whites, is seriously considering a Communist-endorsed downtown march of Negroes and poor whites as a protest against the unfair distribution of food and jobs. Encouraging him as to the advisability of this procedure are Hadley and Green, a white and a black Communist, respectively. Determined to prevent the march, authorities use every device, from review of past favors to threats of physical violence, to persuade Taylor to use his influence to call off the demonstration. Proving stubborn and recalcitrant, Taylor is abducted and mercilessly beaten, but bravely returns to lead a successful biracial march of the indigent and unemployed against their rich oppressors.

"Fire and Cloud" is the only narrative in the collection in which the political and economic philosophy of the author comes to the surface. Racial unity and co-operation with poor whites rather than Communist membership, however, are recommended as an approach to the solution of the problems of the town's trampled and dispossessed; and the lesson which Taylor derives from the demonstration is that "Freedom belongs to the strong!" Competently portrayed is the minister's prolonged struggle between the desire to co-operate with the Reds in an effort to relieve the hunger of the people and his equally strong wish to remain in the good graces of local officials and to cause no innocent bloodshed. Jimmy, the preacher's son, is the new defiant Negro, ready to die rather than suffer brutality and terrorism; while Deacon Smith, distrustful of mass action and genuflective before municipal bigwigs, is a carryover of the traditional handkerchief-head type. The mayor represents the conciliator, and Bruden the autocrat in negotiations with colored people. Hadley, who propagandizes the city to gain relief, tells Taylor that Negro leaders frequently delay the advancement of their people by adopting a course of action sponsored by the dominant white group:

> "That's just it, Reverend. Don't be afraid of their turning you down because you're fighting for your people. If they knew you'd really fight, they'd dislike you; yes? But you can make them give something to *all* of your people, not just to *you*. Don't you see, Taylor, you're standing *between your* people and the white folks. You can make them give something to *all* of them. And the poor, hungry white folks will be with you."

Just before the march takes place, as the following remarks to Jimmy indicate, Taylor becomes convinced that the salvation of the Negro depends upon the organization of a strong popular front:

> "We gotta git wid the *people,* son. Too long we done tried t do this thing our way n when we failed we wanted t run out n pay-off the white folks. Then they kill us up like flies. It's the people, son! Wes too much erlon this way! Wes los when wes erlone. Wes gotta be wid our folks. . . ."

In brief, *Uncle Tom's Children* is a vivid, dramatic protest against Southern prejudice. The horror and tragedy suffered by Negroes in the narratives seem unnecessary in the light of the trivial incidents which cause them. Trespassing to swim on private property, using a stolen boat to transport a pregnant woman to a hospital, being helpless to repel the lust of a graphophone salesman, and planning a rather timid demonstration for food are sufficient to precipitate panic, loathing, murder, and mob violence. The responsibility for Southern turmoil is placed squarely at the doors of white demagogues who seek to maintain the ill-ordered *status quo* and of kowtowing Negro leaders who co-operate with them in this policy.

The second edition of *Uncle Tom's Children* includes "Bright and Morning Star," first published in *The New Masses* on May 10, 1939. Having its locale in the Mississippi River lowlands near Memphis, the narrative sets forth the joint efforts of Negro and white sharecroppers to get equality and justice from their overlords. Among the leaders of the group is Johnny-Boy, whose brother, Sug, has already been imprisoned for radical activities and whose mother, Aunt Sue, has abandoned her all-enduring Christian discipleship in order to do her share toward improving the status of poor people in the South. Johnny-Boy, who believes that black men cannot by themselves successfully oppose wealthy landowners and who recognizes class rather than racial lines of social demarcation, is loved by Reva, daughter of a poor white farmer named Lem. Trouble comes when law-enforcement officers, hearing of a meeting scheduled at Lem's home, seek to get further information on the organization by torturing Aunt Sue and Johnny-Boy. In a desperate move to warn other members of her party, Aunt Sue gives their names to Booker, a neophyte who proves to be a traitor, but thereafter succeeds in killing him before he can betray the loyal members of the party. Angered by the turn of events, the officers shoot Johnny-Boy and his mother in cold blood. "Bright and Morning Star," one of Wright's most partisan efforts, portrays the internal and external hazards of revolutionary political activities in the agricultural Mid-South. The love of Reva for Johnny-Boy is presented without squeamishness, and dying for collectivist principles is viewed as glorious martyrdom.

When reviews of *Uncle Tom's Children* appeared, Wright felt that he "had made an awfully naive mistake" in writing "a book which even bankers' daughters could read and weep over and feel good."[11] Therefore, in the composition of *Native Son* (1940), his next full-length work, he resolved not to be guilty of lachrymatory fiction again:

> I swore to myself that if ever I wrote another book, no one would weep over it; that it would be so hard and deep that they would have to face it without the consolation of tears.[12]

To obtain raw material for this obdurate and intractable novel Wright confessedly dug deep into his experience and compounded a symptomatic hero chiefly out of five social misfits that he had earlier known.[13] The first was a young bully who terrorized the boys of Jackson, Mississippi; the second, about seventeen years of age, showed resentment for the ruling class of the South by refusing to pay for his food, clothing, and housing; the third, whom the whites called a "bad nigger," bluffed his way for a while but was shot fatally during a Prohibition-era liquor raid; the fourth, who smarted under segregation and discrimination in the South, finally lost his mind and was remanded to an institution for the insane; and the fifth, whose fate was unknown but easy to imagine, took spirited delight in riding in the white sections of Jim-Crow street cars and defying conductors to move him. These five disjointed and maladjusted personalities were worked over by Wright's creative imagination until a synthetic character, Bigger Thomas of *Native Son,* emerged.

Considering his twisted and deprived hero in relation to the ideology of the labor movement and revolutionary politics, Wright observed that Bigger Thomases were white as well as black and that there were millions of young men with a similarly conditioned outlook in the various nations of the world:

> More than anything else, as a writer, I was fascinated by the similarity of the emotional tensions of Bigger in America and Bigger in Nazi Germany and Bigger in old Russia. All Bigger Thomases, white and black, felt tense, afraid, nervous, hysterical, and restless.[14]

Thinking in terms of the Bigger of the United States, Wright determined—regardless of anticipated deprecations from prejudiced

Nordics, misunderstanding Communists, and bourgeois Negroes—to exemplify in his hero "a symbolic figure of American life, a figure who would hold within him the prophecy of our future."[15] In using the title *Native Son*, then, the author sought "to show that Bigger Thomas is an authentic American, not imported from Moscow or anywhere."[16]

As the background for Bigger Thomas' activities Wright discarded the South for the black ghetto of Chicago, the sprawling and opulent metropolis of the Mid-West. The author reflected that this high-powered urban environment—with all of its glitter and allurement operating unceasingly "through the newspapers, magazines, radios, movies, and the mere imposing sight and sound of daily American life"—would cause Bigger, "estranged from the religion and folk culture of his race," to revolt even more furiously than he would in the South upon realizing that the full enjoyment of this stimulating scene was hollow mockery and utter impossibility for him.[17] Bigger, having deep-seated yearnings to be an aviator and to participate in weighty military and diplomatic matters, can enter these spheres of life only through ineffectual games of make-believe. His daily experience brings segregation, insult, mistreatment, and injury. Stirred by racial ostracism, he caustically says:

> "Every time I think about it I feel like somebody's poking a red-hot iron down my throat. Goddammit, look! We live here and they live there. We black and they white. They got things and we ain't. They do things and we can't. It's just like living in jail. Half the time I feel like I'm on the outside of the world peeping in through a knot-hole in the fence."

With thoughts like these surging through his mind, Bigger is bored and discontented with his humdrum existence of reading cheap magazines, going to movies, frequenting pool rooms, participating in petty robberies, laughing and talking with the gang, visiting his girl, or just spending time in idleness. In this provocative Chicago environment, then, much more than in the South,

Bigger is ready for any risky adjustment that a neurotic individual—twisted by race, poverty, and family disorganization—can make to safeguard or better his condition. As Wright explains:

> It was not that Chicago segregated Negroes more than the South, but that Chicago had more to offer, that Chicago's physical aspect—noisy, crowded, filled with the sense of power and fulfillment—did so much more to dazzle the mind with a taunting sense of possible achievement that the segregation it did impose brought forth from Bigger a reaction more obstreperous than in the South.[18]

At the beginning of the novel Bigger is living with his pious mother and younger brother and sister in a rat-infested, dilapidated one-room apartment for which the family pays the exorbitant rental fees usually assessed Negro residents in South Chicago. Through a relief agency he gets employment as a chauffeur at the home of Henry Dalton, wealthy owner of Negro property (including the run-down and mouldy tenement in which the Thomases dwell), loyal supporter of the National Association for the Advancement of Colored People, and heavy contributor to institutions of higher education for Negroes. During his first assignment as a chauffeur Bigger secretly takes Mary, Dalton's pro-Red daughter, to meet her Communist sweetheart, Jan Erlone. At the request of the couple, Bigger drives to a Southside cafe and reluctantly joins the lovers in eating and drinking. Afterwards he drives the intoxicated pair about Washington Park until Erlone boards a northbound trolley. Entrusted with attending Mary, Bigger takes her home, where, because of her drunken state, he is obliged to carry her bodily to her upstairs bedroom. Contemplating sexual possession of the girl, he is frightened by the approach of blind Mrs. Dalton. To insure his safety, he unintentionally smothers Mary to death with a pillow and subsequently burns her corpse in the furnace in an effort to remove all incriminatory evidence. To make his innocence appear doubly certain, he craftily involves Erlone and thereafter plans, with the unwilling co-operation of his concubine, Bessie Mears, to extract ransom from the Daltons. Eventually discovered in his guilt, Bigger flees and murders Bessie in order to remove the only person to whom he has confessed the crime, but is finally trapped after a vast manhunt throughout Chicago's Black Belt. In a hate-charged trial Bigger is finally sentenced to death in spite of an able plea for life imprisonment by Boris A. Max, an elderly Jewish lawyer who contends that ill-ordered American society, rather than Bigger himself, is responsible for the heinous and revolting murders committed by the accused. In the closing scene of the book Max appears in Bigger's cell, according to Wright, "to register the moral—or what *I* felt was the moral—horror of Negro life in the United States."[19]

The all-pervading thought of *Native Son* is that a prejudiced and capitalistic social order, rather than any intrinsic human deficiency, is the cause of the frustration and rebellion of underprivileged Negro youth of America. Attention is focused upon the paradoxical policy of Dalton, who contributes heavily to Negro education and simultaneously hems colored Chicagoans in a rotting slum area. Mention is made of the distrust of the Negro for real sympathy and understanding offered by well-intending white people. In Bigger's mother is typified the old-fashioned Negro's willingness to endure the trials and privations of this life because of the prospect of eternal happiness in the hereafter. Emphasis is placed, however, upon the injustices heaped upon the black population of the United States. Referring to American Negroes, Max, who is the author's mouthpiece, says:

"Taken collectively, they are not simply twelve million people; in reality, they constitute a separate nation, stunted, stripped, and held captive *within* this nation, devoid of political, social, economic, and property rights."

Thus limited and restricted, according to Max, the Negro feels resentment and fear for the entire white race and, thus conditioned psychologically, is always capable of viciousness and murder:

"Every time he comes in contact with us, he kills! It is a physiological and psychological reaction, embedded in his being. Every thought he thinks is potential murder. Excluded from, and unassimilated in our society, yet longing to gratify impulses akin to our own but denied the objects and channels evolved through long centuries for their socialized expression, every sunrise and sunset make him guilty of subversive actions. Every movement of his body is an unconscious protest. Every desire, every dream, no matter how intimate or personal, is a plot or a conspiracy. Every hope is a plan for insurrection. Every glance of the eye is a threat. His very existence is a crime against the state."

The slaying of Mary Dalton, therefore, is explained as a natural and inevitable act in a partisan society which considered Bigger guilty even before he took the girl's life. The responsibility for the crime is laid squarely upon the American people who, according to Wright, must decide whether this symbolic national product will ultimately be Fascist or Communist:

"Whether he'll follow some gaudy, hysterical leader who'll promise rashly to fill up the void in him, or whether he'll come to an understanding with the millions of his kindred fellow workers under trade union or revolutionary guidance depends upon the future drift of events in America. But, granting the emotional state, the tensity, the fear, the hate, the impatience, the sense of exclusion, the ache for violent action, the emotional and cultural hunger, Bigger's conditioned organism will not become an ardent, or even a lukewarm, supporter of the status quo."[20]

*Native Son,* the most perdurable and influential novel yet written by an American Negro, is at the same time one of the masterpieces of modern proletarian fiction. Taking as its leading character a traditional "bad-nigger" stereotype usually accepted as a representative Negro by misinformed whites and frequently viewed with nausea by supercilious blacks, the book seeks to show that the individual's delinquency is produced by a distorting environment rather than by innate criminality. Having this purpose, *Native Son* may rightly be regarded as the most significant probing of the plight of the lower-class Northern urban Negro in contemporary American literature. "Like *Grapes of Wrath,*" as Henry Seidel Canby has noted, "it is a fully realized story of unfortunates, uncompromisingly realistic, and quite as human as it is Negro."[21]

The foregoing criticism does not imply that *Native Son* is without blemishes and imperfections. Like certain other authors of proletarian fiction, Wright does not see the whole of life steadily and thoroughly: he sees only a segment of life, and even this limited part he views in its most violent and horrible aspects. To this restricted perspective may be traced the battering redundancy, the morbid melodrama, the overwrought excitement, and the inflated calamities that sometimes appear in his work. In his limited field, nevertheless, he is generally a realistic analyst and thoughtful interpreter of social ills and, above all other American novelists, is the sensitive painter and perspicacious spokesman of the inarticulate black millions of this country.

## IV. *FOLK REALISM*

During the Renascence the Northern metropolis was a more attractive background for the Negro writer of fiction than was the agricultural South. Jean Toomer's *Cane,* which ushered in the Renascence era, presented realistic pictures of folk life in rural Georgia, and Eric Walrond and Claude McKay gave authentic representations of folk life in the West Indies, but these paths were not the popular ones. Novelists of the 1920's were more concerned with caste and color among the urban bourgeoisie and with sex and the cabaret in Harlem than with the experiences of the black masses of the cotton belt.

During the depression decade, however, Negro fictionists, along with their white confreres, manifested a growing interest in the rural South. In *Jonah's Gourd Vine* (1934) and *Their Eyes Were Watching God* (1937) Zora Neale Hurston, an archaeologist and a favorite student of Dr. Franz Boas, treats characters and folklore of Alabama and Florida. George Wylie Henderson's *Ollie Miss* (1935), the first novel by a colored writer to concentrate upon the theme of sharecropping, deals with isolated Negro life in Georgia. George W. Lee's *River George* (1937) not only follows *Ollie Miss* in focusing upon sharecropping but also is the first novel by a Negro to handle at length the exploits of a legendary racial hero.[22] Mercedes Gilbert's *Aunt Sara's Wooden God* (1938), returning to the trite subject of miscegenation and intraracial color prejudice, contains scenes of life in Georgia.

### Zora Neale Hurston

Zora Neale Hurston—who has done important investigations in the folklore of the Southern United States, particularly Louisiana and her native Florida,[23] and of Jamaica and Haiti[24]—is also the author of *Jonah's Gourd Vine* (1934) and *Their Eyes Were Watching God* (1937), novels that reveal an unusual capacity for appropriating folklore to the purposes of fiction. The former work, having its setting in Alabama and Florida, presents as the leading character John Buddy Pearson, the illegitimate son of a white man and a Negro woman. Unjustly governed by his black stepfather, Pearson goes "over de Big Creek" to the plantation of a white boss who remembers the youth's mother as "a well-built-up girl and a splendid hoe-hand" and cannot "see why she married that darky and let him drag her around sharecropping." Given employment, Pearson becomes a valuable worker and the husband of an intelligent girl named Lucy. A series of illicit affairs finally results, however, in a brawl which forces Pearson to flee in order to escape punishment. Eventually settling in Eatonville, Florida,[25] Pearson sends for Lucy and, largely through her wise counsel, becomes a property-owner, a successful preacher, and mayor. His continued marital unfaithfulness, however, hastens the death of his wife. A subsequent marriage with a strumpet leads precipitately to a divorce trial, the repercussions of which force Pearson to give up his church in Sanford. Going to Plant City, the disgraced minister marries a prosperous and respectable widow who guides him to the pastorship of a large church, but an incontinent escapade with an Eatonville slut provokes him to such all-consuming self-condemnation that he drives headlong into a train and meets instant death.

Because of her ability to penetrate what Boas has termed "that affected demeanor by which the Negro excludes the white observer," Miss Hurston produces a more intimate transcript of folk life than that of Julia Peterkin. Convincing are her descriptions of railroad camps with their "hammer-muscling men, singers, dancers, liars, fighters, bluffers, and lovers," of the Northward surge of dark people during the World War I period, and of Negro churches with their emotional religion and corrupt politics. The peculiar idiom of folk speech and the "big old lies" of folk characters are competently handled. Less convincing is the development of character and the analysis of social problems. Racial difficulties never disturb the even tenor of the novel, and the Negro peons of the story are resigned to exploitation and oppression. Andrew Burris, therefore, is possibly correct in his observation that in *Jonah's Gourd Vine* Miss Hurston uses "her characters and the various situations created for them as mere pegs upon which to hang their dialect and folkways."[26]

In her second novel, *Their Eyes Were Watching God* (1937), Miss Hurston displays not only a gift for handling folk material but also a better grasp of character and setting. Janie, an octoroon born out of wedlock, is the heroine of the story. After marrying an elderly farmer in order to please her grandmother, she deserts him in order to elope with Joe Starks to the colored town of Eatonville. Here Starks becomes landlord, storekeeper, and mayor, but develops such an absorption in self that he loses the affection of his wife. After Starks's death Janie is wooed and won by Tea Cake, a happy-go-lucky gambler and itinerant worker with whom she finds love and happiness. Together they enjoy an adventurous life until Tea Cake, bitten by a mad dog during a Lake Okechobee hurricane, contracts hydrophobia. Forced to kill her maddened husband in order to save her own life, Janie is later exonerated and returns to Eatonville.

In addition to painting vivid pictures of social life in Eatonville, gambling dives in Jacksonville, and bean-picking communities in the Everglades, *Their Eyes Were Watching God* mirrors more effectively than does *Jonah's Gourd Vine* the social tension of the Southern scene. Effectively rooting her narrative in the past, Miss Hurston recounts how Janie's slave grandmother, having borne a child by her master, fled from his vengeful wife. The Lake Okechobee hurricane episode, like Richard Wright's "Down by the Riverside" in *Uncle Tom's Children,* illustrates that prejudice thrives in times of disaster. During the fierce storm, for example, whites pre-empt elevated points and afterwards bury their dead individually in pine boxes while ordering Negro fatalities to be dumped wholesale into pits.

*Their Eyes Were Watching God* also studies intraracial color prejudice. Mrs. Turner, a disciple of Nordicism whom Janie meets in the Everglades, brings to mind Olivia Cary of *Comedy: American Style*. Possessing Caucasian features, she idolizes these traits in others and despises Negroid characteristics. Viewing intermixture with horror, she thinks that light-skinned colored people should first seek union with whites or, if this is impossible, should establish a separate and distinct mulatto caste. She admires her brother, who considers Booker T. Washington a "white folks' nigger." Disregarding snubs and mistreatment, she grovels before whiteness and simultaneously subjects dark folk to insult and humiliation.

In general, Miss Hurston is more interested in folklore and dialect than in social criticism. Neglecting the racial tensions which attracted many of those with whom she associated during the Negro Renascence, she usually presents Southern folk life without shame, rancor, or protest.

### George Wylie Henderson

In *Ollie Miss* (1935) George Wylie Henderson becomes the first Negro to write a novel which focuses upon sharecropping. In so doing, however, Henderson avoids racial problems and conflict. Only two white characters are introduced—the one, the sheriff of a small Alabama town, and the other, a store proprietor—and neither is permitted to be obtrusive. The main character of the novel is Ollie Miss, a copper-hued young woman who can plow, hoe, and swing an axe like a man. Though taciturn and tight-lipped, Ollie has a certain fascination over men, especially when she is drinking corn liquor and twisting her slender hips to voluptuous dance rhythms. Deserted by her lover Jule, Ollie gains employment as a sharecropper on the cotton farm of Uncle Alex. Though sought by the males on the place, she remains loyal to Jule, but her faithfulness is not reciprocated. After Jule uses a camp meeting as a pretext for visiting Ollie, Lena, his other woman, tracks him down and slashes her rival with a razor. Upon recovering from her wounds, Ollie refuses either to prosecute her assailant or to marry Jule, although she is about to bear him a child. At the end of the novel Ollie is confidently looking forward to rearing her offspring on a ten-acre tract given her by Uncle Alex.

Life in *Ollie Miss* is unruffled by problems of race. Emphasis is placed upon farm activities, with occasional picnics, ball games, parties, and camp meetings providing a diversion from the workaday routine. The chief discordant influences are the prying meddlesomeness of impertinent gossips and the spirited fights of jealous lovers. Though Henderson's recording of rural life among sharecroppers of the Black Belt is to be commended for its detachment, the story is too much dissociated from the grim realities of Southern life. As Alain Locke observes:

> The depression has broken this peasant Arcady, even in the few places where it still persisted, and while it is humanly interesting and refreshing enough, . . . it is so extinct that our only possible approach to it is the idyllic and retrospective.[27]

## George W. Lee

Like *Ollie Miss,* George W. Lee's *River George* (1937) treats the lives of Negro sharecroppers in the deep South, but here the similarity ends. *Ollie Miss,* evading racial issues, presents black landowners and sharecroppers far removed from the interference of whites. Lee's work, on the other hand, provides a more realistic depiction of Negro tenant farmers in their relations with one another and with white members of the community. Deriving much of its plot from the life of a semi-legendary Mississippi River rouster discussed in Lee's earlier book, *Beale Street: Where the Blues Began* (1934),[28] *River George* offers as a hero a Mississippi college student who hopes that through the practice of law he may help to free his race "from a bitter bondage which did not end with the signing of the Emancipation Proclamation." George is keenly aware of the hardships of the Negro:

> "It is a battle with the majority of the whites, who insist on holding up, as most representative of the Negro, his worst, rather than his best. It is a battle with the majority of the Negroes themselves who crucify their own kind upon a cross of indifference or desire for personal gain through gaining favor with the whites; it is a battle with one's own self in which one is forced to accept life on a lower level and yet keep faith with his highest convictions. It is a battle against despair, life's deadliest sin."

Shunted from his professional ambitions by the death of his father, George assumes support of his mother and becomes a sharecropper on the Beaver Dam Plantation. He gives up his work, however, upon being cheated by the plantation bookkeeper and upon discovering that Ada Smith, the woman he loves, is the mistress of Fred Smith, "a mean-faced, mean-souled white man." George's efforts to organize the Negro tenant farmers of the district lead directly to a fight with Smith, who is determined not to share his concubine "with any nigger." After killing his opponent George flees to Memphis, where he lives with Annie Bell, proprietress of a Beale Street brothel, until detectives learn of his whereabouts. The fugitive next joins the Army with the hope that the Negro, after fighting beside the white man to preserve democracy, will receive justice in America. After the Armistice, however, the activities of the Ku Klux Klan convince him that Annie was right when she said:

"Don't fool yourself. If you go over there to fight and get back here, so far as this man's country is concerned, you'll still be a nigger and you'll still be treated like a nigger."

Returning to America, George spends a short while in Harlem and then, with the hope of getting in touch with his mother and Ada, goes to Vicksburg, Mississippi, which he is forced to leave because of resentment for his officer's uniform. In Memphis he is captured by a Negro detective but makes a daring escape. Getting work as a Mississippi River rouster, he establishes himself as a notorious bad man by defeating Black Bill. During a southward trip on a steamboat George is recognized by three white passengers and later lynched by a Mississippi mob for the murder of Smith.

In its earlier chapters *River George* authentically portrays Negro sharecroppers who work from dawn to dusk throughout the year and derive their chief diversion from Saturday night breakdowns and Sunday religious excesses. Revealing the tension between overlords and peons of the Cotton Belt, the novel shows how black workers are fleeced and oppressed. In an effort to escape the tyranny of the system the tenants in some cases seek to gain equitable settlement and long-time contracts; but migration to Northern industrial centers, where higher wages and better living conditions are available, is the more popular alternative.

Almost as well developed as the sharecropping background is the Beale Street setting, where George lives as a fugitive after fleeing from Beaver Dam Plantation. In this "Blues Heben" river rats, rousters, rustics, and spruce city dandies mingle in an atmosphere reeking with corn liquor and barbecue. With George we visit the Panama, Hammett's Place, the Hole in the Wall, the Monarch, Peewee's Place, and the voodoo headquarters of Mary the Wonder, each of which the author knew firsthand. Less intimately done is the description of Harlem, where George spends two days; and altogether neglected is the presentation of the European scene, where he gives over a year of service in the United States Army. *River George* is chiefly important, therefore, for its exposure of the abuses of the tenant farmer system.

### Mercedes Gilbert

Mercedes Gilbert's *Aunt Sara's Wooden God* (1938) is a study of miscegenation and color prejudice. Unlike most novels handling these themes, this work is neither bitter nor preoccupied with racial issues. Aunt Sara, the last of several generations of mulatto mistresses of men of the aristocratic Gordon family, is the mother of two sons—the older, William, her "wooden god," by her white lover, Franklyn Gordon, and the younger, Jim, by her colored husband, John Carter. She is extremely partial to William: "He was her God. Next to her religion she worshipped him." Groomed by his mother for the ministry, William is sent from Byron, Georgia, his home town, to attend high school in Macon. There he commits a crime and, in an attempt to evade conviction, pins the guilt upon his half-brother, who is imprisoned and sent to the chain gang. Going to a lumber camp with his ex-prostitute mistress, William is fatally wounded in a brawl with another laborer. Though cognizant of the treachery which sent him to the chain gang, Jim does not disillusion doting Aunt Sara by disclosing his half-brother's villainy and lawlessness.

Erskine Caldwell has illustrated that rural Georgia is a treasure-trove of literary material. In *Aunt Sara's Wooden God* Miss Gilbert, though presenting a theme and setting rich with dramatic possibilities, inexpertly portrays Georgia and the folk who dwell there.

## V. *THE NEGRO COLLEGE*

The Negro college has received much incidental treatment in novels and short stories by American Negroes. Prior to World

War I many authors, wishing to provide a complimentary portrayal of racial life and character, gave passing but much too flattering attention to the Negro college. During the Negro Renascence and the depression years several writers probed into the workings of these schools and offered a more realistic rendering of conditions in them. It was not until the appearance of O'Wendell Shaw's *Greater Need Below* in 1936, however, that a full-length novel on Negro college life was published. Unfortunately, this pioneering work is weakened by sensationalism that taxes the credulity of the reader.

### O'Wendell Shaw

O'Wendell Shaw's *Greater Need Below,* the only American novel devoted entirely to the portrayal of life in the Southern state college for Negroes, is a bitter invective against this particular type of institution. Stating that his book is based upon experiences gained during four years of service as a faculty member in such a school as well as upon reports of happenings in similar colleges, the author declares in his foreword that *Greater Need Below* "was not written in an effort to reform these schools of certain conditions as here depicted; rather, the aim is merely to present a few interesting scenes from the 'inside' of a life which must needs be of vital interest to thousands of people." This statement denying motives of reform is not corroborated in the novel, for the author tells a lurid, sensational story which strongly suggests that he desired corrective measures.

Shaw's exposé of the Southern tax-supported school for Negroes is constructed around the early career of Ellen Vance, who, upon completing her studies at a Northern university and observing the limited vocational opportunities for colored teachers in that area, decides to go South to instruct Negro youth because there is "greater need below." Accepting a position at $100.00 per month as head of the Music Department of Avon State College, Ellen finds herself in the most vicious educational system imaginable. In this corrupt school Jesse Sales, treasurer of the institution and also its real boss, makes dates between colored women on the campus and white men in the community. As a result of Sales' activities as a procurer, Madge Conley, Ellen's roommate, is raped by a white citizen and eventually dies of an abortion; and the dean of women is fatally shot because of a belated attempt to expel Gail Hinds, a student, for illicit intercourse with a white man. Other liaisons involve the principal's wife and Madge's ravisher and the principal himself and Gail. After learning too much concerning the private lives of debauched officials, Ellen leaves Avon State College and marries DeWalt Brooks, a former colleague who had earlier resigned because he could not tolerate the school. At the close of the novel DeWalt is head of the Anice Vance College of Practical Negro Education, a school established by Ellen's mother with profits earned from a successful venture in the manufacture of toilet preparations.

Shaw paints a dismal picture of the Negro tax-supported institution. Mention has been made of clandestine sexual relationships involving teachers, students, and white citizens; but this is only one of the many depressing scenes on the author's canvas. State legislators insult Negroes and show inordinate fondness for slave songs. School administrators demonstrate ignorance, inefficiency, intimidation of staff and students, and obsequious deference to white political leaders. Teachers are primarily interested in advanced degrees, Greek-letter organizations, and salary checks. Students are young people determined to get by easily, unconcerned about helping their race, and having little initiative and culture. As an exemplary contrast to this demoralized institution, Shaw proposes a school, such as the one founded by Ellen's mother, "which would not be dependent upon philanthropy from outside the Negro race; thus, one which would be free to disperse an education especially designed for the problems confronting Negroes." Further describing this school, Shaw says:

"There would be no prejudiced white officials out of whom appropriations must be wheedled by way of various and sundry forms of 'bootlicking'! There would be no 'Simon Legrees' constantly brandishing a psychological whip over its purposeful and sincere faculty members! Negro youth would be taught the true meaning of manhood and womanhood; they would leave this institution bubbling over with enthusiasm and initiative—ready to grapple with, and solve, the vital problems of their race!"

In *Greater Need Below* Shaw writes as an embittered propagandist, and his story has the usual exaggerations of biased works. Although there are many inferior colleges for Negroes in the South, it is doubtful that there has ever been one so completely degenerate as Avon State. Perhaps the main service of the book will be to indicate the rich field which the Negro college affords for writers of fiction.

## VI. *FAMILY CHRONICLE*

Negro life in the United States is a rich field for family chronicle. Slavery, emancipation, enfranchisement, disfranchisement, segregation, prejudice, and oppression have given the American Negro family genuine distinctiveness in the national scene and limitless possibilities for fictional treatment. In general, however, writers have neglected this material; and Waters Edward Turpin, the author of *These Low Grounds* (1937) and *O Canaan!* (1939), was the only Negro novelist of the period who was actively at work in family chronicle.

### Waters Edward Turpin

In *These Low Grounds* (1937) and *O Canaan!* (1939) Waters Edward Turpin is the chronicler of the Negro family in the United States. The former novel, depicting four aspiring matriarchs who strive and endure in order that their progeny may have a richer life, is a study of a Maryland family through four generations and as many migrations. Opening in Baltimore just before the Civil War, the narrative launches into the story of Martha, who makes great sacrifices in order to establish her husband in business and give her daughter Carrie an education. Martha breaks under her heavy burden; but Carrie rises from a brothel to become the wife of Jim Prince, a respectable farmer from Maryland's Eastern Shore, and the mother of three children—young Jim, Blanche, and Martha. Though the family gains material prosperity, its happiness is overcast successively by the death of Prince's father, the lynching of a Negro youth, the questionable legitimacy of Martha's birth, the death of young Jim, and the philandering of Prince. Becoming restless and provoked because of her husband's unfaithfulness, Carrie goes to Herdford, where she consorts first with Jake Tillery, who had earlier contributed to the disintegration of her father, and then with Lew Grundy, a married man from the nearby town of Belfort. When Carrie determines to take Martha to visit Prince during the Christmas holidays, Grundy jealously murders his mistress in cold blood.

After Carrie's death Martha becomes the central character. Joining her father and sister in Shrewsbury, she pains them by falling in love with Grundy's son, Jimmy-Lew. After Jimmy-Lew loses his life in an effort to rescue a child from the path of a train, Martha flees to Philadelphia to escape the disgrace of becoming an unmarried mother in her home town. Subsequently acclaimed as a theatrical performer, she undertakes to educate young Jimmy-Lew but dies during his freshman year in college. After graduation Jimmy-Lew marries Ellen Miles, henceforth the most important woman in the action. As teachers the young couple work for the uplift of their people; but Jimmy-Lew is disheartened and embittered by the unfair distribution of educational appropriations, the lynching of a Negro laborer in Shrewsbury,[29] and the spinelessness of colored citizens. Ellen consoles her husband, however, with the following words of hope:

"We've love to give each other, and the right to live here in these Low Grounds, as your grandfather calls them. We belong here as much as the other groups of Americans, Jimmy-Lew. We're no more or less than the other Americans. We're just people . . . all of us . . . North, South, East, West . . . white, black, brown, yellow . . . we're just people . . . Americans. . . . And in our working, our loving, our sorrowing, and our dying we are making the America of Now and Tomorrow, just as we helped to make it Yesterday."

Though Ellen's counsel is optimistic, Jimmy-Lew is not altogether converted,[30] and in general the book strikes a note of futility. Though the first Martha, Carrie, and the second Martha toil bravely, neither they nor their menfolk gain happiness and security; and Ellen, while practical and patient, seems destined to be overcome along with Jimmy-Lew in "these low grounds of sorrow." Nevertheless there is an epical quality in the way these characters struggle in order that they and their progeny may enjoy a better life.

*These Low Grounds* provides authentic depiction of Maryland's Eastern Shore. The oyster- and crab-industry towns are well drawn, and the folkways and dialect of their inhabitants are convincingly rendered. In the representation of the urban scenes of Baltimore, Philadelphia, and New York City, however, Turpin is not skilful. Furthermore, in many instances the novel, neglecting character analysis and social documentation, assumes the nature of a précis, for the author treats summarily such subjects as slavery, the Civil War, Reconstruction, World War I, "the roaring twenties," and the depression. These and numerous other subjects, more adequately handled, would have given the book a firmer footing in American life.

Just as *These Low Grounds* is trail-blazing in its treatment of folk life in the coastal lowlands of Maryland, so *O Canaan!* is pioneering in its study of a Negro family through the World War I migration, the boom years, and the depression. The central character is Joe Benson, a sturdy sharecropper who takes his wife and five children from rural Mississippi to Chicago's South Side. In this urban environment Benson becomes a prosperous merchant and an influential citizen, his wife Christine receives recognition as a respectable matron, his daughter Connie marries a promising young physician, and his son Lem prepares for a professional career as a social worker. The stock market débâcle of 1929, however, wreaks havoc in the lives of the Bensons. Ruined by the crash of a bank in which he had invested his savings, Benson has a nervous breakdown but recovers sufficiently to gain employment as a Pullman porter. During these lean years Christine has an illicit affair with a roomer in the home, Lem succumbs to tuberculosis, Connie accepts a teaching position in order to supplement her husband's income, and young Joe dies of syphilis. The most enterprising member of the family during this dark period is Essie, a daughter who falls in love with Paul Johnson, Jim Prince's youngest grandson, who came from Harlem to seek economic security in Chicago. At first postponing marriage because of their insecure financial condition, the young pair are at length forced to wed because of Essie's pregnancy. Unaware of Benson's success in arranging a tavern business which would have supplied Johnson with the funds necessary for the care of the child, Essie submits to an abortion. At the close of the novel the couple, inspired by the fortitude of Benson, vow to cling to one another while striving forward.

Passing rapidly over the setting of Three Forks, Mississippi—with its poor crops, lynchings, liaisons, and prejudices—*O Canaan!* moves into a treatment of the Negro migration and of racial life in Chicago from the World War I period to the middle thirties. At first fascinated by their new-found Promised Land, the incoming black hordes soon feel the disadvantages of their environment. Forced to pay high rents for overcrowded dwellings because of a pressing housing demand intensified by white resistance to Negro residential encroachment, the hapless migrants suffer as a result of unstable family life, gambling, bootlegging, prostitution, and other social cancers. In this blighted and restricted setting, interracial tension grows increasingly acute until the outbreak of the Chicago riot of 1919, in which Benson's son Sol loses his life.

During the depression conditions are aggravated by unemployment, bank failures, mortgages, starvation, and other forms of human misery. The transplanted unfortunates find in their religion "an emotional cathartic and an anesthesia against the pain of reality." In this grim urban environment, just as in "these low grounds of sorrow," the weak perish. Johnson possibly furnishes a statement of the viewpoint of the author when he remarks: "It's a fight for survival, that's all. You've got to fight to live."

The belated introduction of Johnson into the plot of *O Canaan!* gave Turpin an opportunity to include Harlem on his canvas, for the young hero came to Chicago from New York City. The picture that Turpin paints of Harlem, however, is neither comprehensive nor penetrating. The author is primarily interested in the young colored college men who, shunning the hate-charged atmosphere of the South and seeking the temporary pleasures of a metropolitan center, are described as follows by Johnson:

"And there are thousands of fellows like myself—college-bred, supposedly intelligent, and with abilities, yet they're throwing themselves away—chasing phantoms! They're romanticists instead of being realists, that's the trouble. They want to start big and stay big—scrambling after degrees, unwilling to work up in some drudging occupation which supplies the world's needs. Then when they wind up as failures they very often hide behind the bugaboo of race! . . ."

Like *These Low Grounds, O Canaan!* has a hurried narration that frequently takes on the qualities of a prose outline. "The author's style," as Ulysses Lee observes, "is loose and journalistic—journalistic in the nineteenth century manner. Crises come and go in the space of a few paragraphs of rapid, orchidaceous writing."[31] In *Native Son* Richard Wright shows a power of intensity and documentation that Turpin lacks. Yet Turpin's two novels establish him as a noteworthy chronicler of the Negro family in the United States.

## VII. *THE MIGRANT WORKER*

During the 1930's novelists manifested growing interest in the American migrant worker. John Steinbeck's *The Grapes of Wrath* (1939), which treats the tragic journey of a group of destitute farmers from Oklahoma to California, is indicative of this interest. William Attaway, whose first novel was *Let Me Breathe Thunder* (1939), was more active than any other Negro fiction writer of the period in the presentation of the problems of the transient laborer.

### William Attaway

William Attaway's *Let Me Breathe Thunder* (1939), which shows the influence of John Steinbeck, is primarily concerned with the experiences of Step and Ed, white boys whose outlook upon life has been hardened by underprivileged childhood and precarious vagrancy, and of Hi Boy, a spirited ten-year-old Mexican youngster. The action begins with the arrival of the trio in Seattle, where Step has a fight with the bouncer of an underground dive. Fearing vengeance, the transients board a Northern Pacific passenger train for the wheat lands of Kansas and meet Sampson, a Yakima Valley farmer, who persuades them to accept employment on his farm. Step at once deflowers Anna, Sampson's daughter, and establishes a rendezvous with her at a Yakima house of ill repute maintained by Mag, a colored prostitute. When the migrants finish their work on the farm, Anna arranges a final meeting with Step at Mag's place and is there attacked by Cooper, the Negro woman's "sweet man." In an attempt to shoot her unfaithful lover, Mag inflicts an arm wound upon Anna, who frantically rushes into the street and exposes Step as well as Cooper. Fearing Sampson's reaction, the wanderers catch a Northern Pacific freight and on the next morning find Cooper in the same box car with them. Step wants to throw Cooper from the train, but Ed insists that the Negro be given an opportunity to explain his motives. After Cooper says that he only intended to make Mag jealous, Step relents his fury but demands that the Negro get off at the next stop. As the train moves toward the Montana Rockies, Hi Boy suffers from an infection earlier received when he plunged a fork into his hand to prove his strength and fortitude. After almost freezing in the sleet, the itinerants change to a train en route to Denver, but Hi Boy dies before medical aid can be procured.

In *Let Me Breath Thunder* references to Negroes and racial issues are merely incidental. Nevertheless, among the best realized characters in the book are Mag, Cooper, and Black Face, the last-named being a hobo found by the travelers on a freight during the final lap of their journey to Yakima. The chief merit of the book is its realistic treatment of one of the aspects of the American youth problem. Step and Ed, warped personalities without benefit of home and school background, are doomed even before young manhood to the irregular and unstable life of those who are without settled habitation. Hi Boy, who escaped to join Step and Ed after a Mexican family with whom he was traveling was thrown from a train and arrested for burglary, is probably prevented by early death from acquiring the distorted social perspective of an indurate vagrant. Attaway does not undertake to offer a remedy for the maladjustment which he discloses; he simply describes life as he sees it. Ed laments starvation in the midst of plenty, and Sampson attributes much of the vagabondage of American youth to the depression. Cooper, however, traces social ills to hate:

> "It don't make no difference where you go, they always hating somebody somewhere. All along from Texas through New Mexico they hate Mexes worse'n a snake; down in lower California they get like mad dogs if you mention Japs; I ain't never been far east, but they say that out there everybody hates everybody else."

## VIII. *SUMMARY*

In Negro fiction, just as in other branches of national literature, the depression decade witnessed radical revisions in styles, themes, and attitudes. The Harlem obsession passed with "the roaring twenties," and during the 1930's there appeared a literature that was chiefly realistic, historical, sociological, or proletarian. Self-preening and propagandistic racialism became less prevalent, as writers increasingly took cognizance of basic human and social values. As a result, more than ever before Negro fiction became integrated with the main stream of American literature.

Though limited in volume of output, Negro fiction of the depression period made noteworthy departures from the well-trod paths of earlier years. Bontemps revealed the comparatively untapped resources of Negro history, and Daly suggested the possibilities of a World War I novel from the black man's point of view. In the proletarian school Hughes and Wright became spokesmen for the Negro, and the latter's *Native Son* won general recognition as the best novel by a Negro in American literature. Turning from the cultured bourgeoisie of the metropolitan scene, Miss Hurston, Henderson, Lee, and Miss Gilbert produced transcripts of folk life in the South. Exposing facts and also exaggerating them, Shaw showed the worst aspects of the state-supported college for Negroes. Turpin pointed to the untold wealth of Negro family chronicle. Disentangling himself from racial limitations, Attaway ably explored the problems of the migrant worker, objectively presenting the Negro as an integral rather than as a detached personality in the social order. Because of the efforts of the abler novelists of the depression period, Negro fiction gained a sounder and a stronger foundation upon which to build in future years.

CHAPTER 7

# Conclusion

## I. *RETROSPECT*

ALTHOUGH the Civil War gave the Negro emancipation, the dark years of Reconstruction and disfranchisement proved to him that the long campaign for justice and equality was still to be waged. The Ku Klux Klan dedicated itself to the maintenance of racial absolutism in the South, while segregation and discriminatory legislation practically disrobed the freedman of power and influence. In Southern literature the retrospective romancers of the Thomas Nelson Page school fascinated the country with idealization of the ante-bellum plantation, while the Negrophobe sensationalists of the Thomas Dixon cult demonstrated that the mob spirit could exist in letters as in life. Having won the Civil War, the North gave more attention to industrialism than to social justice.

Forced to become race-conscious by the nature and pressure of their environment, Negro fictionists of the nineteenth and of the first two decades of the twentieth century usually neglected art for propaganda and undertook to provide a literary defense for their people. Viewing slavery from afar, they carried on the Abolitionist tradition by attacking bondage and illustrating the fact that plantation life was not a state of perfect contentment. Generally preferring the equal-rights crusade of Frederick Douglass and W. E. B. DuBois to the conciliatory program of Booker T. Washington, they made impassioned appeals for justice, apologized for the failings and paid tribute to the successes of Negroes, and assailed the citadel of Nordicism. In general, they used the pattern of the vicious white man and the virtuous Negro, the former the victimizer and the latter the victim. In stating their cases these writers were the public prosecutors of racism. Though sometimes manifesting affection for the slaveholding aristocracy, they rarely showed sympathy for poor whites, their fellow sufferers in Southern economy. The race-motivated approach of these authors engendered a frequent use of stereotyped characters and situations as well as a treatment just as one-sided as that of the Negrophobe propagandists.

World War I—causing a large-scale migration of black men to Northern industrial centers, a broadening of Negro experience through travel in the North and in Europe, and the propagation of principles of self-determination for racial and national groups—accelerated the cultural emancipation of the Negro. The Garvey Movement—which glorified blackness, fostered pride in Africa, and agitated for Negro freedom—developed a proud and assertive racialism among the black masses of the country. Almost simultaneously the rediscovery of African art and the disclosure of other complimentary information concerning the racial past spurred an upsurge of race pride among the Negro intelligentsia. This mounting racialism—coupled with a more sympathetic interest of white writers in Negro life, a more liberal attitude of white readers and publishers toward Negro subject matter, a more widespread interest in Harlem, and the appearance of a talented group of young colored writers—made the Negro a national vogue.

The intermingling of writers of both races, though often characterized by a spirit of bohemian camaraderie, brought the Negro author into contact with the leading circles of American literature. Moreover, the less biased handling of Negro materials by white authors modified the channelized and race-motivated approach which Negro writers had customarily used before World War I. Whereas American Negro fiction of pre-World War I years was devoted almost entirely to racial defense and advertisement, that of the Renascence period at least introduced a wider range of creative activity, a greater diversity of techniques and ideologies, and a keener appreciation for universal values. Realistic portraiture was done of Southern folk life, the Mid-Western small town, Harlem, and West Indian peasant experience. Analysis was made of the problems of color and caste among the bourgeoisie of the metropolitan North. Agitation for racial justice was conducted on an international as well as a national or sectional basis. Attention was directed to the primitivistic and exotic aspects of Negro life in Harlem. Rollicking satire was employed to attack the American race problem.

After the economic crash of 1929, however, the literary pendulum began to swing away from the subject matter and attitudes which had been popular during the Renascence period. Bringing sweeping changes, the depression ushered in the dawn of a new era. Under the pressure of the financial crisis and of progressive and radical philosophies, racialism yielded ground to proletarianism, liberalism, and democratic ideology. The Negro author began to look at life from a social rather than from an ethnocentric viewpoint and to understand that suffering is not restrictively racial but broadly human: he began to see that Jeeter Lester, Studs Lonigan, Tom Joad, and Bigger Thomas are each and all victims of social and economic dislocation. As a result of this more comprehensive outlook, Negro writers placed less emphasis upon color and manifested more concern about the problems of the miserable masses than about those of maladjusted mulattoes and the "Talented Tenth." Though continuing to treat chiefly of Negro characters and experience, they often viewed their materials from a liberal perspective that did not betray race-consciousness. The trend from racialism was expedited by several white writers who fearlessly threw the spotlight upon the harshness and tragedy of Negro life.

In brief, American Negro fiction mirrors the life and thought of the emancipated colored race in the United States. Besides analyzing the psychology and recounting the experiences of individual Negroes, these novels and short stories depict the colored race passing through slavery, the Civil War, Reconstruction, disfranchisement, World War I, the "Roaring Twenties," and the depression decade. These works also show the reaction of the Negro mind to the plantation tradition, Nordicism, realism, naturalism, primitivism, regionalism, proletarianism, and other significant movements in American literature. As such, this body of writing, though generally lacking the distinction that qualifies art of universal value and appeal, is an important branch of national literature describing an important aspect of national life from an important point of view.

## II. *PROSPECT*

The American Negro author, like all other writers in the world today, is in an uncertain position. The social order is in flux; the old mode of living is collapsing; the society of tomorrow is not yet definable. Nevertheless, if democratic forces subdue the powers that advocate racial oppression, certain predictions concerning the future may justifiably be made.

First, we may forecast that both white and colored writers will continue to exploit the limitless fictional resources of Negro life in the United States. In the past, authors of both races have traveled the main highways. As a result, there remains a treasure-trove of literary material for those who will leave the roads that have been popular in earlier years. The editors of *The Negro Caravan* were cognizant of this fact when they commented:

> Great areas of Negro life remain unexplored, many of them even untouched. The Negro working class, the various strata of the Negro middle class; urban life in both the South and North (outside Harlem) are some of these areas. Even the fields covered—the rural South and Harlem—still call for interpreters. There are many Harlems, for instance, a long way from Van Vechten's *Nigger Heaven,* that could furnish backgrounds for good novels. There is little fiction dealing with college life, with the Negro professional class, with the Negro church, business, white-collar employment, or with Negroes in entertainment and athletics.[1]

Second, we may predict that the Negro writer will obtain full membership in the American literary fraternity. Up to the present the Negro author has dealt almost entirely with the colored race and its relations in the American social order. To a certain extent this preoccupation has been inevitable, because the circumstances of our national life have practically forced expression from a racial point of view, and necessary, because an artist always writes most effectively about what he knows best and feels deepest. This racial circumscription, however, has handicapped the Negro writer in his dealings with his audience and the major publishers. Langston Hughes, one of the better-known contemporary Negro authors, crystallizes most of the difficulties with the publishing world in the following statement:

> Here are our problems: In the first place, Negro books are considered by editors and publishers as exotic. Negro material is placed, like Chinese material or Bali material or East Indian material, into a certain classification. Magazine editors will tell you, "We can use but so many Negro stories a year." (That "so many" meaning very few.) Publishers will say, "We already have one Negro novel on our list this fall."
>
> The market for Negro writers, then, is definitely limited as long as we write about ourselves. And the more truthfully we write about ourselves, the more limited our market becomes. Those novels about Negroes that sell best, by Negroes or whites, those novels that make the best seller lists and receive the leading prizes, are almost always books that touch very lightly upon the facts of Negro life, books that make our black ghettos in the big cities seem very happy places indeed, and our plantations in the deep South idyllic in their pastoral loveliness. . . . When we cease to be exotic, we cease to sell.[2]

But troubles with publishers are not all: there are also troubles with the audience. On the one hand, many prejudiced white readers strongly object to full and honest treatment of Negro life; and, on the other, a large number of Negroes, rendered hypersensitive by years of discrimination and oppression, shrink from anything other than a flattering portrayal of the race. The criticism of numerous Negro readers, as Sterling Brown indicates, is vitiated by at least four fallacies:

> We look upon Negro books regardless of the author's intention, as representative of all Negroes, i.e., as sociological documents.
> We insist that Negro books must be idealistic, optimistic tracts for race advertisement.
> We are afraid of truth telling, of satire.
> We criticize from the point of view of bourgeois America, of racial apologists.[3]

In spite of the foregoing considerations, the prospect is not dark. A growing number of Negro writers, some of them not now widely known, enjoy an encouraging measure of colleagueship and support in American literary circles. The success of Richard Wright demonstrates that a Negro author having technical skill and a profound message may get his work before an appreciative, nation-wide audience. In addition, the recent publication of Frank Yerby's *The Foxes of Harrow* (1946) and *The Vixens* (1947) and of Willard Motley's *Knock on Any Door* (1947) suggests that Negro writers will increasingly treat other phases of American life than the problems of a segregated minority. These three books, which deal primarily with white characters and were advertised on their merits and without reference to the complexion of their creators, signalize the gradual emancipation of Negro writers from preoccupation with strictly racial subject matter and the developing power of these authors to treat competently not only the various aspects of Negro experience but also the broader life of this country and of the world. In general, therefore, it is reasonable to expect that Negro writers of the future will extricate themselves from the limitations of color and stand independently as artists, interpreting racial difficulties in universal terms and providing a comprehensive representation of life.

# Notes

## *CHAPTER* 1

1. Benjamin Brawley, *A Social History of the American Negro* (New York, 1921), p. 262.

2. *Ibid.*

3. Carter G. Woodson, *The Negro in Our History* (Washington, 1941), p. 431.

4. W. E. B. DuBois, *The Souls of Black Folk* (Chicago, 1902), p. 35.

5. Shields McIlwaine, *The Southern Poor White* (Norman, Oklahoma, 1939), pp. 82-83.

6. Benjamin Brawley, *A Short History of the American Negro* (New York, 1931), p. 150.

7. Woodson, *op. cit.*, pp. 412-13.

8. V. F. Calverton, *The Liberation of American Literature* (New York, 1932), p. 332.

9. Oscar Cargill, ed., *The Social Revolt 1888-1914* (New York, 1933), p. 1.

10. Calverton, *op. cit.*, pp. 105-6; Vernon Louis Parrington, *The Beginnings of Critical Realism in America* (New York, 1933), p. 4.

11. Henry W. Grady, *Complete Orations and Speeches* (New York, 1910), pp. 17-18.

12. Brawley, *A Short History of the American Negro*, pp. 151-52. Also see Woodson, *op. cit.*, pp. 418-19.

13. F. P. Gaines, *The Southern Plantation* (New York, 1924), p. 62.

14. *Ibid.*, p. 77.

15. *Ibid.*, p. 62. The persistence of the agrarian tradition is indicated in its recent defense by Southern intellectuals in *I'll Take My Stand* (1930).

16. Thomas Nelson Page, *The Negro: The Southerner's Problem* (New York, 1904), p. 309.

17. *Ibid.*, pp. 5-6.

18. Thomas Nelson Page, *The Old South* (New York, 1892), p. 344.

19. Thomas Dixon, Jr., *The Clansman* (New York, 1905), p. v.

20. The short stories by Cable, Miss King, Mrs. Chopin, Harris, Miss Crim, and Johnston which are discussed in this section—along with such narratives as Harris' "Blue Dave," "Free Joe and the Rest of the World," and "Mom Bi"; Ruth McEnery Stuart's "The Golden Wedding and Old Easter"; Miss King's "Bayou l'Ombre"; Harry Stillwell Edwards' "De Val-

ley and de Shadder"; Mary Virginia Terhune's "Marthy"; Will N. Harben's "The Whipping of Uncle Henry" and "A Humble Abolitionist"; and Maurice Thompson's "Race Romance"—indicate that scattered Southern stories sometimes vary in different degrees from the popular patterns and puppets of the plantation tradition. In this connection Ben Gray Lumpkin, who has made a classification and enumeration of two hundred Negro characters created by white authors, states:

". . . Many of the Negro characters in the Southern short stories display a degree of independence and spirit, a sense of honesty and reliability, and a pride in accomplishment which are not hinted at by the traditional types. In these respects the Negro characters in Southern fiction cannot be correctly lumped with the conventional, traditional stock types which were developed in other literary forms."

See Ben Gray Lumpkin, *Diversity in the Characters Portrayed in Southern Regional Short Stories of the Nineteenth Century,* an unpublished thesis in the library of the University of North Carolina, p. 350.

21. Booker T. Washington, *My Larger Education* (New York, 1911), p. 106.

22. Booker T. Washington, *Selected Speeches* (New York, 1932), p. 34.

23. Letter to the editor of *The New York World,* September 19, 1895.

24. Grover Cleveland, *Letters 1850-1908* (New York, 1933), p. 413.

25. DuBois, *op. cit.*, p. 52.

26. W. E. B. DuBois, *Dusk of Dawn* (New York, 1940), pp. 88-89.

27. W. E. B. DuBois, "Editorial," *The Crisis,* I (1910), 10.

28. W. E. B. DuBois, *A Pageant in Seven Decades* (Atlanta, 1938), p. 27.

29. Washington, *My Larger Education,* pp. 120-27.

## *CHAPTER 2*

1. Charles W. Chesnutt, "Post-Bellum—Pre-Harlem," *Breaking into Print,* edited by Elmer Adler (New York, 1937), p. 51.

2. The fiction of Mrs. Dunbar-Nelson, Durham, and Ellis will not be further discussed in this chapter because this body of writing does not deal with Negro life and thought in this country.

3. Webb is listed as a Negro in the Schomburg Collection of the New York Public Library, but his racial identity is admittedly a matter of conjecture.

4. In *The Anti-Slavery Harp: A Collection of Songs for Anti-Slavery Meetings* (1848) Brown includes a piece entitled "Jefferson's Daughter."

In *Black Reconstruction in America* (New York, 1935), p. 36, W. E. B. DuBois notes: "Several Presidents of the United States have been accused of racial catholicity in sex."

5. The experiences of Chesnutt with *The Atlantic Monthly* and the Houghton Mifflin Company shed interesting light upon his comment that in his day "a literary work by an American of acknowledged color was a doubtful experiment, both for the writer and for the publisher, entirely apart from its intrinsic merit." Some time after Thomas Bailey Aldrich accepted Chesnutt's conjure tales for *The Atlantic Monthly,* Chesnutt submitted stories of post-bellum Negro life and the first draft of *The House Behind the Cedars* to Houghton Mifflin. Walter Hines Page rejected the latter, however, with "the suggestion that perhaps a collection of the conjure stories might be undertaken by the firm with a better prospect of success." Following the advice of Page, Chesnutt was able to get *The Conjure Woman* accepted. The publishers, however, kept quiet about the race of the author until Page, though demurring "at first on the ground that such an announcement might be harmful" to *The Wife of His Youth and Other Stories of the Color Line,* finally permitted James McArthur of *The Critic* to announce, "as a matter of interest to the literary public," that Chesnutt was a mulatto. *The House Behind the Cedars* was later published in revised form by Houghton Mifflin. Charles W. Chesnutt, "Post-Bellum—Pre-Harlem," *op. cit.,* pp. 51-54.

6. William Dean Howells, "Mr. Charles W. Chesnutt's Stories," *The Atlantic Monthly,* LXXXV (1900), 700.

7. Four of the seven stories in *The Conjure Woman* appeared in *The Atlantic Monthly,* and one of the remaining three, "The Conjurer's Revenge," in *The Overland Monthly.* Two were first printed in the bound volume. *The Conjure Woman* was reprinted in 1929 with a foreword by Colonel Joel Spingarn.

8. Chesnutt admits the similarity of *The Conjure Woman* to Harris' work but insists upon his own originality: "The name of the story teller, 'Uncle' Julius, and the locale of the stories, as well as the cover design, were suggestive of Mr. Harris' Uncle Remus, but the tales are entirely different. They are sometimes referred to as folk tales, but while they employ much of the universal machinery of wonder stories, especially the metamorphosis, with one exception, that of the first story, 'The Goophered Grapevine,' of which the norm was the folk tale, the stories are the fruit of my own imagination, in which respect they differ from the Uncle Remus stories which are avowedly folk tales." Charles W. Chesnutt, "Post-Bellum—Pre-Harlem," *op. cit.,* p. 50.

9. Of his race Chesnutt said: "It never occurred to me to claim any merit because of it, and I have always resented the denial of anything on account of it." *Ibid.,* pp. 53-54.

10. Howells, *loc. cit.*, 700.

11. Concerning the material of his novels Chesnutt wrote: "As a matter of fact, substantially all of my writings, with the exception of *The Conjure Woman,* have dealt with the problems of people of mixed blood, which, while in the main the same as those of the Negro, are in some instances and in some respects much more complex and difficult of treatment, in fiction as in life." Chesnutt, *op. cit.,* p. 54.

12. James Weldon Johnson, *The Autobiography of an Ex-Coloured Man* (New York, 1928), p. vii. Introduction by Carl Van Vechten.

13. The riot was doubtless inspired by the racial clashes which occurred in Wilmington, North Carolina, in 1898.

14. Though avoiding the enunciation of a constructive racial program in his fiction, Chesnutt, in an essay written in 1903, advocated political action and humanitarianism as means of improving the condition of the Negro: "The direct remedy for the disfranchisement of the Negro lies through political action. Aid will also come from the power 'that leads men to do justice to one another.'" Charles W. Chesnutt, "The Disfranchisement of the Negro," *The Negro Problem: A Series of Articles by Representative American Negroes of Today* (New York, 1903), p. 124.

15. Lida Keck Wiggins, compiler, *The Life and Works of Paul Laurence Dunbar* (Napierville, Illinois, 1907), pp. 69-70.

16. William Stanley Braithwaite, "The Negro in American Literature," *The New Negro,* edited by Alain Locke (New York, 1925), p. 42.

17. Parrington, *op. cit.,* p. 325.

18. James Weldon Johnson, *op. cit.,* p. vii.

19. "The Ingrate" is supposedly based upon experiences in the life of Dunbar's father, Joshua Dunbar. Benjamin Brawley, *Paul Laurence Dunbar* (Chapel Hill, North Carolina, 1936), p. 81.

20. This essay, which follows the novel, appears on pp. 301-33. Griggs states that he later intends "to deal with Mr. Dixon's second book [*The Clansman*] bearing on the race problem, it being the hope of the writer to give that matter serious and independent attention." *Ibid.,* p. 298. This investigator has found no record of such a study of *The Clansman* by Griggs.

21. In appended "Notes to the Serious" Griggs, somewhat anticipating Marcus Garvey, declares that the idea of a Negro exodus to Africa is his own dream and not the wish of most American Negroes:

> "The overwhelmingly predominant sentiment of the American Negroes is to fight out their battle on these shores. The assigning of the thoughts of the race to the uplift of Africa, as affecting the situation in America, must be taken more as a dream of the author rather than as representing any considerable responsible sentiment within the race, which, as has been stated, seems at present thoroughly and unqualifiedly American, a fact that must never be overlooked by those seeking to deal with this grave question in a practical manner."

22. Frank Norris, *The Responsibilities of a Novelist* (New York, 1903), p. 25.

23. *The Autobiography of an Ex-Coloured Man* was begun as early as 1905, when Johnson showed the first two chapters of the book to Brander Matthews at Columbia University. Reading the entire manuscript later, Matthews liked the novel and wrote a critical introduction for the first edition. George A. Towns, one of the author's classmates at Atlanta University, was the first to issue a printed statement in proof of Johnson's authorship. For the second edition Carl Van Vechten wrote a critical introduction which noted that the novel was not the story of Johnson's life. James Weldon Johnson, *Along This Way* (New York, 1933), p. 193 and pp. 238-39.

24. Johnson, *The Autobiography of an Ex-Coloured Man*, p. xi.

25. *Ibid.*, pp. vii-viii.

26. *Ibid.*, p. xii.

27. John Chamberlain, "The Negro as Writer," *The Bookman*, LXX (1930), 607.

28. Johnson, *The Autobiography of an Ex-Coloured Man*, p. vii.

29. A publisher's note to the reader suggests that *The Homesteader* treats the most important experience of Micheaux's life:

"... Born thirty-three years ago in Southern Illinois, he left those parts at an early age to come into his larger education in the years that followed through extensive traveling and a varied association. Purchasing a relinquishment on a homestead in South Dakota at the age of twenty, five years later he had succeeded and owned several lands in the country wherein he had settled. Always literarily inclined, he wrote articles for newspapers and magazines as a beginner, and then during his twenty-sixth and twenty-seventh years occurred the conflicting incident that changed the whole course of his life, and gave him more than anything else, the subsequent material for the building of this story.

"Shortly after his first book appeared, and he at last found his calling. He wrote his second book two years later. But the episode that changed his life from ranching to writing was ever in his mind and always so forcibly until he was never a contented man until he had written it—and *The Homesteader* is the story."

## *CHAPTER 3*

1. Especially violent was the riot in East St. Louis, Illinois, in July, 1915. For details see Brawley, *A Short History of the American Negro*, pp. 171-72.

2. W. E. B. DuBois, "Returning Soldiers," *The Crisis*, XVIII (1919), 14.

3. E. Franklin Frazier, "The Garvey Movement," *Opportunity*, IV (1926), 346.

4. Charles S. Johnson, "After Garvey—What?" *Opportunity,* I (1923), 232.

5. Frazier, *loc. cit.,* 347.

6. Johnson, *loc. cit.,* 233.

7. *Ibid.*

8. Albert C. Barnes, "Primitive Negro Sculpture and Its Influence on Modern Civilization," *Opportunity,* VI (1928), 140 and 147.

9. *Ibid.,* 147.

10. Oscar Cargill, *Intellectual America: Ideas on the March* (New York, 1941), pp. 315-16. Cargill notes that Miss Stein began "Melanctha" while posing for a portrait by Picasso. *Ibid.,* p. 314.

11. Barnes, *loc. cit.,* 140.

12. Cargill, *op. cit.,* p. 14.

13. *Ibid.,* pp. 397-98.

14. *Ibid.,* p. 14. Freud, who became popular in the United States after a series of lectures at Clark University in 1909, stimulated an interest in primitivism as an avenue of escape for jaded Americans by attributing many of the neuroses of human behavior to the suppression of the sex instinct.

15. Sterling Brown, *The Negro in American Fiction* (Washington, 1937), p. 115.

16. Langston Hughes, "The Negro Artist and the Racial Mountain," *The Nation,* CXXII (1926), 694.

17. Claude McKay, *A Long Way from Home* (New York, 1937), p. 99.

18. Chesnutt, "Post-Bellum—Pre-Harlem," *op. cit.,* pp. 54-55.

19. Valuable discussions of Harlem and its outstanding personalities are available in Hughes's *The Big Sea* (New York, 1940), James Weldon Johnson's *Black Manhattan* (New York, 1930), Claude McKay's *Harlem: Negro Metropolis* (New York, 1940), and Roi Ottley's *New World a-Coming* (New York, 1943).

20. Hughes, *op. cit.,* p. 225.

21. Hughes, "Harlem Literati of the Twenties," *The Saturday Review of Literature,* XXII (1940), 14.

22. In March, 1925, *Survey Graphic* presented a "Harlem Number" devoted entirely to Negro subject-matter; and in October of the following year *Palms* featured a "Negro Number" edited by Countee Cullen. Throughout the Renascence period, articles by Negroes appeared in the country's leading newspapers and magazines.

23. Hughes, *The Big Sea,* p. 218.

24. DuBois, *Dusk of Dawn,* p. 270.

25. Hughes, *The Big Sea,* p. 235.

## *CHAPTER 4*

1. It is interesting to note the persistence of the campaign against the propaganda of Thomas Dixon. For example, as late as 1924, W. Forrest Cozart was prompted to write a biased and unscholarly history of the Negro because of the libels of Dixon. After reading *The Leopard's Spots* and *The Clansman,* Cozart declares: "I then and there resolved to dedicate the rest of my life in trying to refute those false and unjust charges, and from that day until now I have been diligently working to meet those charges." W. Forrest Cozart, *The Chosen People* (Boston, 1924), p. 11.

2. Jean Toomer, *Cane* (New York, 1923), pp. viii-ix. Foreword by Waldo Frank.

3. "Blood-Burning Moon," the short story in which Louisa is the leading female character, appears in O'Brien's *Best Short Stories of 1923.*

4. W. E. B. DuBois and Alain Locke, "The Younger Literary Movement," *The Crisis,* XXVII (1924), 161.

5. Sterling Brown, *op. cit.,* p. 153.

6. Montgomery Gregory, Review of *Cane, Opportunity,* I (1923), 375.

7. Gorham B. Munson, "The Significance of Jean Toomer," *Opportunity,* III (1925), 262.

8. Toomer, *op. cit.*, p. ix.

9. Jessie Fauset, *The Chinaberry Tree* (New York, 1931), pp. vii-viii. Introduction by Zona Gale.

10. Floyd Calvin, "First Time in History of Big New York Store This Has Been Done," *The Pittsburgh Courier,* May 23, 1931.

11. William Stanley Braithwaite, "The Negro in Literature," *The Crisis,* XXVIII (1924), 210.

12. DuBois and Locke, *loc. cit.,* 162.

13. Calvin, *loc. cit.*

14. *Ibid.*

15. Edwin Berry Burgum, Review of *The Chinaberry Tree, Opportunity,* X (1932), 88.

16. *Ibid.*

17. W. E. B. DuBois, Review of *The Chinaberry Tree, The Crisis,* XXXIX (1932), 138.

18. W. E. B. DuBois, Review of *Quicksand*, *The Crisis*, XXXV (1928), 202.

19. DuBois, *Dusk of Dawn*, p. 264.

20. The highlights of White's career as a prober of mob violence are given in his essay, "I Investigate Lynchings," which is included in V. F. Calverton's *Anthology of American Negro Literature* (New York, 1929),

pp. 389-404. It is interesting to note, in passing, that this anthology is dedicated by Calverton "To Walter White in admiration of his courage in the cause of his people, and in tender appreciation of that fine, inspiring warmth which I have found in his friendship."

21. DuBois, *Dusk of Dawn*, pp. 261-62.

22. *Ibid.*, p. 275.

23. *Ibid.*, p. 280.

24. In *Darkwater* (1920) DuBois had shown a leaning toward international racialism:

"What, then, is this dark world thinking? It is thinking that as wild and awful as this shameful war was, *it is nothing to compare with the fight for freedom which black and brown and yellow men must and will make unless their oppression and humiliation and insult at the hands of the White World cease. The Dark World is going to submit to its present treatment just as long as it must and not one moment longer.*" (Italics by DuBois) W. E. B. DuBois, *Darkwater* (New York, 1920), p. 49.

25. Dewey R. Jones, Review of *Slaves Today, Opportunity*, X (1932), 27.

26. Carl Van Vechten, "The Negro in Art: How Shall He Be Portrayed?" *The Crisis*, XXXI (1926), 219.

27. Gwendolyn Bennett, "The Ebony Flute," *Opportunity*, IV (1926), 357.

28. W. E. B. DuBois, Review of *Nigger Heaven, The Crisis*, XXXIII (1926), 81-82.

29. James Weldon Johnson, "Romance and Tragedy in Harlem," *Opportunity*, IV (1926), 316-17.

30. In the jungle pose Langston Hughes wrote such poems as "Nude Young Dancer," "Dream Variation," "Our Land," "Lament for Dark Peoples," "Afraid," "Poem for the Portrait of an African Boy after the Manner of Gauguin," and "Danse Africaine." Nevertheless, when his patron expressed dissatisfaction because he wrote "Advertisement for the Waldorf-Astoria," he explained:

"She wanted me to be primitive and know and feel the intuitions of the primitive. But, unfortunately, I did not feel the rhythms of the primitive surging through me, and so I could not live and write as though I did. I was only an American Negro—who had loved the surface of Africa and the rhythms of Africa—but I was not Africa. I was Chicago and Kansas City and Broadway and Harlem." Hughes, *The Big Sea,* p. 325.

31. Johnson, *Along This Way*, p. 378.

32. In answer to the charge that he wrote *Home to Harlem* because of the success of *Nigger Heaven*, McKay explains:

"Many persons imagine that I wrote *Home to Harlem* because Carl Van Vechten wrote *Nigger Heaven*. But the pattern tale of the book was written under the title of "Home to Harlem" in 1925. When Max Eastman read it he said, "It is worth a thousand dollars." Under the same title it was entered in the story contest of the Negro magazine *Opportunity*. But it did not excite the judges. *Nigger Heaven* was published in the fall of 1926. I never saw the book until the late spring of 1927, when my agent, William Aspenwall Bradley, sent me a copy. And by that time I had nearly completed *Home to Harlem*." McKay, *A Long Way from Home*, pp. 282-83.

33. W. E. B. DuBois, Review of *Home to Harlem*, *The Crisis*, XXXV (1928), 202.

34. McKay defends his knowledge of low life in these words:

"I knew the unskilled Negro worker of the city by working with him as a porter and longshoreman and as a waiter on the railroad. I lived in the same quarters and we drank and caroused together in bars and at rent parties." McKay, *A Long Way from Home*, p. 228.

35. *Ibid.*, pp. 277-95.

36. *Ibid.*, pp. 278, 288.

37. W. E. B. DuBois, Review of *Banjo*, *The Crisis*, XXXVI (1929), 234.

38. On this point McKay writes: "I was an older man and not regarded as a member of the renaissance, but more as a forerunner. Indeed, some of them had aired their resentment of my intrusion from abroad into the renaissance set-up." McKay, *A Long Way from Home*, p. 321.

39. Before 1940 Bontemps' published juvenile stories were *Popo and Fifina* (1932) with Langston Hughes, *You Can't Pet a Possum* (1934), and *Sad Faced Boy* (1937).

40. Sterling Brown, Review of *God Sends Sunday*, *Opportunity*, IX (1931), 188.

41. Laurence Stallings, Review of *God Sends Sunday*, *The New York Sun*, March 18, 1931.

42. Gwendolyn Bennett, Review of *God Sends Sunday*, *The New York Herald Tribune*, March 22, 1931.

43. Chamberlain, *loc. cit.*, 606.

44. Countee Cullen, "The Negro in Art: How Shall He Be Portrayed?" *The Crisis*, XXXII (1926), 193.

45. Brown, *The Negro in American Fiction*, p. 154.

46. Rebecca Chalmers Barton, *Race Consciousness in American Negro Literature* (Copenhagen, 1934), p. 109.

47. Alain Locke, "The Saving Grace of Realism," *Opportunity*, XII (1934), 9.

48. "Writes First Novel," *The Amsterdam News*, July 9, 1930.

49. The autobiographical content of *Not Without Laughter* is discussed as follows by Hughes:

". . . I grew up with other Negro children of Lawrence, sons and daughters of family friends. I had an uncle of sorts who ran a barber shop in Kansas City. And later I had a stepfather who was a wanderer. We were poor—but different. For purposes of the novel, however, I created around myself what seemed to me a family more typical of Negro life in Kansas than my own had been. I gave myself aunts that I didn't have, modeled after other children's aunts whom I had known. But I put in a real cyclone that had blown my grandmother's front porch away. And I added dances and songs I remembered. I brought the boy to Chicago in his teens, as I had come to Chicago—but I did not leave behind a well-fixed aunt whose husband was a mail clerk." Hughes, *The Big Sea,* p. 304.

50. Cargill, *Intellectual America: Ideas on the March*, p. 511.
51. Alain Locke, "This Year of Grace," *Opportunity,* IX (1931), 49.
52. Alain Locke, "We Turn to Prose," *Opportunity*, X (1932), 43.
53. Alain Locke, "1928: A Retrospective Review," *Opportunity*, VII (1929), 8.
54. Hughes, *The Big Sea*, p. 223.
55. *Ibid.*, p. 247.
56. *Ibid.*, pp. 334-35. Hughes writes that he was early aware of the ephemeral nature of the Negro Renascence:

". . . I had a swell time while it lasted. But I thought it wouldn't last long. (I remember the vogue for things Russian, the season the Chauve-Souris first came to town.) For how could a large and enthusiastic number of people be crazy about Negroes forever?" *Ibid.,* p. 228.

57. *Ibid.*
58. McKay, who is frequently very sarcastic in discussing his confreres, makes the following caustic statement concerning the influence of whites upon his Renascence colleagues:

"Also, among Negro artists there was much of the Uncle Tom attitude which works like Satan against the idea of a coherent and purposeful Negro group. Each one wanted to be the first Negro, the one Negro, and the only Negro *for the whites* instead of for their group. Because an unusual number of them were receiving grants to do creative work, they actually and naively believed that Negro artists as a group would be treated differently from white artists and be protected by powerful white patrons." McKay, *A Long Way from Home,* p. 322.

59. Benjamin Brawley, *The Negro in Literature and Art* (New York, 1929), p. 118.
60. Johnson, *Along This Way*, p. 381.
61. Hughes, *The Big Sea*, p. 247.
62. *Ibid.*, p. 238.
63. McKay, *A Long Way from Home*, p. 321.
64. Carl Van Doren, *The American Novel 1789-1939* (New York, 1940), p. 322.
65. *Ibid.*, p. 322.
66. Brown, *The Negro in American Fiction*, p. 149.

## CHAPTER 5

1. *The New Masses* traces its ancestry back to *The Masses*, which was founded in 1911 under the editorship of Thomas Seltzer. Piet Vleg became editor in 1912, and in the following year the Max Eastman group assumed control. During the World War period *The Masses* was converted into *The Liberator*, which in 1924 merged with *Soviet Russia Pictorial* and *Labor Herald* to form *The Workers Monthly*. *The New Masses* appeared in 1926. See Calverton, *op. cit.*, pp. 450-67.

2. Van Doren, *op. cit.*, p. 349.

3. See Joseph Freeman's critical introduction to Granville Hicks *et al.* (eds.), *Proletarian Literature in the United States* (New York, 1935), p. 9.

4. Van Doren, *op. cit.*, p. 350.

5. Sterling Brown, *op. cit.*, p. 181.

6. Quoted in James W. Ford, *The Negro and the Democratic Front* (New York, 1938), p. 193.

7. Van Doren, *op. cit.*, p. 359.

8. Cargill, *Intellectual America: Ideas on the March*, p. 392.

9. Sterling Brown, *op. cit.*, p. 180.

10. Cargill, *op. cit.*, p. 396.

11. Joseph Warren Beach, *American Fiction 1920-1940* (New York, 1941), p. 143.

12. Alain Locke, "The Negro: New or Newer," *Opportunity*, XVII (1939), 7.

13. Benjamin Brawley, "The Promise of Negro Literature," *The Journal of Negro History*, XIX (1934), 56.

## CHAPTER 6

1. Alain Locke, "This Year of Grace," *Opportunity*, IX (1939), 48.

2. Alain Locke, "The Negro: New or Newer," *loc. cit.*, 6.

3. Sterling Brown, *op. cit.*, p. 189. Brown gives a brief but useful discussion of the treatment of the Negro's past by white and colored novelists in the chapter entitled "Historical Fiction," pp. 189-206.

4. A. B. Spingarn, Review of *Black Thunder*, *The Crisis*, XLIV (1937), 47.

5. Rayford W. Logan, Review of *Drums at Dusk*, *Opportunity*, XVII (1939), 218.

6. Van Doren, *op. cit.*, p. 334.

7. Alain Locke, "We Turn to Prose," *loc. cit.*, 43.

8. Richard Wright, "How 'Bigger' Was Born," *The Saturday Review of Literature*, XXII (1940), 20.

9. An example of Wright's leftist verse is "Between the World and Me." See Granville Hicks *et al.* (eds.), *op. cit.*, pp. 202-3.

10. Alain Locke, "Jingo, Counter-Jingo and Us," *Opportunity*, XVI (1938), 11.

11. Wright, "How 'Bigger' Was Born," *loc. cit.*, 19.

12. *Ibid.*

13. *Ibid.*, 3-4.

14. *Ibid.*, 17.

15. *Ibid.*, 18.

16. Statement by Wright in "Negro Hailed as New Writer," news article in *The New York Sun* for March 4, 1940.

17. Wright, "How 'Bigger' Was Born," *loc. cit.*, 4.

18. *Ibid.*, 17.

19. *Ibid.*, 20.

20. *Ibid.*, 18.

21. Henry Seidel Canby, Review of *Native Son,* The Book-of-the-Month Club *News* (February, 1940), p. 3.

22. During the 1930's novels dealing with legendary heroes were popular. Among such works that appeared during the decade are Roark Bradford's *John Henry* (1931), Walter Blair and Frank J. Meine's *Mike Fink: King of Mississippi Keelboatmen* (1933), Paul R. Beath's *Legends of Febold Feboldson* (1937), and James Cloyd Bowman's *Pecos Bill: The Greatest Cowboy of All Time* (1937).

23. The account of Miss Hurston's findings in Florida and Louisiana is given in *Mules and Men* (1935), which contains an introduction by Franz Boas and ten illustrations by Miguel Covarrubias. The book is divided into two principal parts, the first chiefly concerned with folk tales of Florida Negroes and the second with the formulae and paraphernalia of Louisiana hoodoo practitioners. Moses, who is hailed as the first hoodoo specialist, is treated at length by Miss Hurston in *Moses: Man of the Mountain* (1939). In the Introduction to this volume the author indicates the extent and significance of the Mosaic legend:

> "So all across Africa, America, the West Indies, there are tales of the power of Moses and great worship of him and his powers. But it does not flow from the Ten Commandments. It is his rod of power, the terror that he showed before all Israel and to Pharaoh, and THAT MIGHTY HAND."

24. Miss Hurston describes her West Indian investigations in *Tell My Horse* (1938), which is dedicated to Carl Van Vechten, who is called "God's image of a friend." The book discusses Haitian voodoo and Jamaican folklore, politics, and personalities. The appendix includes songs of worship to voodoo gods as well as other native songs. *Tell My Horse* contains much more social criticism than does *Mules and Men.*

25. Miss Hurston's native village.

26. Andrew Burris, Review of *Jonah's Gourd Vine, The Crisis,* XLI (1934), 166.

27. Alain Locke, "Deep River: Deeper Sea," *Opportunity*, XIV (1936), 9.

28. See *Beale Street: Where the Blues Began* (New York, 1934), pp. 35-55.

29. "The town of Shrewsbury is really Salisbury, ill-famed because of a recent lynching, and Turpin describes this tragedy." Sterling Brown, *op. cit.*, p. 187.

30. In *O Canaan!* Paul Johnson reports that after the Shrewsbury lynching Jimmy-Lew was transferred to a school on the Western Shore because he had shown a hot temper and carried a gun. Especially bitter and militant, Jimmy-Lew tells Paul: "I tell you, we who have been better privileged are forsaking our duty to the downtrodden."

31. Ulysses Lee, Review of *O Canaan!*, *Opportunity*, XVII (1939), 312.

## *CHAPTER* 7

1. Sterling Brown *et al.* (eds.), *The Negro Caravan* (New York, 1941), pp. 144-45.

2. Quoted in Donald Ogden Stewart, *Fighting Words* (New York, 1940), pp. 58-59.

3. Sterling A. Brown, "Our Literary Audience," *Opportunity*, VIII (February, 1930), 42.

# Bibliography

## *FICTION BY NEGRO AUTHORS*


ADAMS, CLAYTON. *Ethiopia, the Land of Promise.* New York, The Cosmopolitan Press, 1917.

ASHBY, WILLIAM M. *Redder Blood.* New York, The Cosmopolitan Press, 1915.

ATTAWAY, WILLIAM. *Let Me Breathe Thunder.* New York, Doubleday, Doran and Company, 1939.

BONTEMPS, ARNA. *Black Thunder.* New York, The Macmillan Company, 1936.

———. *Drums at Dusk.* New York, The Macmillan Company, 1939.

———. *God Sends Sunday.* New York, Harcourt, Brace and Company, 1931.

BROWN, WILLIAM WELLS. *Clotel, or The President's Daughter: A Narrative of Slave Life in the United States.* London, 1853.

———. *Clotelle, or The Colored Heroine: A Tale of the Southern States.* Boston, Lee and Shepard, 1867.

BRUCE, JOHN EDWARD. *The Awakening of Hezekiah Jones.* Hopkinsville, Kentucky, Phil. H. Brown, 1916.

CHESNUTT, CHARLES WADDELL. *The Colonel's Dream.* New York, Doubleday, Page and Company, 1905.

———. *The Conjure Woman.* New York, Houghton, Mifflin and Company, 1899.

———. *The House Behind the Cedars.* Boston, Houghton, Mifflin and Company, 1900.

———. *The Marrow of Tradition.* Boston, Houghton, Mifflin and Company, 1901.

———. *The Wife of His Youth and Other Stories of the Color Line.* Boston, Houghton, Mifflin and Company, 1899.

COTTER, JOSEPH S. *Negro Tales.* New York, The Cosmopolitan Press, 1912.

CULLEN, COUNTEE. *One Way to Heaven.* New York, Harper and Brothers, 1932.

DALY, VICTOR. *Not Only War.* Boston, The Christopher Publishing House, 1932.

DELANY, MARTIN R. "Blake, or The Huts of America: A Tale of the Mississippi Valley, the Southern United States and Cuba," *The*

*Anglo-African Magazine*, I (January-July, 1859), 20-29, 37-43, 69-79, 104-114, 128-139, 161-172, 193-203.
DOWNING, HENRY F. *The American Cavalryman*. New York, The Neale Publishing Company, 1917.
DREER, HERMAN. *The Immediate Jewel of His Soul*. St. Louis, Missouri, The St. Louis Argus Publishing Company, 1919.
DUBOIS, W. E. BURGHARDT. *Dark Princess*. New York, Harcourt, Brace and Company, 1928.
———. *The Quest of the Silver Fleece*. Chicago, A. C. McClurg and Company, 1911.
DUNBAR, PAUL LAURENCE. *The Fanatics*. New York, Dodd, Mead and Company, 1901.
———. *Folks From Dixie*. New York, Dodd, Mead and Company, 1898.
———. *The Heart of Happy Hollow*. New York, Dodd, Mead and Company, 1904.
———. *In Old Plantation Days*. New York, Dodd, Mead and Company, 1903.
———. *The Love of Landry*. New York, Dodd, Mead and Company, 1900.
———. *The Sport of the Gods*. New York, Dodd, Mead and Company, 1902.
———. *The Strength of Gideon and Other Stories*. New York, Dodd, Mead and Company, 1900.
———. *The Uncalled*. New York, Dodd, Mead and Company, 1898.
DURHAM, JOHN S. "Diane, Priestess of Haiti," *Lippincott's Monthly Magazine*, LXIX (April, 1902), 387-466.
ELLIS, GEORGE W. *The Leopard's Claw*. New York, International Authors Association, 1917.
FAUSET, JESSIE REDMON. *The Chinaberry Tree*. New York, Frederick A. Stokes Company, 1931.
———. *Comedy American Style*. New York, Frederick A. Stokes Company, 1933.
———. *Plum Bun*. New York, Frederick A. Stokes Company, 1929.
———. *There Is Confusion*. New York, Boni and Liveright, 1924.
FISHER, RUDOLPH. *The Conjure-Man Dies*. New York, Covici Friede, 1932.
———. *The Walls of Jericho*. New York, Alfred A. Knopf, 1928.
FLEMING, SARAH LEE BROWN. *Hope's Highway*. New York, The Neale Publishing Company, 1918.
FOWLER, CHARLES HENRY. *Historical Romance of the American Negro*. Baltimore, Maryland, Press of Thomas and Evans, 1902.
GILBERT, MERCEDES. *Aunt Sara's Wooden God*. Boston, The Christopher Publishing House, 1938.

GILMORE, F. GRANT. *The Problem.* Rochester, New York, Press of Henry Conolly Company, 1915.

GRANT, J. W. *Out of the Darkness, or Diabolism and Destiny.* Nashville, Tennessee, National Baptist Publishing Board, 1909.

GRIGGS, SUTTON E. *The Hindered Hand, or the Reign of the Repressionist.* Nashville, Tennessee, The Orion Publishing Company, 1905.

———. *Imperium in Imperio.* Cincinnati, Ohio, The Editor Publishing Company, 1899.

———. *Overshadowed.* Nashville, Tennessee, The Orion Publishing Company, 1901.

———. *Pointing the Way.* Nashville, Tennessee, The Orion Publishing Company, 1908.

———. *Unfettered.* Nashville, Tennessee, The Orion Publishing Company, 1902.

HARPER, FRANCES ELLEN WATKINS. *Iola Leroy, or Shadows Uplifted.* Philadelphia, Garrigues Brothers, 1892.

HENDERSON, GEORGE WYLIE. *Ollie Miss.* New York, Frederick A. Stokes Company, 1935.

HILL, JOHN H. *Princess Malah.* Washington, D. C., The Associated Publishers, 1933.

HOPKINS, PAULINE E. *Contending Forces.* Boston, The Colored Co-Operative Publishing Company, 1900.

HUGHES, LANGSTON. *Not Without Laughter.* New York, Alfred A. Knopf, 1930.

———. *The Ways of White Folks.* New York, Alfred A. Knopf, 1934.

HURSTON, ZORA NEALE. *Jonah's Gourd Vine.* Philadelphia, J. B. Lippincott, 1934.

———. *Moses: Man of the Mountain.* Philadelphia, J. B. Lippincott, 1939.

———. *Mules and Men.* Philadelphia, J. B. Lippincott, 1935.

———. *Tell My Horse.* Philadelphia, J. B. Lippincott, 1938.

———. *Their Eyes Were Watching God.* Philadelphia, J. B. Lippincott, 1937.

JOHNSON, FENTON. *Tales of Darkest America.* Chicago, The Favorite Magazine, 1920.

JOHNSON, JAMES WELDON. *The Autobiography of an Ex-Coloured Man.* New York, Sherman, French and Company, 1912.

JONES, J. MCHENRY. *Hearts of Gold.* Wheeling, West Virginia, Daily Intelligencer Steam Job Press, 1896.

JONES, JOSHUA HENRY, JR. *By Sanction of Law.* Boston, B. J. Brimmer Company, 1924.

JONES, YORKE. *The Climbers.* Chicago, Glad Tidings Publishing Company, 1912.
LARSEN, NELLA. *Passing.* New York, Alfred A. Knopf, 1929.
———. *Quicksand.* New York, Alfred A. Knopf, 1928.
LEE, GEORGE W. *River George.* New York, The Macaulay Company, 1937.
MCCLELLAN, GEORGE MARION. *Old Greenbottom Inn and Other Stories.* Louisville, Kentucky, George M. McClellan, 1906.
MCGIRT, JAMES E. *The Triumphs of Ephraim.* Philadelphia, no publisher, 1907.
MCKAY, CLAUDE. *Banana Bottom.* New York, Harper and Brothers, 1933.
———. *Banjo.* New York, Harper and Brothers, 1929.
———. *Gingertown.* New York, Harper and Brothers, 1932.
———. *Home to Harlem.* New York, Harper and Brothers, 1928.
MICHEAUX, OSCAR. *The Conquest.* Lincoln, Nebraska, The Woodruff Press, 1913.
———. *The Forged Note.* Lincoln, Nebraska, Western Book Supply Company, 1915.
———. *The Homesteader.* Sioux City, Iowa, Western Book Supply Company, 1917.
NELSON, ALICE DUNBAR. *The Goodness of St. Rocque, and Other Stories.* New York, Dodd, Mead and Company, 1899.
———. *Violets and Other Tales.* No publisher, 1895.
PAYNTER, JOHN H. *Fugitives of the Pearl.* Washington, D. C., The Associated Publishers, 1930.
PICKENS, WILLIAM. *The Vengeance of the Gods and Three Other Stories of Real American Color Line.* Philadelphia, A. M. E. Book Concern, 1922.
PRYOR, G. LANGHORNE. *Neither Bond Nor Free.* New York, J. S. Ogilvie Company, 1902.
SCHUYLER, GEORGE. *Black No More.* New York, The Macaulay Company, 1931.
———. *Slaves Today.* New York, Brewer, Warren and Putnam, 1931.
SHACKELFORD, OTIS M. *Lillian Simmons, or the Conflict of Sections.* Kansas City, Missouri, Burton Publishing Company, 1915.
SHAW, O'WENDELL. *Greater Need Below.* Columbus, Ohio, Bi-Monthly Negro Book Club, 1936.
THURMAN, WALLACE. *The Blacker the Berry.* New York, The Macaulay Company, 1929.
———. *Infants of the Spring.* New York, The Macaulay Company, 1932.
———, and Furman, A. L. *The Interne.* New York, The Macaulay Company, 1932.

Toomer, Jean. *Cane*. New York, Boni and Liveright, 1923.
Tracy, R. Archer. *The Sword of Nemesis*. New York, Neal Publishing Company, 1919.
Turpin, Waters Edward. *O Canaan!* New York, Doubleday, Doran and Company, 1939.
———. *These Low Grounds*. New York, Harper and Brothers, 1937.
Walker, Thomas H. B. *Bebbly, or the Victorious Preacher*. Jacksonville, Florida, Pepper Publishing Company, 1915.
———. *J. Johnson, or the Unknown Man*. DeLand, Florida, The E. D. Painter Printing Company, 1915.
Walrond, Eric. *Tropic Death*. New York, Boni and Liveright, 1926.
Waring, Robert L. *As We See It*. Washington, D. C., Press of C. F. Sudworth, 1910.
Webb, Frank J. *The Garies and Their Friends*. London, 1857.
White, Walter F. *The Fire in the Flint*. New York, Alfred A. Knopf, 1924.
———. *Flight*. New York, Alfred A. Knopf, 1926.
Wright, Richard. *Native Son*. New York, Harper and Brothers, 1940.
———. *Uncle Tom's Children*. New York, Harper and Brothers, 1938.

## *LITERARY HISTORY AND CRITICISM*

Barton, Rebecca Chalmers. *Race Consciousness and the American Negro*. Copenhagen, Denmark, Arnold Busck, 1934.
Beach, Joseph Warren. *American Fiction 1920-1940*. New York, The Macmillan Company, 1941.
———. *The Outlook for American Prose*. Chicago, The University of Chicago Press, 1926.
———. *The Twentieth-Century Novel*. New York, The Century Company, 1932.
Blankenship, Russell. *American Literature as an Expression of the National Mind*. New York, Henry Holt and Company, 1931.
Boyd, Ernest. *Portraits: Real and Imaginary*. New York, George H. Doran Company, 1924.
Boynton, Percy H. *Literature and American Life*. New York, Ginn and Company, 1936.
———. *More Contemporary Americans*. Chicago, The University of Chicago Press, 1927.
———. *Some Contemporary Americans*. Chicago, The University of Chicago Press, 1924.
Brawley, Benjamin Griffith. *The Negro Genius*. New York, Dodd, Mead and Company, 1937.

———. *The Negro in Literature and Art.* New York, Duffield and Company, 1929.
———. *Paul Laurence Dunbar.* Chapel Hill, North Carolina, The University of North Carolina Press, 1936.
BROWN, STERLING. *The Negro in American Fiction.* Washington, D. C., The Associates in Negro Folk Education, 1937.
———. *Negro Poetry and Drama.* Washington, D. C., The Associates in Negro Folk Education, 1937.
CALVERTON, V. F. *The Liberation of American Literature.* New York, Charles Scribner's Sons, 1932.
CANBY, HENRY SEIDEL. *American Estimates.* New York, Harcourt, Brace and Company, 1929.
CARGILL, OSCAR. *Intellectual America: Ideas on the March.* New York, The Macmillan Company, 1941.
EASTMAN, MAX. *The Literary Mind.* New York, Charles Scribner's Sons, 1931.
EDGAR, PELHAM. *The Art of the Novel.* New York, The Macmillan Company, 1933.
FORD, NICK AARON. *The Contemporary Negro Novel.* Boston, Meador Publishing Company, 1936.
GAINES, FRANCIS PENDLETON. *The Southern Plantation.* New York, The Columbia University Press, 1924.
GARLAND, HAMLIN. *Companions on the Trail.* New York, The Macmillan Company, 1931.
———. *My Friendly Contemporaries.* New York, The Macmillan Company, 1932.
———. *Roadside Meetings.* New York, The Macmillan Company, 1930.
HARTWICK, HARRY. *The Foreground of American Fiction.* New York, American Book Company, 1934.
HATCHER, HARLAN. *Creating the Modern American Novel.* New York, Farrar and Rinehart, 1935.
HERRON, I. H. *The Small Town in American Literature.* Durham, North Carolina, Duke University Press, 1939.
HICKS, GRANVILLE. *The Great Tradition.* New York, The Macmillan Company, 1933.
JACKSON, AUGUSTA V. *The Renascence of Negro Literature 1922 to 1929.* Unpublished master's thesis. Atlanta, Georgia, Atlanta University, June, 1936.
KUNITZ, STANLEY J. *Authors Today and Yesterday.* New York, The H. W. Wilson Company, 1933.
LEWISOHN, LUDWIG. *Expression in America.* New York, Harper and Brothers, 1932.

LOGGINS, VERNON. *I Hear America.* New York, The Thomas Y. Crowell Company, 1937.

———. *The Negro Author: His Development in America.* New York, Columbia University Press, 1931.

MCILWAINE, SHIELDS. *The Southern Poor-White from Lubberland to Tobacco Road.* Norman, Oklahoma, University of Oklahoma Press, 1939.

MICHAUD, REGIS. *The American Novel To-Day.* New York, Little, Brown and Company, 1928.

MUNSON, GORHAM B. *Destinations.* New York, J. H. Sears and Company, 1928.

———. *Style and Form in American Prose.* New York, Doubleday, Doran and Company, 1929.

NELSON, JOHN HERBERT. *The Negro Character in American Literature.* Lawrence, Kansas, University of Kansas, Department of Journalism Press, 1926.

NORRIS, FRANK. *The Responsibilities of a Novelist.* New York, Doubleday, Page and Company, 1903.

PARRINGTON, VERNON LOUIS. *The Beginnings of Critical Realism in America 1860-1920.* New York, Harcourt, Brace and Company, 1930.

PATTEE, FRED. *A History of American Literature Since 1870.* New York, Appleton-Century, 1915.

———. *The New American Literature 1890-1930.* New York, The Century Company, 1930.

QUINN, ARTHUR HOBSON. *American Fiction: An Historical and Critical Survey.* New York, D. Appleton-Century Company, 1936.

REDDING, J. SAUNDERS. *To Make a Poet Black.* Chapel Hill, North Carolina, The University of North Carolina Press, 1939.

SHERMAN, STUART P. *Critical Woodcuts.* New York, Charles Scribner's Sons, 1926.

TAYLOR, W. F. *A History of American Letters.* New York, American Book Company, 1936.

VAN DOREN, CARL. *The American Novel 1789-1939.* New York, The Macmillan Company, 1940.

WHIPPLE, T. K. *Spokesmen: Modern Writers and American Life.* New York, D. Appleton and Company, 1928.

WIGGINS, LIDA KECK, comp. *The Life and Works of Paul Laurence Dunbar.* Napierville, Illinois, J. L. Nichols and Company, 1907.

## *MAGAZINE ARTICLES AND REVIEWS*

BARNES, ALBERT C. "Primitive Negro Sculpture and Its Influence on Modern Civilization," *Opportunity,* VI (May, 1928), 139-140, 147.

BENNETT, GWENDOLYN. "The Ebony Flute," *Opportunity,* IV (September, 1926), 292-293.
———. "The Ebony Flute," *Opportunity,* IV (October, 1926), 322-323.
———. "The Ebony Flute," *Opportunity,* IV (November, 1926), 356-358.
———. "The Ebony Flute," *Opportunity,* VI (April, 1928), 122.
———. Review of Banjo, *Opportunity,* VII (August, 1929), 254-255.
BOTKIN, B. A. Review of *The Walls of Jericho, Opportunity,* VI (November, 1928), 346.
BRAITHWAITE, WILLIAM STANLEY. "The Negro in Literature," *The Crisis,* XXVIII (September, 1924), 204-210.
———. "The Novels of Jessie Fauset," *Opportunity,* XII (January, 1934), 24-28.
BRAWLEY, BENJAMIN. "The Negro Literary Renaissance," *Southern Workman,* LVI (April, 1927), 177-184.
———. "The Promise of Negro Literature," *The Journal of Negro History,* XIX (January, 1934), 53-59.
BRICKELL, HERSCHEL. Review of *Home to Harlem, Opportunity,* VI (May, 1928), 151-152.
BROWN, STERLING A. "The American Race Problem as Reflected in American Literature," *The Journal of Negro Education,* VIII (July, 1939), 275-290.
———. "In Memoriam: Charles W. Chesnutt," *Opportunity,* X (December, 1932), 387.
———. "The Negro Author and His Publisher," *The Quarterly Review of Higher Education Among Negroes,* IX (July, 1941), 140-146.
———. "The Negro in Fiction and Drama," *The Christian Register,* CXIV (February 14, 1935), 111.
———. Review of *Banana Bottom, Opportunity,* XI (July, 1933), 217, 222.
———. Review of *Black Thunder, Opportunity,* XIV (July, 1936), 216.
———. Review of *Gingertown, Opportunity,* X (August, 1932), 256.
———. Review of *God Sends Sunday, Opportunity,* IX (June, 1931), 188.
———. Review of *Native Son, Opportunity,* XVIII (June, 1940), 185-186.
———. Review of *Not Without Laughter, Opportunity,* VIII (September, 1930), 279-280.
BURGUM, EDWIN BERRY. Review of *The Chinaberry Tree, Opportunity,* X (March, 1932), 88-89.
BURRIS, ANDREW. Review of *Jonah's Gourd Vine, The Crisis,* XLI (June, 1934), 166-167.
CALVERTON, V. F. "The Advance of Negro Literature," *Opportunity,* IV (February, 1926), 54-55.

———. "The Negro's New Belligerent Attitude," *Current History*, XXX (September, 1929), 1081-1088.

———. "The New Negro," *Current History*, XXIII (February, 1926), 694-698.

CANBY, HENRY SEIDEL. Review of *Native Son, The Book-of-the-Month Club News* (February, 1940), 3.

CARTER, EUNICE HUNTON. Review of *The Blacker the Berry, Opportunity*, VII (May, 1929), 162-163.

CHAMBERLAIN, JOHN. "The Negro as Writer," *The Bookman*, LXX (February, 1930), 603-611.

CHESNUTT, CHARLES W. "Post-Bellum—Pre-Harlem," *The Crisis*, XXXVIII (June, 1931), 193-194.

DAVIS, ALLISON. "Our Negro 'Intellectuals,'" *The Crisis*, XXXV (August, 1928), 269.

DAVIS, ARTHUR P. Review of *Black No More, Opportunity*, IX (February, 1931), 89-90.

———. Review of *The Conjure Man Dies, Opportunity*, X (October, 1932), 320.

DE ARMOND, FRED. "A Note on the Sociology of Negro Literature," *Opportunity*, III (December, 1925), 369-371.

DUBOIS, W. E. BURGHARDT. "Editorial," *The Crisis*, I (November, 1910), 10.

———. "Fall Books," *The Crisis*, XXIX (November, 1924), 25-26.

———. "Negro in Literature and Art," *Annals of the American Academy of Political and Social Science*, XLIX (September, 1913), 233-237.

———. "Returning Soldiers," *The Crisis*, XVII (May, 1919), 14.

———. Review of *Banjo, The Crisis*, XXXVI (July, 1929), 234.

———. Review of *Black No More, The Crisis*, XXXVIII (March, 1931), 100.

———. Review of *The Blacker the Berry, The Crisis*, XXXVI (July, 1929), 249-250.

———. Review of *The Chinaberry Tree, The Crisis*, XXXIX (April, 1932), 138.

———. Review of *The Fire in the Flint, The Crisis*, XXIX (November, 1924), 24.

———. Review of *God Sends Sunday, The Crisis*, XXXVIII (September, 1931), 304.

———. Review of *Home to Harlem, The Crisis*, XXXV (June, 1928), 202, 211.

———. Review of *Nigger Heaven, The Crisis*, XXXIII (December, 1926), 81-82.

———. Review of *Quicksand, The Crisis*, XXXV (June, 1928), 202, 211.

———. Review of *The Walls of Jericho, The Crisis,* XXXV (November, 1928), 374.
———, and LOCKE, ALAIN. "The Younger Literary Movement," *The Crisis,* XXVII (February, 1924), 161-164.
FORREST, ETHEL A. Review of *Their Eyes Were Watching God, The Journal of Negro History,* XXIII (January, 1938), 106-107.
FRAZIER, E. FRANKLIN. "The American Negro's New Leaders," *Current History,* XXVIII (April, 1928), 56-59.
———. "The Garvey Movement," *Opportunity,* IV (November, 1926), 346-348.
GLOSTER, HUGH M. "Charles W. Chesnutt: Pioneer in the Fiction of Negro Life," *Phylon,* II (First Quarter, 1941), 57-66.
———. "Richard Wright: Interpreter of Racial and Economic Maladjustments," *Opportunity,* XIX (December, 1941), 361-365, 383.
———. "Sutton E. Griggs: Novelist of the New Negro," *Phylon,* IV (Fourth Quarter, 1943), 335-345.
———. "The Van Vechten Vogue," *Phylon,* VI (Fourth Quarter, 1945), 310-314.
———. "Zora Neale Hurston: Novelist and Folklorist," *Phylon,* IV (Second Quarter, 1943), 153-158.
GREGORY, MONTGOMERY. Review of *Cane, Opportunity,* I (December, 1923), 374-375.
———. "The Spirit of Phyllis Wheatley," *Opportunity,* II (June, 1924), 181-182.
HARTH, R. L. "The New Negro," *Independent,* CV (January 15, 1921), 59-60.
HOLMES, E. C. Review of *The Ways of White Folks, Opportunity,* XII (September, 1934), 283-284.
HOLMES, EUGENE. "Jean Toomer—Apostle of Beauty," *Opportunity,* X (August, 1932), 252-254, 260.
HOPSON, JAMES O. Review of *Mules and Men, The Crisis,* XLIII (April, 1936), 124.
HOWELLS, W. D. "Mr. Charles W. Chesnutt's Stories," *The Atlantic Monthly,* LXXXV (May, 1900), 699-700.
HUGHES, LANGSTON. "Harlem Literati of the Twenties," *The Saturday Review of Literature,* XXII (June 22, 1940), 13-14.
———. "The Negro Artist and the Racial Mountain," *The Nation,* CXXII (June 23, 1926), 692-694.
IVY, JAMES W. Review of *Native Son, The Crisis,* XLVII (April, 1940), 122.
JACOBS, GEORGE W. "Negro Authors Must Eat," *The Nation,* CXXVIII (June 12, 1929), 710-711.

JEROME, J. D. Review of *Drums At Dusk, The Journal of Negro History,* XXIV (July, 1939), 355.
———. Review of *Native Son, The Journal of Negro History,* XXV (April, 1940), 251-252.
JOHNSON, CHARLES S. "After Garvey—What?" *Opportunity,* I (August, 1923), 231-233.
———. Review of *The Fire in the Flint, Opportunity,* II (November, 1924), 344-345.
JOHNSON, JAMES WELDON. "The Dilemma of the Negro Author," *The American Mercury,* XV (December, 1928), 477-481.
———. "Negro Authors and White Publishers," *The Crisis,* XXXVI (July, 1929), 228-229.
———. "Race Prejudice and the Negro Artist," *Harper's Magazine,* CLVII (November, 1928), 769-776.
———. "Romance and Tragedy in Harlem," *Opportunity,* IV (October, 1926), 316-317, 330.
JONES, DEWEY R. Review of *Slaves Today, Opportunity,* X (January, 1932), 27.
KERLIN, ROBERT T. "A Decade of Negro Literature," *Southern Workman,* LIX (May, 1930), 227-229.
LEE, ULYSSES. Review of *Let Me Breathe Thunder, Opportunity,* XVII (September, 1939), 283-284.
———. Review of *O Canaan!, Opportunity,* XVII (October, 1939), 312-313.
———. Review of *These Low Grounds, Opportunity,* XV (November, 1937), 347.
LOCKE, ALAIN. "American Literary Tradition and the Negro," *The Modern Quarterly,* III (May-July, 1926), 215-222.
———. "Apropos of Africa," *Opportunity,* II (February, 1924), 37-40, 58.
———. "Beauty Instead of Ashes," *The Nation,* CXXVI (April 18, 1928), 433 ff.
———. "Black Truth and Black Beauty," *Opportunity,* XI (January, 1933), 14-18.
———. "Deep River: Deeper Sea," *Opportunity,* XIV (January, 1936), 6-10; (February, 1936), 42-43, 61.
———. "Dry Fields and Green Pastures," *Opportunity,* XVIII (January, 1940), 410, 28; (February, 1940), 41-46, 53.
———. "The Eleventh Hour of Nordicism," *Opportunity,* XIII (January, 1935), 8-12; (February, 1935), 46-48, 59.
———. "God Save Reality," *Opportunity, XV* (January, 1937), 8-13; (February, 1937), 40-44.
———. "Jingo, Counter-Jingo and Us," *Opportunity,* XVI (January, 1938), 7-12, 27.

———. "The Negro's Contribution to American Art and Literature," *Annals of the American Academy of Political and Social Science*, CXL (November, 1928), 234-247.
———. "The Negro's Contribution to American Culture," *The Journal of Negro Education*, VIII (July, 1939), 521-529.
———. "The Negro: 'New' or Newer," *Opportunity*, XVII (January, 1939), 4-10; (February, 1939), 36-42.
———. "Of Native Sons: Real and Otherwise," *Opportunity*, XIX (January, 1941), 4-9, (February, 1941), 48-52.
———. "The Saving Grace of Realism," *Opportunity*, XII (January, 1934), 8-11, 30.
———. "This Year of Grace," *Opportunity*, IX (February, 1931), 48-51.
———. "We Turn to Prose," *Opportunity*, X (February, 1932), 40-44.
———. "The Younger Literary Movement," *The Crisis*, XXVII (February, 1924), 161-163.
———. "1928: A Retrospective Review," *Opportunity*, VII (January, 1929), 8-11.
LOGAN, RAYFORD W. Review of *Drums At Dusk*, *Opportunity*, XVII (July, 1939), 218-219.
MOON, HENRY LEE. Review of *These Low Grounds*, *The Crisis*, XLIV (December, 1937), 380.
MORRIS, LLOYD. "The Negro 'Renaissance,'" *Southern Workman*, LIX (February, 1930), 82-86.
MORROW, E. FREDERIC. Review of *Uncle Tom's Children*, *The Crisis*, XLV (May, 1938), 155.
MUNSON, GORHAM B. "The Significance of Jean Toomer," *Opportunity*, III (September, 1925), 262-263.
PERRY, EDWARD G. Review of *Ollie Miss*, *Opportunity*, XIII (April, 1935), 123.
SCHUYLER, GEORGE. Review of *American Stuff*, *Opportunity*, XV (December, 1937), 377-378.
SPINGARN, ARTHUR B. "Books by Negro Authors in 1937," *The Crisis*, XLV (February, 1938), 47.
———. "Books by Negro Authors in 1939," *The Crisis*, XLVII (February, 1940), 46, 50.
———. Review of *Black Thunder*, *The Crisis*, XLIV (February, 1937), 47.
STARKEY, MARION L. "Jessie Fauset," *Southern Workman*, LXI (May, 1932), 217-220.
STREATOR, GEORGE W. Review of *The Ways of White Folks*, *The Crisis*, XLI (July, 1934), 216.
TAUSSIG, CHARLOTTE E. "The New Negro as Revealed in His Poetry," *Opportunity*, V (April, 1927), 108-111.

TAYLOR, LOIS. Review of *Infants of the Spring, Opportunity,* X (March, 1932), 89.

THURMAN, WALLACE. "Negro Artists and the Negro," *The New Republic,* LII (August 31, 1927), 37-39.

———. "Nephews of Uncle Remus," *The Independent,* CXIX (September 24, 1927), 296-298.

VAN DOREN, CARL. "Negro Renaissance," *Century,* CXI (March, 1926), 635-637.

WALROND, ERIC. "The New Negro Faces America," *Current History,* XVII (February, 1923), 786-788.

WALTON, EDA LOU. Review of *Quicksand, Opportunity,* VI (July, 1928), 212-213.

WILKINS, ROY. Review of *Ollie Miss, The Crisis,* XLII (April, 1935), 121.

WOODSON, CARTER G. Review of *Tell My Horse, The Journal of Negro History,* XXIV (January, 1939), 116-118.

WRIGHT, RICHARD. "How Bigger Was Born," *Saturday Review of Literature,* XXII (June 1, 1940), 3-4, 17-20.

YOUNG, PAULINE A. Review of *Black Thunder, The Journal of Negro History,* XXII (July, 1937), 355-356.

———. "The Negro in Art—How Shall He Be Portrayed?" (A Symposium), *The Crisis,* XXXI (March, 1926), 219-220; (April, 1926), 278-280; XXXII (May, 1926), 35-36; (June, 1926), 71-73; (August, 1926), 193-194; (September, 1926), 238-239; XXXIII (November, 1926), 28-29.

## *NEWSPAPER ARTICLES AND REVIEWS*

BENNETT, GWENDOLYN. Review of *God Sends Sunday, The New York Herald Tribune* (March 22, 1931).

CAIN, HELEN. "Negro Story 'Rings True,'" *The Memphis Commercial Appeal* (September 7, 1941).

CALVERTON, V. F. Review of *The Blacker the Berry, The New York Herald Tribune* (March 26, 1929).

———. Review of *Plum Bun, The New York Herald Tribune* (May 26, 1929).

CALVIN, FLOYD, JR. "First Time in History of Big New York Store This Has Been Done," *The Pittsburgh Courier* (May 23, 1931).

"Chesnutt to Publish First Novel in Twenty Years," *The Pittsburgh Courier* (June 30, 1928).

DAVIS, ARTHUR P. Review of *Black Thunder, The Norfolk Journal and Guide* (February 29, 1936).

HOWELL, CLARK. Letter to the Editor, *The New York World* (September 19, 1895).
JONES, DEWEY. Review of *Home to Harlem, The Chicago Defender* (March 17, 1928).
"Negro Hailed as New Writer," *The New York Sun* (March 4, 1940).
Review of *Nigger Heaven, The New York Herald Tribune* (August 22, 1926).
STALLINGS, LAURENCE. Review of *God Sends Sunday, The New York Sun* (March 18, 1931).
"Writes First Novel," *The Amsterdam News* (July 9, 1930).

## *ANTHOLOGIES*

ADLER, ELMER, ed. *Breaking into Print*. New York, Simon and Schuster, 1937.
BROWN, STERLING A., *et al.*, eds. *The Negro Caravan*. New York, The Dryden Press, 1941.
CALVERTON, V. F., ed. *Anthology of American Negro Literature*. New York, The Modern Library Publishers, 1929.
CARGILL, OSCAR, ed. *The Social Revolt 1888-1914*. New York, The Macmillan Company, 1933.
CROMWELL, OTELIA, *et al.*, eds. *Readings from Negro Authors for Schools and Colleges*. New York, Harcourt, Brace and Company, 1931.
CUNARD, NANCY, ed. *Negro Anthology*. London, Wishart and Company, 1934.
FEDERAL WRITERS' PROJECT. *American Stuff*. New York, Viking Press, 1937.
HICKS, GRANVILLE, *et al.*, eds. *Proletarian Literature in the United States*. New York, International Publishers, 1935.
JOHNSON, CHARLES S., ed. *Ebony and Topaz*. New York, *Opportunity*, 1927.
JOHNSON, JAMES WELDON, ed. *The Book of American Negro Poetry*. New York, Harcourt, Brace and Company, 1922. Second edition, 1931.
LOCKE, ALAIN, ed. *The New Negro*. New York, Alfred and Charles Boni, 1925.
NELSON, JOHN HERBERT, ed. *Contemporary Trends*. New York, The Macmillan Company, 1933.
WOODSON, CARTER G., ed. *Negro Orators and Their Orations*. Washington, D. C., Associated Publishers, 1925.

## *BACKGROUND MATERIAL*

BRAWLEY, BENJAMIN. *A Short History of the American Negro*. New York, The Macmillan Company, 1931.

———. *A Social History of the American Negro*. New York, The Macmillan Company, 1921.

CABLE, GEORGE W. *The Grandissimes*. New York, Charles Scribner's Sons [1880].

———. *Old Creole Days*. New York, Charles Scribner's Sons [1879].

CLEVELAND, GROVER. *Letters 1850-1908*, edited by Allen Nevins. New York, The Houghton Mifflin Company, 1933.

COZART, W. FORREST. *The Chosen People*. Boston, The Christopher Publishing House, 1924.

DIXON, THOMAS, JR. *The Clansman*. New York, Grosset and Dunlap, 1905.

———. *The Leopard's Spots*. New York, Doubleday, Page and Company, 1902.

DUBOIS, W. E. BURGHARDT. *Black Reconstruction in America*. New York, Harcourt, Brace and Company, 1935.

———. *Darkwater*. New York, Harcourt, Brace and Company, 1920.

———. *Dusk of Dawn*. New York, Harcourt, Brace and Company, 1940.

———. *A Pageant in Seven Decades*. Atlanta, no publisher, 1938.

———. *The Souls of Black Folk*. Chicago, A. C. McClurg and Company, 1902.

EMBREE, EDWIN R. *Brown America*. New York, The Viking Press, 1935.

FORD, JAMES W. *The Negro and the Democratic Front*. New York, International Publishers, 1938.

GRADY, HENRY W. *The Complete Orations and Speeches*, edited by Edwin DuBois Shurter. New York, Hinds, Noble and Eldredge, 1910.

HOWELLS, WILLIAM DEAN. *An Imperative Duty*. New York, Harper and Brothers, 1892.

HUGHES, LANGSTON. *The Big Sea: An Autobiography*. New York, Alfred A. Knopf, 1940.

JOHNSON, CHARLES S. *The Negro in American Civilization*. New York, Henry Holt and Company, 1930.

JOHNSON, JAMES WELDON. *Along This Way*. New York, The Viking Press, 1933.

———. *Black Manhattan*. New York, Alfred A. Knopf Company, 1930.

KING, GRACE. *Balcony Stories*. New York, The Macmillan Company, 1925.

LEE, GEORGE W. *Beale Street*. New York, Vail-Ballou Press, 1934.

McKAY, CLAUDE. *Harlem: Negro Metropolis.* New York, E. P. Dutton and Company, 1940.
———. *A Long Way from Home.* New York, Lee Furman Company, 1937.
MAYS, BENJAMIN E. *The Negro's God.* Boston, Chapman and Grimes, 1938.
———, and NICHOLSON, JOSEPH W. *The Negro's Church.* New York, Institute of Social and Religious Research, 1933.
MYRDAL, GUNNAR, *et al. An American Dilemma.* 2 vols. New York, Harper and Brothers, 1944.
OTTLEY, ROI. *New World a-Coming.* Boston, Houghton Mifflin Company, 1943.
PAGE, THOMAS NELSON. *In Ole Virginia, or Marse Chan and Other Stories.* New York, Charles Scribner's Sons, 1887.
———. *The Negro: The Southerner's Problem.* New York, Charles Scribner's Sons, 1904.
———. *The Old South.* New York, Charles Scribner's Sons, 1892.
———. *Red Rock.* New York, Charles Scribner's Sons, 1898.
STEWART, DONALD OGDEN. *Fighting Words.* New York, Harcourt, Brace and Company, 1940.
TOURGEE, ALBION W. *Pactolus Prime.* New York, Cassell Publishing Company [1890].
———. *A Royal Gentleman, and 'Zouri's Christmas.* New York, Fords, Howard, and Hulbert [1874].
TWAIN, MARK. *The Tragedy of Pudd'nhead Wilson.* Hartford, American Publishing Company, 1894.
VAN VECHTEN, CARL. *Nigger Heaven.* New York, A. A. Knopf, 1926.
WASHINGTON, BOOKER T. *My Larger Education.* New York, Doubleday, Page and Company, 1911.
———. *Selected Speeches,* edited by E. Davidson Washington. New York, Doubleday, Doran and Company, 1932.
———. *Up from Slavery.* New York, Doubleday, Page and Company, 1901.
———, *et al. The Negro Problem.* New York, J. Pott and Company, 1903.
WOODSON, CARTER GODWIN. *The Negro in Our History.* Washington, The Associated Publishers, 1941.

# Index